WRITING
PERSUASIVE
BRIEFS

WRITING PERSUASIVE BRIEFS

GIRVAN PECK

MEMBER, CALIFORNIA BAR

LITTLE, BROWN AND COMPANY
BOSTON   TORONTO

Library of Congress Catalog Card No. 84-080192
ISBN 0-316-69666-8

FG

Published simultaneously in Canada
by Little, Brown & Company (Canada) Limited
Printed in the United States of America

To Nancy
and to
Tally, Larry, Christie, Sheila,
Todd, Jimmy, and Alex

IN MEMORIAM

Girvan Peck, our partner for twenty-two years, was a lawyer's lawyer and a valued friend. He possessed the genius for simplifying that is the hallmark of a brilliant legal mind. He was also a gentleman in the figurative and literal sense of that word.

Girvan died shortly before this book was published. But every word in it is his. The book is an outgrowth of Girvan's own extensive litigation experience and his work in our firm's Legal Writing Program, which he headed for many years.

Writing the book was a labor of love for Girvan. Characteristically, Girvan considered it but a modest contribution to the art of advocacy that he practiced so well. Those of us practicing lawyers who have read the manuscript, however, know that it will become a standard in the field. As such, it is a fitting legacy from its author, a man whose loss diminishes our firm and the profession.

MORRISON & FOERSTER
May 21, 1984
San Francisco

Girvan Peck evinced many of those qualities that make working with authors such a distinct pleasure and honor.

Although, unlike many books, his came to us as an essentially complete manuscript, he was always willing to listen to editorial advice. He was scrupulous in his attention to those oft-neglected chores that make the difference between a fair book and an excellent book. Most of all, however, he believed strongly in the persuasive power of good legal writing and practiced its principles assiduously. It is from Girvan's faith in his book that we derived the most satisfaction during the short period in which it was our privilege to know him.

LITTLE, BROWN AND COMPANY
LAW DIVISION
May 21, 1984
Boston

CONTENTS

Contents

FOREWORD

Most attorneys, I suspect, have learned how to write briefs by doing it, aided by comments and criticism from associates or partners. That was my experience, and I still recall the statement of one of the senior partners when I was starting to write my first brief in support of an appeal. "The first thing you have to do is show the court that your client has a bloody nose." I also recall the time when I wrote an answering brief in a case where the petitioners were attacking the validity of a newly adopted charter amendment creating a health service system for San Francisco's employees. One point raised was that it was unconstitutional for the city to withhold money from the employees' earnings to pay salaries to the employees who were elected directors of the system. I had written what I thought was a reasonably brief analysis, refuting the point. The same partner struck it out and substituted the following: "The salaries of the directors are like the snakes in Ireland. The charter does not provide for them." What more was there to say?

This kind of education in brief writing is better than none, but not all that it should be. It is fragmented and haphazard, and may or may not be available when it is needed. That is why I think that Girvan Peck's book is so valuable.

Drawing upon what he has learned from his own extensive experience, he has pulled together the wisdom and the suggestions of many other masters of the subject. The book is well organized and full of useful information and suggestions, reinforced by carefully chosen examples. I expect it to become the *vade-mecum* of every lawyer who has to write a brief. Doesn't that include us all?

Ben C. Duniway
Senior United States Circuit Judge
San Francisco
November 1983

PREFACE

This book grew out of the author's experience in putting together a training program for his law firm. The idea was to teach the younger lawyers to write better briefs and, incidentally, better memoranda, letters, and contracts.

Whoever approaches such an assignment must deal with the fact that law students and younger lawyers have begun to acquire the bad habits of their seniors. Already they look with favor on conceptual and pompous words; they are attracted to the involved sentence and the shapeless paragraph; they are tempted by the argumentative footnote: in short, they want to expound as they think lawyers do. The first task of the teacher, accordingly, is to demonstrate that advocates are not required to write in impenetrable legalese, but can write clear and memorable prose, and that their briefs will be more effective if they do so.

At the same time the teacher must try to guide his charges to an understanding of the process of persuasion. Here again there is much for them to unlearn. Students or young lawyers may have the impression from their own experience that an oral or written argument is a kind of verbal combat, whereas it is in fact an exercise in artful salesmanship. If they have experience debating, budding lawyers may liken the process of persuasion to a debate, in which the contestants receive points for demonstrated rhetorical skills. In a legal argument, however, what wins is a demonstrably attractive case, vividly brought to life by the advocate, just as in a horse show, points are not awarded to the skilled rider but to the horse. Frequently students or recent graduates will write as if addressing their professors or the academic community at large. This, of course, is what they are used to, but in a brief they must direct their prose toward specific individuals who have the mission of deciding concrete cases. They must learn to write for judges.

In a brief the techniques of writing and persuasion complement each other. Analytically they are separable, but the advocate's persuasive arts will not reach his readers unless his prose is skillful, and his prose will not be effectively directed unless he understands the process of persuasion. Each technique is indispensable. Each is an integral part of any successful brief.

In this book the essentials of effective writing are presented first, followed by an introduction to the elements of persuasion. These fundamentals are then applied first to the different parts of a brief and then to different kinds of briefs. At the end there is a discussion of the methods with which lawyers prepare, draft, revise, and edit their work.

In researching the book I found no other with a similar format, but did find a variety of useful source materials. These will be found in the notes to each chapter and in the bibliography at the end of the book. The most helpful sources, taken as a group, are the articles and addresses written by judges. Their authors are not only experienced; they are, after all, the advocate's audience, and accordingly their precepts and preferences are uniquely authoritative. The reader will find such judicial comments liberally quoted in the text.

This book could not have been written without the generous support of my colleagues at Morrison & Foerster. James J. Brosnahan encouraged me to teach and to write and to publish. I had the benefit of comments on portions of the manuscript from James P. Bennett, James J. Garrett, Alan Cope Johnston, John M. Kelly, and Douglas C. White, and the stimulation of questions and further comments from numerous students at my seminars on the same subject. The firm's library staff was untiringly helpful. Ruth Johnson typed it all—each draft and each of the interminable revisions—with her expert touch and her usual good cheer. To all of these generous people, my thanks once again.

G.P.

WRITING
PERSUASIVE
BRIEFS

1
THE NATURE
OF BRIEF WRITING

The law is nothing if not traditional, and accordingly lawyers cling to archaic terms like "brief" and "memorandum of points and authorities," although both have become misnomers. Today, as we know, a brief is not necessarily short, for it may be as long as a book, and it is not in any sense a memorandum or a summary of an argument to follow. It is a written argument, and in fact is the only complete and definitive argument made by the advocate to the court. Instead of being a mere collection of references arranged for the convenience of the judges, it is, throughout, an essay in persuasion, or advocacy reduced to writing.

On an appeal it is the oral argument that is now, in practice, brief and limited in scope.[1] Gone are the expansive orations, lasting for hours or days, which once were the pride of the advocate. The oral argument is now usually reduced to a matter of minutes. It still may be illuminating, and sometimes it will be decisive, but its function has changed. Increasingly judges are using the time allotted to oral argument for key questions and informal colloquy. They know where to find the complete and documented arguments of the advocates. These are to be found in the briefs.

THE BRIEF AS THE PRIMARY ARGUMENT

The brief has emerged from its obscurity to assume a leading role in the communication of arguments to judges. It is not a

1. Peck, Time for Oral Argument, 4 Litigation 39 (1978); Vanderbilt, Forensic Persuasion, 7 Wash. & Lee L. Rev. 1, 16-17 (1950).

summary or abbreviated argument, but is complete. It is not in question-and-answer form, but is in an orderly exposition. Frequently a brief has the capacity to establish the issues and direct the oral argument, as a play or a script controls the actors. Always it is available, permanently and without change, until the judicial decision is made.

As Judge Goodrich of the United States Court of Appeals for the Third Circuit put it in a symposium,

> It is hard to overstate the importance of the brief on an appeal. Oral argument will be discussed later. It is important, too. But it is made only once in nearly all instances and it is inevitable that some of its effect will be lost in the interval between the time the argument is made and the court opinion appears. . . . But the brief speaks from the time it is filed and continues through oral argument, conference, and opinion writing. Sometimes a brief will be read and reread, no one knows how many times except the judge and his law clerk.[2]

The same may be said of any important brief in a trial court. On a major motion the oral argument is often important, but the briefing may be decisive in the end. The wise advocate knows that a brief must be capable of standing alone, as if no oral argument will be permitted or taken seriously. He cannot afford to assume otherwise.

For advocates who take pride in speaking well, and in using to the full an expressive face and an appealing or perhaps commanding personality, the realization that these attributes may not affect the outcome is unwelcome, but unavoidable. To the extent they must rely on their brief they must rely on the written word alone. Advocates cannot converse with the judges; they cannot see from their expressions whether the judges are bored, distracted, or hostile; they cannot command attention by modulating their voices or pounding on the lectern. If by their prose they fail to communicate effectively, or if their points are missed altogether, they may never know it.

2. Goodrich, A Case on Appeal—A Judge's View, in A Case on Appeal 1, 10-11 (1967). Justice Marshall has expressed similar views: Marshall, The Federal Appeal, in Counsel on Appeal 139, 146 (Charpentier ed. 1968).

Accordingly lawyers must find ways to write so clearly and emphatically that the court cannot misunderstand them, and cannot fail to be impressed with the convincing force of their written argument.[3]

If advocates are to do this well, they must call on abilities they may never have fully developed. It is one thing to analyze the issues, the facts, and the law and to see where the most effective arguments lie. For this lawyers are presumably well schooled. It is another matter for advocates to organize and express arguments in writing so that their readers, the judges and clerks, will follow them surely and easily, point by point, with a sense of mounting conviction. For this lawyers may have little training. They may have written essays in college or law school, but they will have been graded primarily on their knowledge displayed and not the skill of their expression. In practice lawyers may have become expert in constructing pleadings or interrogatories, contracts, conveyances, or wills; such lawyerly skills do not help them write a brief. Now they need the abilities of a writer whose business it is to communicate for a living. Like the author of a best-selling book on current political or economic issues, advocates must know their subject, but they must also produce prose that attracts the attention of their readers and persuades them. When lawyers sit down to write a brief, they are being paid for such skills. Like it or not, they are professional writers.

Many lawyers, including some of the finest minds in the legal profession, have never achieved professional skills in writing. Their briefs may be well researched and well organized, but one strains to understand them. Their words are pompous and dull, their sentences long and involved, their paragraphs marked off seemingly at random; there is no con-

---

3. "A writer commits this error [of subjectivity] when he thinks it enough if he himself knows what he means and wants to say, and takes no thought for the reader, who is left to get at the bottom of it as best he can. This is as though the author were holding a monologue; whereas it ought to be a dialogue; and a dialogue, too, in which he must express himself all the more clearly inasmuch as he cannot hear the questions of his interlocutor." Schopenhauer, On Style, in The Writer's Art by Those Who Have Practiced It 317 (Brown ed. 1921).

4

tinuous march, step by step, through statement and argument. It is only by persistent effort that the reader can disentangle such prose, and at the end he is still left with strands of thought that do not seem to fit in any logical sequence.

Judges will read such briefs, but not happily. They must try to understand the arguments on both sides of an issue, and to this extent they are a captive audience. But judges are also human and there are limits to their time and energies. No rule requires them to spend three times as much effort on one side of an argument as the other, merely because one presentation is confused and the other is clear. Nothing can force them to grasp concepts that are obscurely expressed, or to remember later what they only dimly perceived in the first place. Judges offer the writer an audience, but it is up to the brief writer to engage their minds. Judge Kaufman of the Second Circuit put it in a nutshell when he wrote,

> Language is the lawyer's scalpel. If he cannot use it skillfully, he is apt to butcher his suffering client's case.[4]

What judges want to see in a brief is a reliable, clear, and persuasive guide to a decision. They have stated the desired elements many times in speeches and articles: Briefs should be accurate and not overstated; they should be complete, so that the judge will have the party's entire position clearly laid out. At the same time briefs should be concise and not discursive; they should be simply and clearly expressed; they should be argumentative, where argument is called for, and partisan within the limits of accuracy and honesty.[5]

4. Kaufman, Appellate Advocacy in the Federal Courts, 79 F.R.D. 165, 170 (1978).

5. "Every appellate advocate must state facts and law candidly and accurately. This is an uncompromising absolute." Godbold, Twenty Pages and Twenty Minutes — Effective Advocacy on Appeal, 30 Southwestern L.J. 801, 816 (1976); "The lawyer's greatest weapon is clarity, and its whetstone is succinctness." Prettyman, Some Observations Concerning Appellate Advocacy, 39 Va. L. Rev. 285, 288 (1953).

"A properly prepared brief will be so meticulously prepared, so complete, that the judge will be neither forced nor tempted to do his own research, either through the record for facts or through the library for cases." Id.

In substance this is merely to say that briefs should be well written, for any writer in any field who wishes to persuade an audience to a point of view will practice these principles. Still it is significant that judges emphasize such points. Clearly they are dissatisfied with the prose they are often required to read. They are reminding the bar that advocates are writers as well as lawyers, and that their writing skills leave much to be desired.

BRIEF WRITING AS AN ACQUIRED SKILL

Judges have also pointed out, entirely correctly, that writing is an acquired skill.[6] It is not easy to write well, but with concentrated attention the lawyer can become proficient. Good writing, as Ambrose Bierce put it, is essentially "clear thinking made visible,"[7] and thus is a skill well within the reach of lawyers. Lawyers as a group have a broad education, a facile mind, and a large vocabulary, all of which are major assets for the developing writer. They have the basic equipment, like a natural athlete who takes up a new sport; now all they need to do is learn the sport itself.

How does the lawyer set about doing this? The first requisite is a proper state of mind. The advocate needs to take writing techniques seriously. The written expression of thoughts must be as important as the thoughts themselves. He must understand that thinking and writing are indivisible; style is the end product of thought, and a good style can only emanate from the thoughts themselves.[8] As E.B. White phrased it in *The Elements of Style:*

6. See, e.g., notes 10 and 11 *infra*.

7. Bierce, Write It Right: A Little Blacklist of Literary Faults 13 (1971).

8. "Nothing is easier than to write so that no one can understand; just as, contrarily, nothing is more difficult than to express deep things in such a way that everyone must necessarily grasp them." Schopenhauer, *supra* note 3, at 306.

Young writers often suppose that style is a garnish for the meat of prose, a sauce by which a dull dish is made palatable. Style has no such separate entity; it is nondetachable, unfilterable. The beginner should approach style warily, realizing that it is himself he is approaching, no other; and he should begin by turning resolutely away from all devices that are popularly believed to indicate style — all mannerisms, tricks, adornments. The approach to style is by way of plainness, simplicity, orderliness, sincerity.[9]

So long as advocates think of writing as a frill, or as mere polish to be applied to fact summaries or case briefs, they cannot begin to succeed. They must decide that each sentence and each paragraph in their written arguments will be fully grasped by their readers, and then must work on the text until no judge can misunderstand them. Judge Prettyman of the District of Columbia Circuit put it well in a law review article:

I said at the outset that appellate persuasion is an art. But it is an art which, like many another, can be learned. One need not be born a genius to succeed at it. How does a lawyer acquire proficiency at this art? The answer is quite simple. It is: By work. . . .

What do we mean by "work"? We mean several things. I mention four:

First: Learn to write. I say this to young lawyers, and I say it to the older ones too, even to those as ancient as I. Can you write a sentence in English — a sentence in which a thought is stated so clearly and simply that it is easily understood and cannot be misunderstood? Rarely is ability to write such sentences a natural gift. It is acquired. You write, and rewrite — four, six, eight times. Those crystal-clear sentences that you sometimes see are rarely flashes of genius. They are the product of long, weary trying, and trying, and trying — either on the particular sentences or in years of constant cultivation.[10]

The "years of constant cultivation" Judge Prettyman referred to may be thought of as the second requirement for

9. Strunk and White, The Elements of Style 69 (3d ed. 1979).
10. Prettyman, *supra* note 5, at 301-302.

any aspiring writer. Anyone can learn merely by noticing how other writers obtain their effects. What kinds of words do they use, and what do they avoid? How do they order their thoughts? When a passage is powerful and memorable, what makes it so? Justice Jackson, himself a masterful advocate and then Supreme Court Justice, emphasized in a lecture the value of cultivating one's interest in language.

> The advocate will read and reread the majestic efforts of leaders of his profession on important occasions, and linger over their manner of handling challenging subjects. He will master the short Saxon word that pierces the mind like a spear and the simple figure that lights the understanding. He will never drive the judge to his dictionary. He will rejoice in the strength of the mother tongue as found in the King James version of the Bible, and in the power of the terse and flashing phrase of a Kipling or a Churchill.[11]

Here is the elegant prose of a lawyer who never stopped learning to speak and to write.

A third practice, requisite for the writing of briefs or any prose, is the habit of listening to the words we write. Barbara W. Tuchman, the prize-winning historian, relates that when she was in college her history thesis was "badly written." Later, as her readers know, she learned to write extremely well. She recalls

> One learns to write, I have since discovered, in the practice thereof. After seven years' apprenticeship in journalism I discovered that an essential element for good writing is a good ear. One must *listen* to the sound of one's own prose. This, I think, is one of the failings of much American writing. Too many writers do not listen to the sound of their own words.[12]

Lawyers who write briefs can listen to the sound of their own prose, and in fact they must listen if they are to write

11. Jackson, Advocacy Before the Supreme Court: Suggestions for Effective Case Presentations, 37 A.B.A.J. 801, 863-864 (1951).
12. Tuchman, Practicing History 16 (1981).

effective briefs. They should listen, as Mrs. Tuchman listens, for the sound of their words as they would affect the intelligent general reader. At the same time they should have in mind their own particular readers—the judge or panel of judges who will decide their case. If they make a habit of listening they will hear the awkward sounds, and change them. In time they will develop a good ear for clear, understandable language.

When a lawyer listens to his own brief he may assume, if he wishes, that the judge reading it will be as alert as the judge described by Judge Godbold of the Fifth Circuit in a recent article.

> Whether in his library or on the bench, the judge is trying with every ounce of his capacity to traverse the path from issue to answer. Every intellectual pore is open to receive help and guidance from what the lawyers say and write.[13]

It may be safer, however, to assume that judges are like other busy people who bear heavy responsibilities. Every intellectual pore cannot be open all of the time, and may not be when the brief is actually read.

The prudent brief writer will bear in mind that the case loads of judges everywhere are on the increase. In some courts the burden is crushing; judges know they cannot give adequate attention to each case, and they have repeatedly so warned the legislatures and the bar; still there is no relief in sight. Therefore, the brief writer should assume the worst case and suppose, for example, that the judge has heard three arguments in the morning, one of which was inadequately prepared and the others ponderously dull; in the afternoon he has read two briefs on other cases, both of which were long-winded, vituperative, and largely irrelevant to the issues. Now it is the end of a long day. The judge is tired and irritable. Only the realization that a stack of other briefs, petitions, and motions are waiting nearby has caused him to pick up the present brief. He feels he must read it, but he longs to go home.

13. Godbold, *supra* note 5, at 808.

Now the lawyer tests his draft. He plays the part of the judge and he reads his brief as the judge would, not for pleasure but as a duty, and skeptically. What is the judge saying to himself as he goes? Perhaps he is muttering, "I don't follow this. . . . What's this mean? . . . Why is that case relevant? . . . I don't understand. . . . I don't see that he's answered the point. . . ."

Or perhaps the judge has now become interested, despite his fatigue, and he is saying to himself, "I see . . . yes, that's very clear. . . . I hadn't though of that. . . . That's true . . . that seems unanswerable. . . ." The surprising fact is that the writer can usually predict his reader's reactions—provided he listens.

If the writer senses that his reader may not understand a phrase or a sentence or a paragraph, the red flag goes up. Something is wrong. Perhaps he has not expressed directly and simply what he means, or perhaps he has not yet thought through exactly what he means. Now he knows he will have to come back and rewrite. But at least he has pinpointed a trouble spot, by the simple process of listening with a sensitive ear.

If the brief writer will cultivate these habits—the habit of working at writing for its own sake, the habit of reading forensic prose for the stylistic lessons it teaches, the habit of listening to the sound of his own prose—he will have started down the road to writing well.

What remains is the study of writing techniques themselves. Here the self-analysis of professional writers helps us, because they often have written about how good prose is produced. The principles they teach are the subjects of the chapters to follow.

THE PLAN OF THIS BOOK

A well-written brief is, first of all, a work of effective expository writing. We cannot express a convincing argument unless we have gained the basic skills of narrating facts and explaining ideas. Beyond that, a brief should be deliberately constructed as a piece of forensic writing, or rhetoric, which means that it should be designed and executed to be convincing to its readers. Expository skills are the indispensable foundation, but the purpose of the finished structure is to persuade.

Each of these skills should be considered in order. To put it in another way, it is best to review first the skills that make for clear exposition, then the principles of effective persuasion, and only then the application of those skills and principles to the writing of the various parts of a brief. These, at least, are the author's own conclusions, and they have controlled the plan of this book.

Accordingly, the chapters that immediately follow deal with the essentials of expository writing. They are concerned with Words and Phrases (Chapter 2), Sentences and Paragraphs (Chapter 3), and Continuity in Exposition (Chapter 4). In these chapters the reader will find examples of good and bad writing, and in particular legal writing, along with the views of the author and others on what makes for clarity, readability, and emphasis.

In Chapter 5, we deal for the first time with the Elements of Persuasion, or what makes for a convincing argument. In this chapter, the reader will find an analysis of the subject, and, again, a variety of examples of persuasive and nonpersuasive techniques.

Chapters 6, 7, and 8 are designed to build on the principles expressed in the previous chapters and to apply successively to the main parts of a brief—Defining the Issues, Factual Statements, and the Argument. Excerpts taken from effective briefs illustrate both the function of each part of the brief and the way each dovetails with the other parts.

In Chapter 9 we deal with the principal varieties of briefs in different courts and before agencies, and with some of the main differences among opening, responding, and reply briefs.

Chapter 10, entitled "Methods of Writing and Editing," largely concerns mechanics—how the writer organizes materials, gets out a first draft, and then revises and rewrites the draft, all with an eye to a deadline.

The Nature of Brief Writing

Each chapter of the book can be read separately, but not without some loss of understanding, for each depends in part on the preceding chapters. The best way to use the book is to skim it or read it through first to get the sense of it, and then return to the parts that seem most useful.

2
WORDS AND PHRASES

Each word in a brief counts. If it is clear and it fits, it moves the thought along. If it is vivid and especially apt, it does more, for then it illuminates the sentence and the paragraph in which it appears. Such a word lingers in the mind.

As a group, lawyers are not particularly skilled in the use of ordinary words. They use legal words accurately because they are required to do so; as professionals they cannot afford to misuse technical terms. But lawyers do not take ordinary words seriously because they do not think of themselves as professional writers. The result is that when they try their hand at an essay in persuasion, like a brief, they have no clear perception of the qualities and functions of the words available to them. They are about to design and build a house without a working knowledge of their building materials.

Like anyone else, however, lawyers can become conscious of ordinary words. If they start to examine them for clarity and color, as they might seashells or pieces of jade, lawyers can learn to appreciate their structure, their beauty, and their extraordinary diversity. As any collector does in time, they become connoisseurs.

Choosing words and phrases of good quality is not easy, but it is not nearly as difficult as many tasks lawyers are called on to perform. Once a person examines the elements of language, common-sense principles of word selection become apparent:

- Words are intended to communicate ideas so that someone else will understand them.
- Words that communicate nothing, or interfere with communication, are better omitted.

- Clear-cut, simple words communicate ideas better than vague or complex words.
- Concrete, colorful, and memorable words communicate ideas better than abstract, drab, and forgettable words.

The more a writer understands and practices these principles, the better will be his choice of words. If he chooses his words well, he has the components of good prose laid out before him. From such building blocks he can shape strong sentences and then fit them together in neatly constructed paragraphs. But the writer must start with the words themselves.

WORKING WORDS

A good writer will choose words and phrases for their ability to perform. Like the director of a play or the coach of a team, he must work with a limited number of players. If the group is to be successful, each player chosen must perform a function and perform it well or a substitute will be sent in. There is no room for the incompetent or the slacker. The object is to fill each position with a strong team player and each prominent role with a star.

Verbs especially should be chosen with particular care because they are the action words, the words that supply motive power to the sentence. If the writer can find a verb that pinpoints the action to be described, it may carry the sentence. A good verb needs no adverb or any other qualifying language, but it does the job by itself. The good writer does not like to waste words. For example

Wordy	*Succinct*
She worked laboriously on her brief for two weeks.	She labored on her brief for two weeks.
The child was taken away against her will.	The child was kidnapped.

As a scientist, he had a contemptuous opinion of astrology.	As a scientist, he despised astrology.
Cortez caused Mexico to be brought under the control of his forces.	Cortez conquered Mexico.

Some writers consistently weaken their prose by avoiding working verbs, using instead a weak, neutral verb and then a noun that derives from the verb they should be using.[1] Their prose would be strengthened if they would use the verb itself. Consider the following examples:

Verb avoided	*Verb used*
The court stated its disapproval of the *Smith* case.	The court disapproved the *Smith* case.
The plaintiff also included in her prayer for relief a request for punitive damages.	The plaintiff also prayed for punitive damages
Congress has effected a reduction in welfare benefits.	Congress has reduced welfare benefits.
Whenever she saw her father she experienced a trembling sensation.	Whenever she saw her father she trembled.

Other writers weaken their verbs by using the passive voice instead of the active. At times the passive voice may be entirely proper, as when the identity of the person who acts is unimportant.

1. *See also* Chapter 3, pp. 41-42. A very helpful treatment of this subject, demonstrating the importance of using the action verbs themselves rather than "nominalizations," is contained in Williams, Style: Ten Lessons in Clarity & Grace 7-32 (1981).

William Zinsser in his book On Writing Well: An Informal Guide to Writing Nonfiction 100 (1976) uses the phrase "concept nouns" to describe the same bad habit, giving various examples of "dead sentences" that "have no people in them" and also no "working verbs."

The steel was fabricated in France, the engine was built in ‖ Germany, but the body was made in Milan.

At other times the passive voice may be preferable, as when the writer wants to stress that it does not matter who is to perform the act in question.

Just ask the General Industries Corporation to do it, and it ‖ will be done.

Normally, however, the use of the passive voice merely results in an awkward prepositional phrase, beginning with "by" or some equivalent, or else results in omitting the name of the actor.

The contract was intended by Smith to be terminable. (Sim- ‖ pler to say, "Smith intended the contract to be terminable.")
The contract was intended to be terminable. (Does not say ‖ who so intended.)

A good, practical rule to follow is to prefer the active verb, and to fall back on the passive form only when the writer wishes to avoid or deemphasize the identity of the actor.

Nouns, like verbs, can express the principal thought in a sentence. If they are chosen with enough care, they may need no adjectives, just as some verbs require no adverbs. Consider, for example, the following sentences:

Wordy	*Succinct*
He had a choice of one difficult course of action or another.	He was faced with a dilemma.
From then on the regiment was subject to such orders as he might issue in his capacity as its commander.	From then on the regiment was under his command.

The way Smith conducted himself was not a true indication of the way he actually felt at the time.	Smith's conduct was mere pretense.
The result was that the crowd became so terrified it was out of control.	The result was panic.

Even in the case of abstract and complex ideas, nouns can sometimes be found that by themselves will express the essence of the writer's idea. For example

The glory that was Greece, the grandeur that was Rome.

Abstract nouns may be used to summarize a concrete example, as in the following:

Just because we have the freedoms guaranteed by the Bill of Rights does not mean we can do whatever we want. Liberty is not to be confused with license.

When you are as helpless as a dealer in Jim Smith's position and you get a notice like this from the company, what can you do? This is not persuasion; this is coercion.

Each of the key nouns in the examples above was chosen to express an idea contrasting with another (*glory* v. *grandeur*, *liberty* v. *license, persuasion* v. *coercion*), and each is capable of standing alone without further elaboration. The result is succinct and emphatic.

Does all of this mean that adjectives and adverbs can be dispensed with altogether? No, it means merely that they are subsidiary in function and secondary in importance. When adjectives and adverbs are needed, as they often are no matter how carefully the writer selects nouns and verbs, they too should be precise. Their purpose, after all, is to furnish a description more definite than could be achieved with nouns and verbs alone, as in the following:

Holmes's opinions were frequently elliptical and occasionally cryptic.

My opponent has danced around the subject lightly, but I'm going to come to grips with it, and not so politely.

When adverbs are used to modify adjectives that in turn modify nouns, or to modify other adverbs that in turn modify verbs, the result is usually an ungainly pile, with the adverb contributing nothing but surplus weight, and perhaps smothering the words underneath. Consider the examples below:

An automobile can be a *reasonably* lethal weapon.

Williams was a *somewhat* untrustworthy witness.

Mayer is a *most* outstanding officer.

In this respect the letter was *very* ambiguous.

The court's holding is *quite* clearly to the contrary.

This was a *fairly* confidential memorandum.

DDT is a *relatively* poisonous chemical.

The admissions in the exhibit are *extremely* damning.

The argument is *simply* absurd.

The argument is *just* ridiculous.

The argument is *totally* nonsensical.

The argument is *utterly* fallacious.

In these examples the italicized extra adverbs add nothing, but instead detract from the adjectives they modify. All should be omitted.

CONCRETE WORDS—METAPHOR AND SIMILE

A reader of prose will grasp and remember an idea if it is brought home to him in concrete, personal terms. Concrete illustrations often consist of sentences or paragraphs, but they may also be conveyed by a single word or a phrase. Such words are not merely working words, accurate and clear to the intellect; they penetrate to the reader's senses, experience, and emotions. These are the words that the reader not only understands but feels.

When describing a group or combination of facts, the writer's first inclination may be to characterize it with an adjective, an adverb, or a descriptive phrase. This will make for brevity, but the description may be more vivid if concrete examples are chosen and used to symbolize or epitomize the rest of the facts.

In her last days, she became very weak.	In her last days, she was scarcely able to lift a cup or a spoon to her lips.
The witness repeatedly testified that he had no recollection.	The witness repeatedly answered, "I don't recall."
The buyer's inspectors found the merchandise was defective.	The buyer's inspectors found that patterns were mismatched, seams crooked, buttons missing.

Highlighting a wholly abstract concept seems at first blush more difficult. The writer, however, can illustrate an abstraction with a concrete idea that expresses a functionally similar concept. For example

Jones's employment was terminated after 20 years.	Jones was out on the street after 20 years.
When shown the November 10 memorandum, the witness sought to qualify his earlier testimony.	When shown the November 10 memorandum, the witness backtracked.

Despite all warnings from its bankers, the company unheedingly proceeded with its hiring program.	Despite all warnings from its bankers, the company marched ahead with its hiring program.
If the court should so hold, it will effectively preclude enforcement by the police.	If the court should so hold, it will put the police in a strait jacket.

Judges in their opinions, like lawyers in their briefs, have often turned to concrete expressions as the most vivid means of describing abstract concepts. Consider, for example, the following much-quoted passage from Justice Cardozo's opinion in *Meinhard v. Salmon:*

Many forms of conduct permissible in a *workaday* world, for those acting *at arm's length,* are forbidden to those *bound by fiduciary ties.* A trustee is held to something stricter than the *morals of the market place.* Not honesty alone but the *punctilio* of an honor the most sensitive, is then the standard of behavior. As to this there has developed a tradition that is *unbending* and inveterate. Uncompromising *rigidity* has been the attitude of courts of equity when petitioned to *undermine* the rule of undivided loyalty by the "disintegrating erosion" of particular exceptions. [Citation] Only thus has the level of conduct for fiduciaries been kept at a level higher than that *trodden by the crowd.* It will not consciously be lowered by any judgment of this court. (Emphasis added.)[2]

Precisely because they are often abstract, legal concepts need concrete illustrations; metaphors and similes used to express them must also be phrased in concrete language. In this way the concepts can be made to come alive. The legal writer can find the raw materials for such illustrations anywhere, but the most logical sources are in the language of combat and competition, for the law deals with controversy; in language describing structural components, for the law deals with logi-

2. *Meinhard v. Salmon,* 249 N.Y. 458, 164 N.E. 545, 546 (1928).

cal structures; and in the language of the visual arts and show business, for the practice of law often resembles both of these.

Suppose, for example, that a brief writer is dealing with a case in which his opponent, a large company, seeks to acquire his client, a smaller company. A hostile bid has been made, and the battle is on. The brief writer might describe the buyer's practice of seeking out promising acquisitions in terms that derive from hunting and fishing. Some examples are

> on the trail of, quarry, prey, sniff out, beat the bushes, in its sights, bird in the hand, in the bag, caught in a trap, lure, hook, barb, bait, harpoon, play the fish, reel it in, land it, in the net

If the brief writer contends that the acquiring company has misrepresented the facts to his client's shareholders, the regulatory authorities, and the public, he may want to draw on the language of the visual arts and show business to make this point. Some examples are

> with a broad brush, free form, colored, lack of perspective, foreshortened, out of focus, highlighted, blurred, touch up, finishing touches, framed, cast of characters, backdrop, quick change, mask, veil, masquerade, double talk, play to the galleries, magician, vanishing trick, direct the show, stage, orchestrate, write the script

If the brief writer wishes to describe the takeover battle itself he has at his disposal words and phrases from the language of war, personal combat, and competitive sports. Some examples are

> skirmish, barrage, lay seige to, pitched battle, blitz, counterattack, maneuver, flanking movement, ambush, sniped at, guerilla warfare, camouflage, sabotage, evasive action, sparring, fast footwork, body blow, low blow, counterpunch, knockout punch, bare-knuckled, toe hold, strangle hold, hammerlock, alley fight, no holds barred, back to the wall, fight to the finish, game plan, kick off, end run, play hardball, pitch a curve, steal a base, obstacle course, marathon

In describing the structure of the law, and the defects in his opponent's arguments, the writer may turn to the language of building construction, machinery, or the human body. For example

blueprint, foundation, underpinning, arch, keystone, framework, threshold, partition, paper over, patch up, shore up, hinge on, weak link, free wheeling, coupled with, linchpin, kingpin, skeleton, backbone, heart, skin deep

When and how should the writer use concrete metaphors and similes to describe abstract ideas? The answer is: sparingly and carefully. Too many figures of speech make for ornate and confusing prose. Careless use of them may result in mixed metaphors ("The witness Smith did not get up to bat until the second act in this extended trial.") or else in obscure or far-fetched illustrations. If the concrete metaphor or simile is not wholly clear by itself, the writer may feel it prudent to state the idea first in abstract but concise terms and then follow with a concrete expression for color and emphasis, as in the following example:

General Industries failed to anticipate the impact of foreign competition. Its management continued, with blinders on, to design and produce the same products.

Properly used, however, concrete words and phrases are the ones that illuminate ideas and make them memorable.

WORDS TO BEWARE OF OR TO AVOID

Traditionally lawyers have used archaic and pompous phraseology in pleadings, contracts, conveyances, and wills. In these instruments archaisms may do little damage, but the disease can spread. If the lawyer is not careful, he or she will unwittingly use them in briefs and oral argument, where they will certainly result in stilted prose. Common examples, to be purged wherever possible, are as follows:

said, aforesaid, aforementioned

herein, hereat, hereafter, hereunder, hereinabove, hereinafter, heretofore

therein, thereat, thereafter, thereunder, thereinbefore, thereinafter, theretofore

wherein, whereat, whereafter, whereunder, whereinafter, wherefore

The phrase "the instant case" is best changed to "the present case" or merely "this case." "Supra" and "infra" are usually unnecessary, but if needed they should be explicit: "See page 21 *infra*." The words *former* and *latter* require the reader to reread the sentence and are thus best avoided. The expression *and/or* is unnecessarily vague.

Brief writers also borrow from the phraseology common in other legal documents the lawyer's habit of unnecessary specificity with names. It is an insult to the judge's intelligence to write at the beginning of a brief, "James A. Doe, the plaintiff herein (hereafter referred to as 'Doe')," when the judge is quite capable of inferring that "Doe" is the same man just named as "James A. Doe." It is also unnecessary, and sounds something like an advertisement, to refer repeatedly to the full name of the client, especially in capital letters: "GENERAL WIDGET COMPANY, INC. rejects any such argument in its entirety. GENERAL WIDGET COMPANY, INC. contends, on the contrary, that. . . ." In briefs as in any expository prose, surnames or abbreviations are preferable to monotonous repetition, provided that references are clear. The same can be said of pronouns. They should be freely used except when the reader might be uncertain of the person or entity referred to (see page 29 infra); only then will it be advisable to insert a proper name.

Closely related to legalisms are the pompous and trendy words that seem to be an occupational disease with many government officals, professors, businesspeople, and lawyers. In one of his opinions, Judge Duniway of the Ninth Circuit, whose own prose is notably direct and lucid, described such terms with some exasperation in the following way:

> The agents involved speak an almost impenetrable jargon. They do not get into their cars; they enter official government vehicles. They do not get out of or leave their cars, they exit them. They do not go somewhere; they proceed. They do not go to a particular place; they proceed to its vicinity. They do not watch or look; they surveille. They never see anything; they observe it. No one tells them anything; they are advised. A person does not tell them his name; he identifies himself. A person does not say something; he indicates. They do not listen to a telephone conversation; they monitor it. People telephoning to each other do not say "hello"; they exhange greetings.[3]

Lawyers use too many of such terms. They tend to pick out lengthy words of Latin derivation and use them where simple words would do better. For example

ameliorate	*for* improve *or* get better
deceased	*for* died *or* dead
effectuate	*for* bring about
elucidate	*for* explain
eventuate	*for* happen
expedite	*for* speed
implement	*for* carry out *or* do
indicate	*for* say
initiate	*for* start
rehabilitate	*for* restore or improve
remunerate	*for* pay
finalize *or* terminate	*for* end
utilize	*for* use
verbalize	*for* express

Not all of these words are pure jargon, but all are pretentious and dull. The reader must concentrate in order to tell

3. *United States v. Marshall,* 488 F.2d 1169, 1171, n.1 (9th Cir. 1973).

one word from another, and when he does he is disappointed that all those syllables have so little content. Sharp, simple words are better. The reader does not stumble over them but grasps them right away, which means that he can go on immediately to the thought they express.

Vague words should ordinarily be avoided. Occasionally they cannot be escaped: A lawyer must use words like *reasonable* in a contract now and then for the very purpose of evading specificity, and at times when he writes a brief he must be deliberately vague, for sometimes the facts are uncertain or the law ambiguous. Too often, however, lawyers use words in an imprecise sense from habit. They use words like *nature, character, aspect, facet, factor, manner, situation, reaction, oriented, involved, liberal, strict,* and *meaningful* because these are familiar and comfortable. Usually some more specific word can be found and substituted, with a resulting gain in clarity.

Vague words and phrases are all too commonly used in describing relationships, where specificity would be helpful. The following phrases are among the more frequent offenders:

> along these lines, as to, as regards, concerning, in connection with, in regard to, in relation to, in respect to, in terms of, in the case of, in the instance of, referencing, referring to, regarding, relative to, respecting, similarly, similar to, with reference to, with regard to, with relation to, with a view to.

Such phrases often do no more than suggest that somewhere a logical relationship can be discerned, if the reader will search for it. It is better, of course, to do this work for the reader and to specify the relationship itself: *in answer to, next in order was, the result was, an example of this line of cases is, an analogous argument was made in,* and so forth.

Superfluous or redundant words merely bloat a sentence. Lawyers are accustomed to redundant language in the legal instruments they draft, but they should avoid it in briefs. The following are examples of redundant phrases in which one word or the other should be omitted:

claims and causes of action
precisely and exactly
wholly and totally
secondly and furthermore

Sometimes an adjective or adverb is used that adds nothing to the word it modifies, as in the following:

true facts
binding contract
obviously apparent

Sometimes the superfluous modifying language purports to define a word that needs no such definition, as in the following:

consensus of opinion
later in time
short in height
many in number

It is easy enough to write redundancies like these, but it is also easy enough, in checking a text, to find and remove them.

Not infrequently lawyers make out-and-out mistakes in the meaning of words. The following words are often confused in briefs and other legal writings:

adapt	adopt
averse	adverse
affect	effect
appraise	apprise
between	among
blatant	flagrant, obvious
censor	censure
complement	compliment
contrary	converse, opposite
counsel, counselor	council, councilor
	consul
deprecate	depreciate

discreet	discrete
flaunt	flout
forceful	forcible
illusion	delusion
infer	imply
ingenious	ingenuous
parameter	perimeter
peremptory	preemptive
practicable	practical
rebound	redound
regretfully	regrettably
therefore	therefor
trustee	trusty
undoubtedly	indubitably

Whatever words the brief writer is not sure of, he should of course check in a dictionary. The dictionary habit is a good one, and not only for accuracy: It may lead the writer to a similar word, better than the one he had in mind.

TROUBLESOME PRONOUNS

Pronouns are necessary as a means of avoiding wearisome repetition, but they also invite awkwardness and error. The person or thing to which the pronoun refers must be clear, otherwise the pronoun will become a major source of ambiguity. In normal conversation, we hear many sequences like this:

"Sally was talking to Cynthia and you know what *she* said? *She* saw Bob the other night. And you know what *she* said? *She* said . . ."

The same sort of ambiguity can creep into a brief. For example

The witness testified that in his conversation with Bob ‖
Lawson *he* said . . .

In both of these examples, it is not clear from the context to
whom the pronouns refer. Lawyers must avoid ambiguities
like this. They can and should use pronouns, but they must
first establish the person to whom the pronoun refers, so that
the reader has no doubt of the reference. When writers introduce a new reference they must establish it and differentiate it
from the old one. For example

Dr. Smith testified that in his conversation with Bob Lawson ‖
he told Lawson not to worry. In his opinion, he advised
Lawson, the treatment was going very well. Lawson, however, was skeptical. He told the doctor that he trusted his
views but that as a patient he had the right to an honest,
candid prognosis.

All that is really necessary is that writers watch out for uncertain references when using pronouns. If they are sharply
aware of the problem they will get into the habit of testing
each pronoun to see that the reference is unmistakable. If it is
not, they will supply further identification as necessary.

Pronouns, unlike names, have subjective and objective
forms, and these are sometimes misused. The most common
error is in the use of "I" and "me." For example

She took Jack and I out to dinner. ‖

The pronoun *I* is one of the objects of the verb "took" in this
sentence. She did not take "I" out to dinner; she took "me."
Thus the sentence should be

She took Jack and me out to dinner. ‖

Some speakers and writers, perhaps in doubt as to the correct
form of the pronoun, use *myself* instead

She went to the meeting with Jack and myself. ‖

Here, however, the writer does not intend to emphasize himself with the exclusive word *myself*. All he intends to say, and therefore should say, is

‖ She went to the meeting with Jack and me.

The word *myself*, being unintended, is merely confusing.

One other note about pronouns: The English language unfortunately does not provide us with a gender-neutral form of the singular pronouns "he" and "she," so that if we want a neutral pronoun to use, we find there is none. The ancient custom has been to use the male pronoun on such occasions. For example

‖ When some judge reads this, he is unlikely to be convinced.

In this example the writer does not know whether "some judge" will be a man or a woman; he has no neutral pronoun to use and so, by custom, he uses the male form. The unintended result is the sexist implication that the unknown judge will probably be male. He can avoid this by writing, for example, "A judge reading this is unlikely to be convinced."

There is, however, no fully satisfactory answer to the problem of the universal *he*. It is no solution to use the feminine pronoun in the same situation ("When some judge reads this, she is unlikely to be convinced") for this will merely suggest, misleadingly, that the writer has in mind a female judge. Nor is it a solution to use the word *person*, for that word sounds awkward when substituted for a pronoun ("When some judge reads this, that person is unlikely to be convinced"). Often the use of *he* or *his* in a neutral sense can be avoided by using plural nouns, so that the appropriate pronouns become *they* and *their*.

Perhaps someone will coin a gender-neutral pronoun in the near future. It would promptly become one of the most useful words in the language.

3

SENTENCES AND PARAGRAPHS

The sentence is best thought of as part of the paragraph, much as the arm or the leg is part of the human body. Sentences do express limited ideas that stand on their own, but in expository writing it is the paragraph that expresses the fully articulated thought. Sentences are subsidiary to it. They are used to introduce the thought, to illustrate it and support it, to point out qualifications and contrasts and distinctions, to restate it and to summarize it, but they are all servants to the dominant thought of the paragraph.

Once the writer has grasped the concept that the paragraph is his working unit of thought, he senses a new freedom in his composition, for he finds that he has no need to overload his sentences. If he has a whole paragraph to work with, no one sentence need be long or complex. The writer breaks down his thought into segments, arranges them in a logical order, and sets each one off as a sentence. At that point he is writing in paragraphs.

By using the paragraph effectively the writer avoids the confused, overloaded sentences so common in the writing of many lawyers and other professional people. Consider the following examples:

> Even more remarkable, however, is that the court below, without comment on the action of the trial court in finding . . . , finds that the jury could have disregarded the testimony of . . . , . . . , and . . . , to say nothing of . . . , which is not mentioned in the decision, and to accept the testimony of. . . .
>
> The uncontested facts were such that something other than . . . must be called for if there is to be any requirement of . . . whether it be . . . or . . . that must be proved.

These two sentences are adapted from briefs filed in the Supreme Court of the United States. The root problem in each is that the sentences are overloaded with logically different and separable thoughts. The author has not taken full advantage of the paragraph — that useful device that sets off the subparts of thought separately and distinctly, and yet at the same time shows the unity of the whole.

THE STRUCTURE OF THE PARAGRAPH

There is no set format for a paragraph, but in expository writing, at least, there is a fairly typical structure. Normally a paragraph will start with some kind of introductory sentence that leads into the main topic without fully defining it. The next sentence may expand on the first, or state the reason behind it, or distinguish it from some other idea, so that the topic is made clear in the reader's mind. Next may come illustrations, citations, or any other support for the central thought. At the end the writer will often provide a climax in the form of a pithy conclusion designed to drive home the essential point.

Whatever the format chosen, the purpose of the paragraph is to lead readers by the hand to the writer's destination. The writer should guide readers to the central idea, explore it with them, and then leave them with a vivid picture of the idea as seen from the writer's own perspective.

We can best see how paragraphing works if we use an example based on a simple set of facts. Suppose we write out the facts in the following sequence of sentences:

Hart Manufacturing Company advertised in its brochure that the Superwidget was "rated at 1500 r.p.m." O'Neil Distributing Company described the Superwidget in its catalog as "capable of performing at 1500 r.p.m. in normal operation." Paul Jones, Sales Manager for O'Neil, stated to plaintiff's buyer that he could "count on the Superwidget to deliver 1500 r.p.m." Plaintiff found that under actual operating conditions the Superwidget could operate at only 700 r.p.m.

Each of the sentences above is in itself adequately clear, but there is still something seriously wrong with the sequence as a paragraph. It is very dull, for one thing, because the sentences have no variety. More importantly, the central point is not made evident. Each sentence appears to stand for a separate thought, for the reader is nowhere told how the four sentences are intended to fit together. He has been left to puzzle it out for himself.

Many unskilled writers attempt to hint at the logical relationships among sentences by supplying "connectives," such as *moreover, furthermore, additionally, similarly, indeed, however, thus,* and *therefore.* These help, but not very much. Let's try the sequence above with connectives added but no other changes and see how it reads.

Hart Manufacturing Company advertised in its brochure that the Superwidget was "rated at 1500 r.p.m." Moreover, O'Neil Distributing Company described the Superwidget in its catalog as "capable of performing at 1500 r.p.m. in normal operation." Indeed, Paul Jones, Sales Manager for O'Neil, stated to plaintiff's buyer that he could "count on the Superwidget to deliver 1500 r.p.m." However, plaintiff found that under actual operating conditions the Superwidget could operate at only 700 r.p.m.

How does this read? Better, but the sequence is still monotonous. It still lacks clarity because connectives by themselves are incapable of spelling out logical relationships. The reader has not yet been told expressly what the first three sentences have in common, or how they contrast with the last. Now suppose, instead, that we come right out and make clear what the relationships are.

The defendants have repeatedly misrepresented the capacity of the Superwidget. Hart, the manufacturer, advertised its product as "rated at 1500 r.p.m." O'Neil, the distributor, more specifically described the machine in its catalog as "capable of performing at 1500 r.p.m. in normal operation." Paul Jones, O'Neil's Sales Manager, gave plaintiff's buyer his personal assurance that he could "count on the Superwidget to deliver 1500 r.p.m." All these representations proved to be false. Under normal operating conditions, as the plaintiff later discovered, the Superwidget could deliver no more than 700 r.p.m.

In this version the writer has not only analyzed but expressed the relationships among the facts he describes, and has subordinated his sentences to his central idea. Now he has written a paragraph.

The simplest kind of paragraph for a lawyer to write is probably the one that sets forth a legal principle. First he introduces the principle, then illustrates it with authorities, then states some expanded conclusion. The following is a carefully constructed example, drawn from the dissenting opinion of Hughes, C.J., in *Morehead v. New York ex rel. Tipaldo.*

> We have repeatedly said that liberty of contract is a qualified and not an absolute right. "There is no absolute freedom to do as one wills or to contract as one chooses.... Liberty implies the absence of arbitrary restraint, not immunity from reasonable regulations and prohibitions imposed in the interests of the community." [Introductory sentence; quotation expanding on the idea.] The numerous restraints that have been sustained have often been recited. [Citations omitted.] Thus we have upheld.... [Sentence introducing illustrations to come, followed by long sentence setting forth illustrative cases themselves.] The test of validity is not artificial. It is whether the limitation upon the freedom of contract is arbitrary and capricious or one reasonably required in order appropriately to serve the public interest in the light of the particular conditions to which the power is addressed. [Expanded conclusion, phrased negatively and then positively, for emphasis.][1]

1. *Morehead v. New York ex rel. Tipaldo,* 298 U.S. 628-629 (1931).

The progress of this paragraph from beginning to end is clear and unmistakable. Each sentence has its function, and each leads to the next. The order of the sentences and the structure of each is dictated by the purpose of the paragraph as a whole.

The same general format may be used when the writer is advocating a principle on the basis of logic rather than authority. An idea is introduced, expanded on with reason or illustration, and then summarized with a conclusion. The following example derives from the brief for appellants in *Kahn v. Shevin,* here quoted with bracketed comments.

> The division of the widowed population into two distinct classes, self-sufficient men and disabled women, is hardly tenable in this latter half of the twentieth century. [Introductory sentence, suggesting conclusions to follow.] Widowhood may have a devastating impact on a man whose age disqualifies him from pursuing economic opportunities, and who must cope with loss of myriad services once performed for him by his spouse. On the other hand, many women, during marriage, are self supporting and may contribute importantly to the support of their families. Hardly atypical is the older couple with a wife in good health who assumes financial responsibility for an ailing husband. Moreover, widowed women do not constitute a clear economic class. On the contrary, the Florida population undoubtedly includes a substantial number of affluent widows who need a tax exemption far less than widowers of limited means. [Examples to prove the point.]
>
> In short, Fla. Stat. §196.191(7) reflects a stereotypical view of the economic roles of men and women which does not correspond with reality for millions of persons in the United States. [Conclusion, expressed at beginning of following paragraph.][2]

Different formats are used when the writer is expressing distinctions and contrasts. Now he shapes his paragraphs and sentences according to the twists and turns of his thought, sharply warning the reader at each fork in the road. A good illustration of an effective paragraph from a summary of ar-

2. U.S. Supreme Court No. 73-78, October Term 1973.

gument appears in the government brief filed in *Vance v. Bradley,* here quoted with bracketed comments.

> In attacking the Foreign Service mandatory retirement age, appellees in this case advance an argument slightly different from that rejected by the Court in *Murgia.* [Introduction leading into topic and suggesting conclusion.] Appellees do not contend that the Constitution bars Congress from establishing a mandatory retirement age for Foreign Service employees. Nor do they maintain that Congress could not rationally choose to set that age at 60. Rather they argue that the equal component of the Due Process Clause precludes the legislature from establishing one mandatory retirement age for Foreign Service personnel and another for Civil Service personnel. [Sentences designed to isolate and pinpoint opponent's argument, in preparation for conclusion.] Appellees are wrong. [First brief statement of conclusion.] The Congressional decision to create different retirement systems with different mandatory retirement ages for the Foreign Service and the Civil Service is supported by an articulated rational basis and should be sustained. [Expanded conclusion.][3]

In this example, the authors limited their first sentence to a lead-in to the topic, which excluded all unnecessary details. The next three sentences could have been phrased in one, but separation of the ideas permits clarity and emphasis ("Appellees do not contend. . . . Nor do they maintain. . . . Rather they argue. . . ."), so that the reader will have no doubt of the argument's limited scope. The next sentence is extremely short, to state an emphatic conclusion. It calls for an explanation, but that is immediately supplied in the following and final sentence.

A comparable example of a paragraph in which an opposing point of view is examined and rejected appears in the opening brief of petitioner in the criminal case of *Leary v. United States.* Dr. Timothy Leary's attorneys argued that his privilege against self-incrimination had been violated, so as to provide a complete defense to a drug charge.

3. U.S. Supreme Court No. 77-1254, October Term 1978.

The Court of Appeals held that Petitioner by taking the stand and explaining his acquisition and transportation of marihuana waived his privilege (392 F.2d at 222). This holding is untenable. Petitioner testified as to the facts surrounding his possession of marihuana because of the presumption of illegality arising from his mere possession of marihuana under 21 U.S.C. §176a. If defending himself against the importation count amounts to an effective waiver of the privilege with respect to the tax count, then the Fifth Amendment privilege can be destroyed simply by the Government's joinder of an importation count and a tax count.[4]

Here Leary's attorneys describe the holding about which they complain and state that it is untenable (first two sentences), then state why Leary was forced to take the stand and thus did not willingly waive his privilege (third sentence), and finally point out that the result of the holding would be a routine destruction of the privilege (fourth sentence). Each sentence leads logically to the next, and to the conclusion that the procedure followed was unconstitutional.

For the reasons already suggested, a mere summary or digest of a case is not an effective paragraph in a brief. Too often judges are served up paragraphs that read like the following:

In *Smith v. Arnold,* the plaintiff claimed. . . . The evidence showed. . . . On these facts the court held. . . .

After reading such a paragraph a judge is left with nothing but questions. Why is the case relevant? What is the impact of the case? What, if anything, am I supposed to notice and remember and relate to the case before me? Effective brief writers will never merely digest a case. Instead they will discuss the case in such a way as to make a relevant point, and construct the paragraph to emphasize that point. For example

Directly on point in this respect is *Smith v. Arnold.* There, as here, the evidence was. . . . The court rejected an argument

4. U.S. Supreme Court No. 65, October Term 1968.

similar to appellant's argument here and held that.... ‖
Thus the case is persuasive authority that.... ‖

In this example the writer has not left the court to puzzle out the relevance of the cited authority. The relevant point is clearly expressed and defined.

How long should paragraphs be? There is no rule, because it all depends on how long it takes to express a simple thought. A paragraph may consist of a short sentence or two, as when the writer wishes to flag a major transition. For example

The plaintiff, however, need not rely on these common-law ‖
principles alone, for in the present case his rights are addi- ‖
tionally guaranteed by the United States Constitution. ‖

On the other hand a paragraph may be longer than a printed page and still not bore the reader. If, however, the expression of a single thought will make a paragraph of a page or more, the writer should try to invent some logical way to subdivide it. For example, he can use a connective to tell the reader that a new stage has been reached, although the general direction remains the same:

Two years later this Court reached the same conclusion ‖
in.... ‖
The reasoning of the court in the *Brown* case is worth sepa- ‖
rate emphasis. ‖

In this way paragraphs can be kept to a reasonable length, and the reader can follow the point-to-point progression of the argument.

THE STRUCTURE OF THE SENTENCE

Once a paragraph is mapped out, the writer constructs the sentences that are its component parts.

The first goal is to be concise, for needless words interfere with structure and clarity. Professor Strunk said it all in his timeless "little book," in the following perfectly chiseled paragraph:

> Vigorous writing is concise. A sentence should contain no unnecessary words, a paragraph no unnecessary sentences, for the same reason that a drawing should have no unnecessary parts. This requires not that the writer make all his sentences short, or that he avoid all detail and treat his subjects only in outline, but that every word tell.[5]

One common type of verbiage, particularly prevalent in legal writing, is the unnecessary introduction to the sentence proper. Consider the following examples:

It would appear (it would seem) that. . . .

It is (would appear to be, would seem to be) the case that. . . .

It is submitted (suggested, concluded) that. . . .

It is significant (important, interesting) to note that. . . .

It should be emphasized (pointed out) that. . . .

It is to be hoped (expected, should come as no surprise) that. . . .

It is the fact (the evidence, the law) that. . . .

It is our view (opinion, contention, assertion) that. . . .

It is not to be doubted (denied, gainsaid) that. . . .

Preliminarily (at the outset, as a threshold matter) it should be stated that. . . .

Moreover (furthermore, additionally) it should be recalled that. . . .

5. Strunk and White, The Elements of Style 23 (3d ed. 1979). Others have expressed the same point; *e.g.*, "As in architecture an excess of decoration is to be avoided, so in the art of literature a writer must guard against all rhetorical finery, all useless amplification, and all superfluity in general; in a word he must strive after *chastity* of style." Schopenhauer, On Style, in The Writer's Art by Those Who Have Practiced It 315 (R. Brown ed. 1921).

Finally (in summary, in light of the law, in view of the evidence) the conclusion is inescapable that. . . . ‖

Such preliminaries usually serve only to postpone the main thought of the sentence, in which case they are better omitted.

Other common types of wordiness are the unnecessary adjectives and adverbs, and the redundant phrases dealt with in the preceding chapter. The writer snuffs these out mainly by experimenting with their omission: If I delete this, how will it read? If a word or phrase contributes nothing it is stricken, and the sentence is immediately clearer and stronger than before.

What's left of a sentence, after the fat is pared off, should be structurally simple. The skeleton should show.

The essential working words in a sentence are the subject, the verb, and the object if there is one. These elements should appear to the reader at a glance. If they do not, the sentence will be shapeless and therefore unclear.

But many professional people avoid the key words in their writings. They hide the true subject, writing "It is considered that . . ." instead of "We think . . ." so as to avoid saying who is actually doing what. They write in passive verbs instead of active verbs, or convert their verbs into lengthy noun forms strung together with forms of the verb "to be" or equivalent ("She experienced a trembling sensation" instead of "She trembled"). The result is that the bare bones of a simple sentence are hidden away in a shapeless mishmash of professionalese. Consider, for a moment, the simple and memorable words from John F. Kennedy's inaugural address:

Ask not what your country can do for you; ask what you can do for your country. ‖

In professionalese such a thought might appear as something like this:

The preferred inquiry is not as to the benefits accruing to individuals that may be derived from national programs, ‖

41

but instead relates to the services to be rendered by individuals that may be promotive of national programs.

In this version the essential elements of the Kennedy sentence ("ask," "can do," "you," "your country") have disappeared. The skeleton is gone, and so is the shape, the clarity, and the force of the sentence.

At least half the task of writing clearly is being concise and keeping the key elements of the sentence in plain view; but the writer must also put the sentence's words in an understandable sequence. Clarity depends on the words themselves, but it also depends on the order in which the words appear.

Most important is the placing of the key words. A sentence will be clearer if the subject is placed near the verb and the verb is placed near the object, for then the reader will grasp the essence of the sentence at once. Lengthy inserts between the key words interrupt the sequence and obscure the thought. If possible, therefore, the writer will place nonessential material elsewhere, typically at the beginning or the end of the sentence. When this is not possible, the writer may need to split up the sentence. In the following examples the sentence on the left in each case is interrupted and disorganized; the one on the right represents a reordered and improved version.

Disorganized	*Improved*
Jones on October 10, 1981, accompanied by Smith and two other highly placed officers, toured the Panco facilities.	On October 10, 1981, Jones toured the Panco facilities, accompanied by Smith and two other highly placed officers.
The parties, with their counsel in attendance except in the case of Mr. White, who was a lawyer by training, executed the written, duly authorized instrument on December 1.	The parties executed the written, duly notarized instrument on December 1. All were represented by counsel except for Mr. White, who was himself a lawyer by training.

Descriptive words and phrases should be placed as close as possible to the words they modify, so that the reference is clear.[6] If they are near some other word, the reader may mistake the reference altogether. In the following pairs the sentence on the right has been reordered to provide a clear reference.

Reference unclear	*Reference clear*
He was the son of Samuel Black, who died intestate in 1980.	The son of Samuel Black, he died intestate in 1980.
The president stated that he hoped all stockholders would support his actions at the annual meeting.	The president stated at the annual meeting that he hoped all stockholders would support his actions.

If the subject of the sentence is very long it will in itself delay the introduction of the verb so as to make the sentence hard to follow. For example

The language of the Court in *Schmidt v. Wanamaker* to the effect that a contract will be vitiated by fraud and the holding in *Carley v. Blum* that the breach of the covenant in that case was not fraudulent are not inconsistent.

Here there is nothing inserted between the subject (the two clauses ending with the word *fraudulent*) and the verb (*are*), but the reader must wait until almost the end of the sentence to find out what the verb is, and thus to understand the point of the sentence. The writer's thought will be much easier to follow if the sentence is recast so that the key thought (*are not inconsistent*) appears at the beginning.

There is no inconsistency between the language of *Schmidt v. Wanamaker,* to the effect that a contract will be vitiated by

6. Further discussion of word placement, with examples, is given in Gowers, Plain Words: Their ABC 180-188 (1972).

fraud, and the holding of *Carley v. Blum,* that the breach of the covenant in that case was not fraudulent.

Now the reader has the central thought from the beginning, and knows what to look for in the remainder of the sentence.

In longer sentences the secret of clarity lies in a logical and visible structure: The relationship of each clause and phrase to the others must be made apparent, or the reader may not follow the thought.[7] A simple example of the extended sentence is the parallel sequence, as in a listing of similar things or similar thoughts. More complex thought sequences require more care, but their structure can be clearly illustrated if the writer will provide specific guidance to the reader at each major turn. Loose connections like *and, but, which* and *that* are usually insufficient. For example

The witness Goldstein testified on direct that when he talked to police officers after the accident it was already "almost dark," and passing cars "already had their lights on," which was a few minutes after the accident and which came from a concededly impartial witness.

Here the *which* conjunctions are loose and ambiguous. For greater clarity, the logical relationships among the clauses should be made express, as in the following:

The witness Goldstein testified on direct that when he talked to police officers after the accident it was already "almost dark," and passing cars "already had their lights on": a relevant observation, for Goldstein observed the darkness a few minutes after the accident, and a trustworthy observation, for Goldstein was concededly an impartial witness.

7. A very helpful chapter on "Sustaining the Longer Sentence" is contained in Williams, Style: Ten Lessons in Clarity & Grace 79-105 (1981). *See also* Goldfarb & Raymond, Clear Understandings: A Guide to Legal Writing 95-99 (1982).

In this example clarity is improved by first picking a word to refer to what the witness noticed (*observation*), then picking words to describe the two characteristics of the observation (*relevant* and *trustworthy*), and then setting these characteristics forth in parallel fashion.

As a rule, writers should take care to vary the structure of their sentences. They should avoid a series of complex sentences, and similarly should break up a string of simple, declarative ones. A variety of sentence formations will do away with monotonous sing-song.

There are times, however, when a succession of identical sentence structures will be very useful for emphasis. The writer wishing to stress the similarity of ideas can pound the point home by deliberate repetition of words in the same order. In the following sentences those on the left are phrased without repetition, whereas in those on the right repetition is used for emphasis.

Repetition not used	*Repetition used*
As a child the defendant did not have a happy home life. After his father left the home to enter the Army, his mother became an alcoholic and accordingly ignored the child.	As a child the defendant did not have a happy home life. His father abandoned him for the Army. His mother abandoned him for alcohol.
The defendant made no attempt to brake his car as the intersection approached. When he saw the child step off the curb he failed to sound his horn. After that, when the child ran out on the roadway, there was apparently no effort on his part to turn his car to the left or the right.	The defendant made no attempt to brake his car as the intersection approached. He made no attempt to sound his horn as he saw the child step off the curb. He made no attempt to turn to the left or the right as the child ran out into the roadway.

EXPRESSION THROUGH ORDER AND SEQUENCE

The order of words in sentences and paragraphs is itself a form of expression. One arrangement of words may imply similarity of ideas; another may suggest contrast. With one sequence the writer will emphasize a word or phrase; with a different sequence he can shift the emphasis elsewhere. Words change in shade and color like chameleons depending on where they are placed.

The importance of word order can be illustrated with a single example. In February, 1861, Abraham Lincoln addressed an audience in Springfield, Illinois as he was about to leave for Washington. The final words of his speech were designed to express his sadness in leaving his childhood home, perhaps for the last time. Here is how he arranged his words:

> No one, not in my situation, can appreciate my feeling of sadness at this parting. To this place, and the kindness of these people, I owe everything. Here I have lived a quarter of a century, and have passed from a young to an old man. Here my children have been born, and one is buried. I now leave, not knowing when or whether ever I may return, with a task before me greater than that which rested upon Washington. Without the assistance of that Divine Being who ever attended him, I cannot succeed. With that assistance I cannot fail. Trusting in Him who can go with me, and remain with you, and be everywhere for good, let us confidently hope that all will yet be well.[8]

Notice how Lincoln emphasized the importance of his birthplace by referring to it at the beginnings of three successive sentences ("To this place. . . . Here. . . . Here. . . .") and how he used a parallel structure to point a contrast ("Without the assistance. . . . With that assistance. . . ."). These are simple

8. Bartlett, Bartlett's Familiar Quotations 521 (15th ed. 1980).

words, but they become moving and memorable when arranged with such skill.

The brief writer will find it useful to become familiar with the following three techniques commonly used in arranging words for emphasis and force:

1. the placement of key words at the beginning or the end of sentences for emphasis
2. the placement of key words at the end of one sentence and the beginning of the next, so that they are opposed to each other and suggest contrast
3. the use of parallel word structures in order to emphasize the similarity of parallel thoughts

In a simple sentence the beginnings and the endings are the showcases. They attract the reader's attention because they are marked by full stops. Accordingly, if we wish to stress a word or phrase we normally place it at the beginning or the end of a sentence rather than in the middle. Consider, in the following set of sentences, the differences in emphasis.

The company in one year lost $10 million.
The company lost $10 million in one year.
In one year the company lost $10 million.
The issue is a narrow one on this appeal.
The issue on this appeal is a narrow one.
On this appeal the issue is a narrow one.

Normally a subordinate clause in a sentence is placed first, so that the main clause follows and is stressed by its placement at the end. Compare, for example, the following two sentences:

The cases are in principle the same, although there are some differences in the factual context.
Although there are some differences in the factual context, the cases are in principle the same.

47

In a parallel series, the words, clauses, or sentences should lead to the most important element in the series, so as to form a climax. Compare the following examples:

> The witness responded in one of three ways: he could not remember the meetings at all, he could not remember the conversations, or he could not remember the parties present.
>
> The witness responded in one of three ways: he could not remember the parties present, he could not remember the conversations, or he could not remember the meetings at all.

We can create further emphasis by inverting the normal word order of a sentence (subject-verb-object), placing the object first and thus emphasizing it.[9] Consider, for example, the emphatic effect of the inversions in the second sentences of the following pairs:

> He could tolerate laziness or even stupidity. He could not forgive disloyalty.
>
> He could tolerate laziness or even stupidity. Disloyalty he could not forgive.
>
> He invariably treated his daughters with affection. He adored his son from the day he was born.
>
> He invariably treated his daughters with affection. His son he adored from the day he was born.

Here the writer emphasizes a chosen word or a phrase ("disloyalty" and "his son") by placing it before the verb rather than after it.

Writers use the same principle—that words can be emphasized by placing them first or last in a sentence—when they set a key word or phrase at the end of one sentence in opposition to the first word or phrase in the next. Such a back-to-back placement signifies an abrupt change or contrast in

9. Further useful examples are given in Weihofen, Legal Writing Style 125 (2d ed. 1980).

meaning. Sometimes the opposed words are identical, as in the following examples:

It may not have achieved monopoly; monopoly may have been thrust upon it.
There is no such evidence anywhere in the record. The record, in fact, is all to the contrary.

The writer may also signal a distinction or contrast by juxtaposing words that sharply differ in meaning.

By then 85 percent of the market was in the control of this one giant corporation. No other company, none in the United States or abroad, controlled as much as 2 percent.
So much for the defendant's rights under the local ordinance. Under the Constitution of the United States his rights are broader.
General Industries has concentrated its predatory pricing practices on its major competitors. The smaller companies it does not bother with.

The third useful device, perhaps the most useful of all the devices in the lawyer's tool box, is the parallel structure. Parallel phrases, sentences, and clauses permit the brief writer to hold up one idea (phrased in a given sequence) against another idea (phrased in the same sequence) and then to compare or contrast them point for point. The similarity or dissimilarity will stand out because the parallel sequence invites a clear-cut comparison. The following are examples of parallel structures.

Ask not what your country can do for you; ask what you can do for your country.
Publicly he supported a policy of peace; privately he ordered preparations for war.
In that case, the plaintiff was a construction worker with limited education, who had no experience in business

transactions. In this case the plaintiff is an executive with an advanced degree, whose job it is to conduct business transactions.

In each of these examples the words are so ordered that the point-for-point comparison is clear.

Because briefs routinely require emphasis, contrast, and comparison, each of these three techniques is especially adaptable to brief writing.

PUNCTUATION AND TABULATION

Punctuation exists to promote clarity. Therefore if the writer thinks a pause should be indicated, a comma should be inserted, regardless of what the style books may say. If successive sentences are linked together in a train of thought, the writer should consider using semicolons, and should not reject them as old-fashioned: They do have a function. And if the argument leads to a conclusion or an example to be stated immediately (as in the preceding sentence), the author should not hesitate to use a colon.

Underlining is usually a confession of weakness in prose. If the writer chooses effective words, and chooses an effective structure for paragraphs and sentences, there will seldom, if ever, be a need to underline anything except a subhead or a case citation. Relying heavily on underlining results in less emphasis, not more.[10] As Judge Friedman of the United States Court of Appeals for the Federal Circuit has recently put it in an article:

10. "Italics should be sparingly used, exclamation points practically never, and capitalized boldfaced type not at all; rather the emphasis should result from the contents and the arrangement of the thoughts." Tate, The Art of Brief Writing: What a Judge Wants to Read, 4 Litigation 11, 12 (Winter 1978).

Effectiveness is lost by extensive capitalization, underlining, boldface type, or italics. These devices are helpful only if used on those rare occasions that emphasis dramatically drives a point home or draws an important contrast. But if every third sentence is underlined, there is no emphasis at all.[11]

Underlining usually means that the writer wants to emphasize a word, a phrase, or a sentence but does not know to do so otherwise. If a word does not stand out on its own, the remedy is to pick a better one, reorder the words in the sentence, or add detail or emphasis. But the underline itself is merely confusing and disruptive when applied to ordinary words and phrases, as in the following:

Appellants have never admitted that Smith met with Jones on May 20. Smith's testimony was that he did not meet with Jones on that day. Jones testified that he met with Smith in May but the actual date he could not remember.

In this example, is the writer's meaning different than it would be if the underlining were omitted? If so, what is the difference? Perhaps there is some other meaning, but if so it is better to specify it and forget the underline. For example

Appellants have never admitted, in any brief in response to any interrogatory or request for admission, that Smith met with Jones on May 20. Smith's testimony was clearly to the contrary: "I know I did not meet with him on that day. I was in Denver" (R.T. 545). Jones testified: "I believe I met with Mr. Smith sometime during May, but I have no record of the date" (R.T. 1372).

Only rarely—once or twice in a brief, if at all—is it useful to underline any part of the text. The best place to save it for is a key sentence, which constitutes the fulcrum of an entire argument or exposition. Even then the question remains

11. Friedman, Winning on Appeal, 9 Litigation 15, 17 (Spring 1983).

whether the underlining adds or detracts: Would the reader find it helpful or not?

The brief writer should beware of parentheses, dashes, question marks, and exclamation points because they are distracting.

Parentheses, or dashes or double dashes, are commonly used to enclose a thought outside the mainstream of a sentence. For example

> The difficulty with this argument (as we have already briefly mentioned under Point III above) is that it is supported by no authority.
>
> The witness Caldecott testified — if his testimony on this point or any other point can be believed — that he was not present at the time.

Digressions like this are distracting. The reader is asked to pull his attention away from the principal thought in his sentence, momentarily, and then direct it back again, all in a very brief period. He may not like being pulled and pushed; he may choose not to make the effort. In any case the resulting prose is unnecessarily difficult to follow.

The writer should be wary of questions unless they are purely rhetorical. He should follow the guiding principle of the cross-examining attorney, which is never to ask a question unless he knows what the answer must be, or, to put it another way, he should make all his questions rhetorical. The true question, which admits of more than one answer, has no place in a brief. The writer's purpose is not to pose questions, but to answer them.

Exclamation points, like underlines, should almost never be used. The writer can show surprise or emphasis with much greater force and clarity by choosing appropriate words. Using an exclamation point is no more than a way to blow off steam.

Lists and tables can be helpful, but they can also be overused. Whenever clear-cut categories exist, and the writer thinks it important that the reader have them clearly in mind, some kind of tabulation will be visually helpful. Consider the numbered list in the following example:

In the case of *Shapiro v. Bidwell* the Supreme Court reached three distinct holdings:
  1. ...
  2. ...
  3. ...
Only the last of these concerns us in the present case.

A tabulation is not a substitute, however, for logical organization. Thus to label a series of sentences or paragraphs with arbitrarily assigned letters or numbers does not help the reader: It makes him wonder if there is some significance to the letters or numbers that he has been unable to see from the text.

Not to be overlooked as a mechanical device is the use of two texts side by side on a page, as when the reader is asked to compare them word for word. Examples are drafts of contracts, drafts of legislation, and differing answers of witnesses. In these instances the physical arrangement of the two texts on the page is visually helpful to the reader and also underlines the writer's thought.

In general mechanical crutches added to a text are suspect. The writer should first try to choose and arrange words themselves so clearly and emphatically that they stand by themselves and need no artificial supports.

SUMMARY AND AN EXAMPLE

In this and the preceding chapter we have discussed the utility of concise expression, of vivid words and phrases, and of logical paragraphs and sentences; we have also discussed the importance of avoiding artificialities of all kinds.

These elements of style can be illustrated by selecting a

well-known paragraph and, in a leap into pure fiction, imagining how it might have evolved. Suppose, if the reader will, that he is a leader of a nation at war. He wants to write a speech stating the current policy of his country, and so he asks an assistant to draft a paragraph defining it. The next day the assistant hands him the following text:

> It is to be understood that the policy of this nation from this point in time onward shall be to engage the enemy by means of military action wherever any offensive operations are conducted by said enemy, not only in the initial phases but the later phases, and that, pursuant to the aforesaid policy, this nation will not, in any future time frame, be prepared to entertain proposals for negotiated solutions dependent upon the capitulation of our Armed Forces.

This paragraph accurately states the policy in question, but the wording is not what the political leader had in mind. His first thought is that the text has a number of extra words, which he proceeds to delete as follows:

> ~~It is to be understood that~~ the policy of this nation ~~from this point in time onward~~ shall be to engage the enemy ~~by means of military action~~ wherever any offensive operations are conducted by said enemy, not only in the initial phases but the later phases, and ~~that, pursuant to the aforesaid policy, this nation will not~~, in any future time frame, ~~be prepared to~~ entertain proposals for ~~negogiated solutions dependent upon~~ the capitulation of our Armed Forces.

The result looks like this:

> The policy of this nation shall be to engage the enemy wherever any offensive operations are conducted by said enemy, not only in the initial phases but the later phases, and not, in any future time frame, entertain proposals for the capitulation of our Armed Forces.

Despite these deletions, the leader decides, the text lacks force. Why? Well, in large part because it avoids simple and specific words. So he takes the remaining text and writes it out on one side of a page; on the other side he replaces the puffed-up phrases of the original with clear-cut working words, as follows:

The policy of this nation shall be to	We shall
engage the enemy	fight the enemy
wherever any offensive operations are conducted	everywhere
not only in the initial phases but the later phases	and at every step
and not, in any future time frame	and never
entertain proposals for the capitulation of our Armed Forces	surrender

Here is the result:

We shall fight the enemy everywhere and at every step and never surrender. ‖

Now, at least, he has a sharp, concise statement. It could stand as it is, but the leader decides that this should be the heart of the speech he is planning. Accordingly for this passage he wants emphasis. He needs concrete words that will bring home vividly to each of his countrymen the nature of the battles they may expect to fight. At the same time he needs the rhetorical power that comes from repetition, so that his words will roll out with the force of a drumbeat. If his name is Winston Churchill, and if the occasion is the eve of the Battle of Britain, this is what he writes:

We shall not flag or fail. We shall go on to the end. We shall fight in France, we shall fight on the seas and oceans, we shall fight with growing confidence and growing strength in the air, we shall defend our island, whatever the cost may be, we shall fight on the beaches, we shall fight on the landing grounds, we shall fight in the fields and in the streets, we shall fight in the hills; we shall never surrender.[12]

Now he has a text that will move his listeners. In fact, as we know, it moved the whole free world.

12. Churchill, Speech on Dunkirk, House of Commons, June 4, 1940, as quoted in Bartlett, Bartlett's Familiar Quotations 744 (15th ed. 1980).

4
CONTINUITY
IN EXPOSITION

The paragraphs in a brief may be thought of as steps along a path. Each is a separately articulated thought, but each is also part of a logical and continuous progression. The reader should have a sense that he is being guided in a purposeful direction, from the chosen beginning of his walk to its carefully planned destination.

The writer obtains obtains such continuity in large part by arranging his paragraphs in a logical sequence. The more he can set them out in a direct line, each closely placed in logic to the next, the less he will need to guide the reader from step to step. Where, however, the direction must be altered, as at turning points in his exposition, he provides signals, in words and phrases, to make sure that the reader comes along with him.

Because briefs deal with inherently complex sequences of thought, sure-handed guidance is especially important. Once the judge who reads the brief misses a connection his mind is at large; he has temporarily lost the sequence. He may later find it, but only with difficulty, and only with some sense of annoyance. The brief writer should make every effort to avoid any such mishap.

ORGANIZING PARAGRAPHS IN SEQUENCE

Lawyers are skilled at thinking in logical progressions, but they do not always express them clearly, simply, and step by step. At times they take too large a leap, failing to set in place the intervening stepping stones. At other times they insert detours, without realizing that the reader cannot readily follow them and still return to the principal sequence. In both these ways brief writers can lose the sense of continuity that keeps a reader's attention.

Frequently a writer will omit some logical intervening step between paragraphs because to him it is implicit and obvious. He may forget that the reader does not know, as the author does, where the chosen path will lead. What is obvious to him is not obvious to his reader at all, but must be expressed.

To guard against such omissions the writer will do well to develop the habit of testing each transition between paragraphs. Is there a break in thought here? Is there a gap? If the drafter is not sure of the answer, there is nothing like experimenting with an intervening paragraph to spell out whatever transition in thought there may be. This can tell the writer whether he is belaboring the obvious or has located a significant break in the argument's progression. If an intervening paragraph is needed to fill a gap the writer may wonder how he could have overlooked such an omission in the first place, but he need not be surprised. It is a normal experience in brief writing for the author's mind to leap ahead, leaving gaps large and small, and it is a routine task in revising briefs to spot such gaps and fill them in.

Brief writers also commonly make the opposite mistake. Instead of omitting a logically necessary paragraph they include an extra one that does not contribute to the progression of thought. The extra paragraph may be mere surplusage, in which case it slows down the reader's progress but does not divert him from the path. Much more serious is the logically unrelated paragraph, which the writer has misguidedly inserted into an otherwise logical sequence. Often the paragraph begins with an introductory clause such as "It is interesting to note that . . ." or "It may be noted in passing that . . .", or, still more revealingly, "While not relevant to the present argument, it should be pointed out that. . . ." Usually the writer permits himself such a digression because he has in mind some fact or authority that he feels should be in the brief somewhere, but he has not found an appropriate place for it.

When a brief writer is tempted to disgress from his planned thought sequence he should ask himself the hard question: "Which is more important, this isolated information or the continuity of my argument?" He then must be ruthlessly honest in giving his answer, which usually means he will set the material aside. Perhaps he will later find a good place for it or build a new and separate argument around it, or perhaps he will find that it is not worth preserving and therefore will omit it entirely. In the meantime, however, he should cast it aside, and clear the roadway for his thought.

The impairment of continuity will not be wholly avoided by dropping the extraneous material into a footnote. Either the footnote will be ignored or it will be noticed. If it is noticed it will distract the reader at least momentarily.

As a general rule, the only way to write in a continuous flow of thought is to omit extraneous material entirely. If it will not fit a sequence, out it goes. If it will confuse the reader, out it goes. If it is merely of passing interest, out it goes.

SIMPLE TRANSITIONS

When paragraphs are laid out in a clear and logical sequence they do not require elaborate introductions. Each new paragraph follows by a simple step from the one before. Nevertheless, a word or a phrase or a sentence will help the reader to take that step.

Transitional words should be specific enough to guide the reader's thought from one topic to the next. Their purpose is not merely to signal a stop or a pause: the reader can see for himself that a new paragraph is coming. What he wants and needs, if he is to proceed easily from thought, is a preview of the writer's new direction.

For this reason mere numbers placed before paragraphs, as "first," "second," "third," etc., are not helpful as transitions unless the numbers have some independent significance, which they normally do not. Numbers may give some sense of organization, but only superficially, for the numbers are unrelated to the thought itself. Thus if the writer puts down

First, ... (and then writes a paragraph dealing with a factual argument)

Second, ... (and then writes an argument based on reason)

Third, ... (and then writes a discussion of the cases)

the ordinal numbers express nothing. A preview of the new paragraph is needed, which will link it in some way with the paragraph before. For example

Appellants' argument cannot be squared with the evidence in this case. They ignore the fact that ...

Logically, as well, appellants' argument is indefensible. Their premise appears to be ...

Not surprisingly, appellants' illogical argument finds no support in the law. The key case they have cited ...

At this point the writer is providing helpful transitions.

"Connective" words placed at the beginning of paragraphs are hardly more expressive than numbers. Suppose, for example, that we read successive paragraphs introduced as follows:

The trial court erred in admitting the testimony of Jones that ...

Moreover, Mr. Jones's testimony was that ...

Furthermore, Jones's testimony was contrary to Smith's, which stated that ...

However, the trial court found that ...

Here the "connectives" do not signal the thought to follow. They do not really connect. With a little effort, the writer can do far better.

> The trial court erred in admitting the testimony of Jones that . . .
>
> Even if properly admitted, Jones's testimony did not support the finding because it was limited to . . .
>
> On the other hand, Smith testified specifically, and contrary to the finding, that . . .
>
> Although the only evidence on the subject matter of the finding was Smith's testimony summarized above, the trial court found that . . .

Now the writer is providing transitions that guide the reader from one paragraph to the next.

In a statement of facts, transitions are relatively simple. If the writer's exposition is proceeding in chronological order, as in the following examples, transitional sentences will typically signal the passage of time.

> It was not until four years later, in May 1981, that Carter again met with Pierce to discuss the possible acquisition.
>
> By the following afternoon the directors had issued a policy statement.
>
> From then on, no further mention was made of the proposal on either side.
>
> On the same morning Maxfield put in a call for the Chairman of the Board.

If, however, the exposition moves from one topic to another, and the time period is the same, the writer will invent transitions designed to guide the reader from subject to subject. For example

> Meanwhile the defendants were already on Flight 232, on their way to Zurich.

At the same time, at the suggestion of Dr. Weaver, Mrs. Bellamy made a series of visits to a psychiatrist.

Aggressive sales techniques such as these were supported by a new and massive advertising campaign.

In a legal argument the relationship among paragraphs is often more difficult to convey than it is in a statement of facts, for the thought is largely abstract and the transitions may be subtle. All the more reason exists, therefore, to make the attempt. The more common types of transitions, drafted to reflect the logical relationships between paragraphs that are typically found in an argument, are illustrated below.

Similarity
Parallel on its facts is the recent decision in *Ripley v. Comstock.*

All of the ensuing correspondence is in the same vein.

Dissimilarity
Alone in this series of cases is the contrary decision of the court in the *Gault* case.

The new machine developed in Germany is radically different in design.

Comparability
A more conclusive authority is the new decision in this Circuit, *Cohen v. McIntyre.*

Of all the plaintiff's witnesses, the most emphatic on the point was John Allison.

Extended Thought
Not only did Mayer read the letter before it was mailed; he helped to compose it.

If the parties' intent was clear enough in 1978, it became unmistakable afterwards.

In these circumstances, the trial judge had no choice but to make the ruling complained of.

More Specific Thought

The prejudicial nature of the evidence so admitted deserves special mention.

The *Flynn* case so relied upon by appellant merits particular analysis.

Conflicting Thought

This testimony was directly contradicted by the witness Smith.

To the contrary, the courts of this state have never so held.

Limited Concession

Whether or not the Court rules in appellant's favor in this respect, the judgment should be affirmed.

To be sure, there are a few early decisions to the contrary, but each has been distinguished or discredited.

New Direction in Thought

Appellant's position is without merit for an entirely different reason.

So much for appellant's theory of laches; his theory of estoppel is even less supportable.

COMPLEX TRANSITIONS

A transition between thoughts may often extend beyond the wording of a single introductory sentence. It may take up two or more sentences in a paragraph, or all of it. It may include the closing words of the last sentence of the preceding paragraph, as well as the first words of the next.[1]

A change in thought may be signaled emphatically by using

1. One good way to link paragraphs is to repeat a key word from the prior paragraph in the succeeding paragraph. Useful examples are given in Brooks and Warren, Modern Rhetoric 277-279 (2d ed. 1958).

the first two sentences of a paragraph, one negative and one positive, to stress the point of difference. For example

> This was not the holding in *Robinson v. Lathrop*. The court in *Robinson* decided the case entirely on a vested rights theory.
>
> This may be appellant's reading of the *Garfield* case. It is not, however, the interpretation placed upon it by the commentators.
>
> The witness never once made any such statement. All he said, at any point in this testimony, was that Cox looked like someone he had seen before.
>
> The policy does contain such a clause setting forth such exceptions. But it also includes an endorsement specifically designed to limit those exceptions.

An especially useful technique, which makes for a smooth and sure transition between paragraphs, is to begin the shift in thought at the end of one paragraph and follow it more specifically at the beginning of the next. In this way the reader can be warned and generally prepared for a change in direction. He will expect it and perhaps anticipate where it will take him. Then, as he starts the new paragraph, he receives the signal itself. For example

> ... These, in summary, are respondent's contentions in opposition to the petition.
>
> Respondent never addresses the central point set forth in the petition.
>
> ... As the result of these evidentiary rulings, the way was open for plaintiff to resolve the claimed ambiguities in the contract by parol testimony.
>
> Plaintiff, however, never offered testimony from those most familiar with the contract negotiations.
>
> ... After her release from the hospital, Mrs. Cartwright displayed no additional symptoms, but she grew progressively weaker.

> In May of the next year Mrs. Cartwright died of a coronary occlusion.
>
> . . . By this time the "doctrine" of the *Allen* case was so riddled with exceptions that there was little left of the original holding.
>
> The *Allen* doctrine sustained its mortal blow in *Calloway v. Kentucky.*
>
> . . . It was at this point that the company management began a reappraisal of its employment policies.
>
> In 1972 the company for the first time began to hire minorities on a preferential basis.

This technique, which might be called the double transition, is well illustrated by the opinion in *Cabell v. Markham.* The defendants had argued for a literal interpretation of a statute. The court responded, in an opinion by Learned Hand, J., that such a reading was "unreasonable" and "really nonsense," in a paragraph concluding as follows:

> . . . The defendants have no answer except to say that we are not free to depart from the literal meaning of the words, however transparent may be the resulting stultification of the scheme or plan as a whole.

At this point the reader is prepared for the court's emphatic reply, commencing at the beginning of the next paragraph.

> Courts have not stood helpless in such situations; the decisions are legion in which they have refused to be bound by the letter, when it frustrates the patent purpose of the whole statute.[2]

This introductory sentence was followed by a discussion of the authorities, which of course supported the court's view and demolished defendants' argument.

A good example of the use of complex transitions in the exposition of an entire argument may be found in the opinion

2. *Cabell v. Markham,* 148 F.2d 737, 739 (2d Cir. 1945).

of Rehnquist, J., in *Chrysler Corp. v. Brown.* The question was whether Chrysler could enjoin an agency from disclosing information held in its files. The Supreme Court held, among other things, that the Freedom of Information Act did not expressly or impliedly permit such an injunction. Its opinion begins by stating that the point had not previously been decided, but adds, at the end of the first paragraph, a broad hint of what is to come.

> . . . We have, moreover, consistently recognized that the basic objective of the Act is disclosure.

The Court then summarizes Chrysler's contentions in a paragraph, ending with a preview of its reasoning and decision.

> . . . In fact, [Chrysler's] conclusion is not supported by the language, logic, or history of the Act.

In the next two paragraphs the Court deals with the language of the Act, using introductory sentences as follows:

> The organization of the Act is straightforward. . . .
> That the FOIA is exclusively a disclosure statute is, perhaps, demonstrated most convincingly by examining its provision for judicial relief. . . .

Next the Court deals with its second reason, as previously introduced, stating that the Act need not logically be interpreted to bar the disclosure of exempted material. Then comes the third point, which the Court begins with a straightforward introductory sentence

> This conclusion is further supported by the legislative history.[3]

Now the Court is ready for its conclusion, which has already been signaled repeatedly for the reader.

A more extended example of the use of complex transi-

3. *Chrysler Corp. v. Brown,* 441 U.S. 281, 290-294 (1979).

tions is afforded by a passage from the Respondents' Brief in *Niemi v. National Broadcasting Company, Inc.,* in which counsel were distinguishing a case much cited by their opposition. *Niemi* was a tort claim brought by a minor who had been sexually assaulted by other girls following the telecast of a dramatic presentation that, among other incidents, depicted a similar assault. The network defended on First Amendment grounds, pointing out that nothing in the telecast urged its viewers to imitate the criminal act they had witnessed in the show. The appellants relied heavily on an earlier case in which a radio station had been held liable for acts committed by listeners following a broadcast. The respondents dealt with that decision in the following section of their brief, as set forth below with interspersed commentary.

> Throughout the proceedings in this case appellant has insisted that the California Supreme Court's decision in *Weirum v. RKO General, Inc.,* 15 Cal. 3d 40, 539 P.2d 36, 123 Cal. Rptr. 468 (1975), somehow renders the First Amendment inapplicable to this case. For much the same reasons as those set forth immediately above we believe that *Weirum* is simply irrelevant to these proceedings. Because of the importance appellant evidently attaches to the *Weirum* decision, it will be considered at some length.

[Paragraph introducing *Weirum* case, ending with statement that case will now be considered in detail.]

> *Weirum* involved a promotional radio contest designed to advertise the radio station KHJ. In connection with that contest, a KHJ radio announcer urged listeners to drive to a designated location at which a cash prize would be awarded to the first to arrive. As described by presiding Justice Files, dissenting from the Court of Appeal's decision (which was reversed by the California Supreme Court):
>
>> KHJ, by the conditions of its contest, and by the exhortations of its announcer, invited and encouraged youthful contestants to race through the public streets, and rewarded the swiftest with cash prizes. (119 Cal. Rptr. 151, 158 (1975))

[Paragraph stating facts of *Weirum* case, ending with key quote to the effect that listeners wre exhorted, invited, and encouraged to speed in their automobiles.]

Responding to these exhortations, which the California Supreme Court characterized as "repeated importuning" (15 Cal. 3d at 48, 539 P.2d at 41, 123 Cal. Rptr. at 473) two teenage drivers exceeded legal speed limits and forced another car off the road, killing its driver, whose widow brought suit against both other drivers and the radio station. In the course of an opinion which considered, in the main, whether a claim against the radio station could be upheld in such circumstances as a matter of negligence law, the Supreme Court also held that a claim against RKO based upon the giveaway contest was not barred by the First Amendment. "The First Amendment does not sanction the infliction of physical injury merely because achieved by word, rather than act." (15 Cal. 3d at 48, 539 P.2d at 40, 123 Cal. Rptr. at 472.)

[Note how paragraph keys to the one before ("Responding to those exhortations") and then keys into the paragraph following with the quotation concerning injuries "achieved" by words.]

As should be evident, this holding goes no further than the type of case discussed above; it has no impact here. *Weirum* did not involve, as does this case, a dramatic broadcast. The giveaway contest which the Court found unprotected by the First Amendment was rather described as an "attempt . . . to generate a competitive pursuit on public streets, accelerated by repeated importuning by radio to be the very first to arrive at a particular destination." (15 Cal. 3d at 48, 539 P.2d at 41, 123 Cal. Rptr. at 473) In that context the Court ruled that the First Amendment did not preclude tort liability for injury "achieved" as a result of the contest.

[Point foreshadowed in previous paragraph now driven home; injuries "achieved" by words are those that directly result from urging or importunings in the broadcast.]

Thus, as Judge Dossee recognized, liability in *Weirum* is consistent with the distinction between sanctions imposed on expression and sanctions imposed on speech intended and directed to lead the listener to certain actions. For this reason, *Weirum* does not affect the application of the First Amendment to the claim here. It is one thing to impose upon broadcasters an obligation to avoid self-promotional contests which *urge* listeners to *act* by participating in inherently dangerous activities. It is quite another to suggest that the First Amendment permits the imposition of liability with respect to the telecasting of a drama because someone allegedly "got the idea" for a criminal act from seeing — or hearing about — a scene not intended to "urge anyone to do anything unlawful," *Street v. New York*, 394 U.S. 576, 591 (1969).[4]

[Concluding paragraph, pointing contrast between *Weirum* principle and principle applicable to dramatic shows in which no one is urged to commit an unlawful act.]

Transitions such as those just illustrated deserve to be carefully drafted and freely used. They do not create organization by themselves, but they powerfully illuminate it, and so guide the reader through the inevitable twists and turns of argument.

HEADINGS AND SUBHEADINGS

At some stage in the construction of his argument the writer will reach a clear-cut stopping point. He is through with one logical sequence of ideas and has summarized his position for the reader. He is ready to move on to another sequence. Similarly he may reach logical stopping points in his statement of facts. He has summarized the evidence in one topic, and is ready to deal with the next.

At each of these points the brief writer should consider

4. *Niemi v. National Broadcasting Company, Inc.*, Cal. Ct. App. (1st Dist., Div. Four) No.1 Civil 46981.

inserting a heading or a subheading, not merely to signal a change in the direction of his thought but to provide the court with a convenient reference point. The heading should not only state the topic to follow but should be included in the table of contents, so that the court can readily turn to it. When so used, headings are a valuable aid.

Headings and subheadings, however, are no more than frames for the successive pictures that the writer paints. Each picture should be complete without them. The reader should be able to follow each section of the brief, each logical sequence from its introduction to its conclusion, without any headings at all. The headings will neatly set off each section, but they are no substitute for continuity, clarity, and emphasis in the text itself.

Thus, for example, in a memorandum in support of a motion for summary judgment in *Tsakopoulos v. County of Sacramento* the author ended one section of his brief and began another with the following sequence of text, subhead, and renewed text:

> Thus, a plaintiff's complaint of "obnoxious odors" must be grounded on the theory of nuisance. However, he is barred from relief for nuisance by way of damages or injunction by section 731a because he has failed to allege facts or demonstrate that Sacremento Rendering Company's operations are unreasonable or injurious.

D. Plaintiff's Act Does Not Fall Within The "Offensive Odor" Exception to Section 731a

This third part of section 731a relates specifically to offensive odors. It provides, "[n]othing in this act shall be deemed to apply to the *regulation and working hours* of canneries, fertilizing plants, refineries and other similar establishments whose operation produce offensive odors." (Emphasis added.) However, this exception to section 731a is inapplicable in this case.[5]

5. *Tsakopoulos v. County of Sacramento*, Cal. Sup. Ct. Sacramento Co., No. 257976.

When overused, headings can be disruptive and a detriment to continuity. Thus if a sequence of thought proceeds naturally from its introduction to a logical conclusion it will usually be a mistake to introduce subheadings merely because the sequence proceeds for several pages or merely because the sequence passes through different phases or stages as it goes. The reader may assume that the heading signals an end to the sequence, when it is not so intended. Headings, in short, should be inserted only at the logical stopping points in the text.

The writer should also make sure that headings express the essence of the accompanying text as nearly as possible. If they do not, they will be misleading, as newspaper headlines are misleading when they overstate a news story. The writer cannot afford this. If a judge reads a heading and then finds it is not supported by the text, he will begin to doubt the trustworthiness of the brief as a whole.

In a word, headings and subheadings should be dictated by the text itself. They cannot be allowed an independent life in which to roam free, attracting the reader's attention as they go. They must be used only to set off a distinct portion of the text, and so phrased as to express the essence of it.

5

THE ELEMENTS OF PERSUASION

A brief should be designed and written so that it will, by itself and without the aid of oral argument, persuade the judges and clerks for whom it is written. Because the brief constitutes the only complete argument the advocate will make to the court, the writer cannot afford to draft it merely as a source of information, like a reference work or a law review article, and then rely on oral argument to carry the burden of persuasion. The brief itself should do the job.

How, in general, does the brief writer approach the task of persuasion? Over 2000 years ago, Aristotle identified the three major elements of rhetoric, or persuasion, as follows:

Ethos, the element in which the speaker establishes his own character and credentials, and hence his believability

Pathos, the element in which the speaker appeals to his listeners' emotions, so that they are disposed to decide in his favor

Logos, the final element, in which the speaker provides the logical reasons why his side of the issue should prevail[1]

In a brief, all three elements should be convincingly established.

Brief writers establish their own character and credentials, or the element of *ethos,* primarily by being accurate and honest in what they say. They build confidence on the part of judges by making each statement trustworthy. Remembering that a case need not be perfect but only better than an opponent's, they do not risk forfeiting the trust of the judges with exaggerations or evasions at any point.

The second element of rhetoric, *pathos,* is established by

1. See, e.g., Ross, Aristotle 271 (5th ed. 1949).

74

painting a sympathetic picture of the client and the client's cause. Throughout the brief, by their statement of facts and by their approach to the argument, successful brief writers demonstrate to the court the individual equities and the overall policies of the law that favor their position. Their aim is to induce the judges to want to decide for their client if there is any legally justifiable way to do so.

Last, brief writers supply judges and their clerks with the element of *logos*—the most logical and precedential reasons that support a favorable decision. Collectively, these reasons appear as the Argument of the brief. Together they furnish the raw materials for an opinion, if one is called for, or in any case the reasoned basis for a decision.

These remain the essential elements in the art of persuasion. Persuasion is an art, and accordingly lawyers differ on its finer points. But judges and most effective advocates will agree on its fundamentals, which remain essentially unchanged since the time of Aristotle.

UNDERSTANDING THE JUDGES

Persuasion begins with sensitivity. The writer or speaker seeks to understand his audience: who they are, what they want, what they need. If he can do this, he can take the next step, which is to shape a convincing brief; but if he does not understand his audience, he is communicating in a vacuum.

Advocates may differ from automobile salespeople, but they can learn from them. The good salesman has no doubt of his first step. When a potential customer walks in, he approaches, introduces himself, and immediately starts to size up his prospect. He notes at once how the customer dresses and talks, and whether that person is looking at the engine or the upholstery or the price sticker. A word here, a question there, and the salesman has his profile. A few more words, a few more questions, and he can guess what the customer really wants and will actually will buy. The salesman's antennae are sensitive because his livelihood depends on keeping them so.[2]

If the advocate is to be persuasive, he or she will be no less sensitive. The advocate will find out all he can about the individual judges who will decide his case: what decisions they have made before on similar issues; what they may have written in opinions or public statements; what has been their education, their prior professional experience, their religious and political affiliations, their hobbies and interests; what other lawyers who know them have to say about them. This information he will bear in mind when he writes his brief. It may not affect the logical progression of his argument, but it may influence what he chooses to highlight or emphasize. Certainly it will shape his ultimate decision on how to appeal to the court's sense of equity and justice. The court, after all, consists of individuals. If the advocate is to persuade them, he must persuade them as individuals.[3]

The advocate must also be careful not to ignore the clerks or staff attorneys on whose labors judges increasingly rely.[4] Some, like the four clerks now permitted to each justice of the Supreme Court of the United States, are typically young; others, like the three allotted to each Federal circuit judge, the two assigned to each Federal district judge, or the varying numbers assigned to state court appellate judges, may be permanent staff members. Some clerks have strong political persuasions to the left or the right, which may or may not be the same as those of the judges themselves; some have a marked desire to change the law in one direction or another, which may not be shared at all by the judge they assist. Clerks' predilections may be difficult or impossible to discover, but reasonable assumptions may be made about them that may affect the

2. "An appellate advocate is a salesman. His skill in advocacy is shown by how well he 'sells' his wares." Gurfein, Appellate Advocacy, Modern Style, 4 Litigation 8 (Winter 1978).

3. "To enter a courtroom without awareness of the particular judge's performance in the very area of the law under discussion is, in my view, to court disaster." Rifkind, Appellate Courts Compared, in Counsel on Appeal 163, 171 (Charpentier ed. 1968).

4. See Kester, The Law Clerk Explosion, 9 Litigation 20 (Spring 1983).

tone and content of the brief. For example, it may be a safe assumption that a young law school graduate will be less concerned with precedent than the judge to whom he or she sends a memorandum; if so, an ingenious and novel argument may be justified. Then again, when the issue in a case is between subordinates and their supervisors, the clerk may relate to the one and the judge more readily to the other; if so, the brief should be careful not to offend the sensibilities of either.

Apart from whatever is possible to guess about individual readers, the advocate should know the characteristics of judges as a group. They share a specialized vocation, and therefore have much in common. Judges are professional buyers of ideas. As such they are professionally skeptical, for they listen to salespeople every day. Nevertheless they will pay attention to a good presentation, not only because they are required to make a decision one way or another, but because they depend on the advocates for both sides to provide essential facts and ideas. Judges are proud of their high calling, but they also have great respect for other members of the bar. They never stop hoping that each advocate who appears before them will merit their respect and earn their admiration.

Judges wield great power in individual cases, but their powers, nevertheless, are sharply limited. Accordingly, judges urge lawyers to recognize both their powers and the limits of those powers. A trial judge will be impatient if an advocate fails to focus on the authorities from higher courts in his jurisdiction, for he has no choice but to obey them. Appellate judges wearily reject the advocate's attempt to retry a case merely because he has lost it below, for they have no power to do so.[5] At the same time, judges sitting on courts of last resort are particularly sensitive to the broad impact of any opinion they may write. Accordingly, they invite the advocate to address not merely the immediate case but also the merits of the rule of law they are asked to affirm or modify.[6]

When the brief writer has thought through what he knows about the judges on his court, and found out what he can

5. See Chapter 9, pages 162-163.
6. See Chapter 9, pages 165-166.

about them individually, and what he can find out or safely assume about their clerks or staff attorneys, he will have a good sense of what he must do to persuade his readership. He may never have met them or seen them, but he will still be acquainted with how they think and what facts and authorities and arguments will be most convincing. With this in mind he can plan his approach. It may or may not persuade them, but at least he will be talking their language.[7]

EQUITY AND SOCIAL POLICY

The goal of the judge is not merely to reach a decision supported by a rule of law, but to dispense justice to the parties. Accordingly he will be uncomfortable with an argument based on precedent alone, unless it is clear to him where the equities lie. Often he is not required to follow the precedents cited in such an argument; there are overlapping rules of law and conflicting precedents that could also serve as the basis for decision. Accordingly he searches for those rules that will do justice and equity. Here, too, he looks to counsel for guidance. He can read the authorities, but he wants the advocate, with his fuller understanding of the parties and their dispute, to tell him which of his options will bring about a just result.[8]

The judge's clerk or staff attorney who first reads the briefs and then writes a memorandum to the judge may also be

7. "If the places were reversed and you sat where they do, think of what you would want to know about the case. How and in what order would you want the skein unravelled? What would make easier your approach to the true solution? These are questions the advocate must unsparingly put to himself. This is what I mean by changing places with the court." Davis, the Argument of an Appeal, in A Case on Appeal 97 (4th ed. 1967).

8. "Now the kind of help that a judge needs in deciding cases is very simply expressed: He wants a just result in this case by a just procedure." Breitel, A Summing Up, in Counsel on Appeal 193, 202 (Charpentier ed. 1968).

expected to care about the apparent equities. Perhaps it cannot be safely said that the staff person is more concerned with individual justice and less concerned with the structure of the law than the judge who must live with his decision, but at least there is no reason to believe the opposite. The clerk will learn of the equities with interest, and presumably they will affect the memoranda he prepares.

If the just and equitable result becomes evident to the judges and their clerks through the process of briefing and oral argument, they will try to find a way to reach that result. As Judge Gurfein of the Second Circuit has written,

> It is still the mystery of the appellate process that a result is reached in an opinion on thoroughly logical and precedential grounds while it was first approached as the right and fair thing to do.[9]

The key word here is "first." The judges and their staffs will first form an impression of where the equities are from scanning the briefs. Analysis of the authorities and the hearing of the oral argument follow later, and still later the opinion is written, all against the background of the judges' and clerks' first impressions of the case. Under these circumstances it is not entirely surprising or mysterious that judges will so often find logical and precedential grounds to reach the result that they have already decided is "the right and fair thing to do."

For the advocate this lesson is unmistakable. Because judges will normally read or scan the briefs first, then hear oral argument, and then analyze the issues and decide, the brief writer has an invaluable opportunity. In the brief itself, and right from the beginning of it, he should give the judges and their clerks the impression that his client's position is just and fair. From then on his brief and his oral argument need only show them the way to rationalize the result they already desire to

9. Gurfein, *supra* note 2, at 9. Judge Gurfein concludes, "If there is any legitimate way to argue the equities it should be done, though not in the style of jury summation."

reach. If he can do this successfully, his opponent's arguments must bear the incomparably greater burden of showing the judges and their staffs that there is no acceptable way for them to reach the result they want.

The question then is not whether the brief writer should point out the justice in his client's position, but how. What will appeal to the judges as "right and fair," and when and how can such equitable considerations be effectively expressed?

In part, the circumstances that appeal to judges and their clerks are those that would appeal to anyone. The advocate depicts his client as a sympathetic individual, or a responsible and forward-looking company, or an even-handed agency of the government. The client's opponent, unfortunately, lacks such characteristics, as the evidence all too clearly shows. The dispute itself is one-sided. For the plaintiff a great wrong has been committed, which cries out for redress, whereas for the defendant there is no wrong, and it is regrettable that the court's time and energy should be lavished on such a storm in a teacup.

Such, simplistically stated, are the equities for the individual parties, but the advocate also must be concerned with the effects of the decision on nonparties. Appellate judges, and particularly judges in courts of last resort, are acutely aware that hard cases can make bad law. The precedents they set in the interest of doing justice in one case may come back to haunt them in a series of others. Accordingly judges must consider the equities as applied to the categories and classes of parties affected; they must adopt rules of law they can live with. As Chief Justice Vanderbilt of New Jersey wrote,

> Counsel should hesitate to rest his case on mere technicalities, however strongly they may be embedded in earlier decisions. He should never feel safe unless he can and does demonstrate the reasonableness and utility of the rule he is advocating.[10]

To put it another way, the advocate must deal with the policy of the law, and the social policies that the law affects, when-

10. Vanderbilt, Forensic Persuasion, 7 Wash. & Lee L. Rev. 1, 24 (1950).

ever he appeals to judges who have the power to influence such policies.[11]

The experienced advocate starts to evaluate the equities of his case from the moment he is retained because he knows they will shape his strategy. At the same time he starts to persuade himself of the justice of his client's position, because he knows he will be expressing it at every turn. This is not to say that in his heart of hearts he is totally convinced that his client should win. The advocate is not the judge. But he will, like any good salesman, know each appealing feature of the case he advocates and each weakness of his opponent's case, and he will be wholly convinced, at the least, that these features deserve the consideration of the court.

When he comes to write a brief the advocate uses the appealing features of his case as an equitable setting for his argument. He does not so much push them to the forefront as allow them to show through, for he is already persuaded of their importance. All he needs is some legitimate reason to refer to or suggest them. Accordingly, whenever the equities have some bearing on the issues before the court—directly or as relevant background that could influence the decision—the advocate will permit them to shape his argument, his statement of the facts, his choice of words, so that the judges will glimpse his point of view. He is convinced that they should understand what is right and fair from his client's perspective.

As an illustration of the advocate's way of thinking about a

11. The potentially decisive importance of major social policies is illustrated by the various opinions in *Steelworkers v. Weber*, 443 U.S. 193 (1979). On the one hand was the language of Title VII of the Civil Rights Act of 1964, which appeared to prohibit discrimination against whites as well as blacks; on the other was the nation's policy of trying to right a history of social wrongs suffered by blacks. The opinion of Justice Blackmun, concurring, shows how the majority of the Court decided. As he put it (443 U.S. at 214), "Strong considerations of equity support an interpretation of Title VII that would permit private affirmative action to reach where Title VII itself does not."

He then concluded (443 U.S. at 215), "In short, the passages marshaled by the dissent are not so compelling as to merit the whip hand over the obvious equity of permitting employers to ameliorate the effects of past discrimination for which Title VII provides no direct relief."

case, let us imagine that the brief writer is concerned with a motion to suppress in a robbery case. For the prosecution, the motion is one of those regrettable though perhaps inevitable impediments to the cause of justice. The defendant is clearly guilty of the crime charged and a conviction is a foregone conclusion if the motion is defeated. In this instance, the police officers had reason to suspect what the search might discover and, once it was made, their suspicions were amply justified. Accordingly the brief for the prosecution stresses the facts showing guilt and measures the reasonableness of the search by the salutary results achieved.

For the defense the underlying considerations are wholly different. What is at stake is a constitutional principle far transcending in importance the outcome of any one criminal case. It is not the defendant's guilt or innocence but the conduct of the police that the motion puts in issue. Therefore, the defense brief stresses the intent of the policemen when they made the challenged search and any arbitrary or outrageous incidents of the search. Throughout, the brief seeks to isolate the search itself from irrelevant issues of guilt or innocence, which will never be reached if the motion is granted.

As a different illustration of the advocate's technique, let us suppose an antitrust case. A merchant opens a discount store but major suppliers refuse to sell to him, whereupon he sues them for treble damages. The issues on the merits are whether the manufacturers and distributors have conspired to fix prices and effect a boycott, and whether the discounter has been damaged as a result. The equities, however, are broader.

For the plaintiff and his attorney the merchant is a small business trying to compete in a world of giants. He tries to retail goods at low prices for the benefit of the public; the suppliers try to stop him to keep their prices high. The inference of conspiracy is obvious, because the suppliers would surely want the benefit of his high volume. The inference of damage is clear, because he has been forced to do without the prestige merchandise he wanted to buy. The policy of the antitrust laws must now be vindicated. Big companies must be taught that they cannot use their combined power to stop the discount store.

The mind-set of the defense attorneys is diametrically opposite. Their clients sell quality merchandise bearing famous brand names, and accordingly want their goods showcased through major stores, which provide trained salesmen and full services. Each defendant has reached the separate business judgment that a discount store would be undesirable for its business purposes, and each has a right to make that choice independently. The defendants' freedom to trade as they wish is to be protected. That freedom should not be infringed by the unreasonable demands of the discounter. The antitrust laws were not intended to confer on discount stores any special privilege to force unwilling suppliers to sell to them, and they should not now be so construed.

Each side thus develops a set of equitable considerations that give a different emphasis and color to the evidentiary facts. Neither side is misstating the facts, but each is looking at the case from a wholly different point of reference. Each has a different perspective to offer to the court.

Once adopted by the parties, such equitable considerations will appear again and again in the briefs. In motions on the merits in the trial court—for preliminary injunction, for summary judgment, for judgment notwithstanding the verdict— the briefs will touch on or at least suggest the equities. Again they will appear in briefs on appeal dealing with the merits, as when the issue concerns the sufficiency of the evidence, the adequacy of key instructions, or the correctness of major evidentiary rulings.

At each of these points the advocate's brief will project his own equitable setting for the case. He may or may not set aside a separate section to argue it, for it may not be directly relevant, but he will make sure that the court sees the case the way he sees it. He will ask the judges to adopt, for the moment, the partisan viewpoint of his client, confident in the knowledge that his adversary will do likewise, and that only in this way can the court truly understand the bedrock issues, and the fundamental impact of the decision it is asked to make.

PERSUASIVE ATTITUDES

When judges read a brief they do not need to be told that a dispute is in progress, or that each party is outraged with the position of the other, or that counsel may have developed personal quarrels of their own in the course of the litigation. All of this they have seen all too often. What the judges need is a reliable basis for a decision. They are grateful to the advocate who provides them one, and who declines to feud with his opponent or to snipe at judges who have ruled against him.

The seasoned advocate accordingly reins in his emotions, as well as his mind, so that he can concentrate on the factual, legal, and equitable issues. He knows that an argument in court is not an occasion for anger, like a squabble among bad-tempered relatives. He recognizes that he is not engaged in a debate, in which he gains points for clever dialectics. His purpose is to show the judges that his side of the question before the court is the meritorious side. If he does that, he wins.

Understanding the rules of the game, the advocate will recognize that it is bad tactics to downgrade his adversary. It is not the lawyers' arguments that are on trial, but the issues. If the advocate belittles his adversary, he necessarily suggests that the opposing argument must be poorly made, and could be much stronger. But if he praises his adversary's skills, he suggests that the opposing argument is as strong as it can be made: The weakness is not in his adversary's argument, but in his case.

At the same time the advocate will convince himself, as a good salesperson does, that he has something important and valuable to sell. His adversary's product, unfortunately, is less desirable for a series of reasons that he stresses in a point-by-point comparison. The judges he addresses are sophisticated buyers who need only to be alerted to the merits of the product he has for sale; happily it offers them exactly what they need, and their decision should be simple.[12]

Such attitudes make for effective advocacy. There are others, however, that create unpersuasive briefs. Some of them are all too common.

Some brief writers fail to recognize that judges have the power to make decisions whereas advocates do not. The brief writer may be learned and he may know his case, but if he lectures the judges, on his own authority and in the tones of a professor to a student, they will resent it. If they are told they "must" reach a certain decision or conclusion, or that they "cannot" reach another, they might well regard the lawyer's imperative as a challenge to do otherwise. They will accept the commands of legislatures and higher courts but they are not prepared to obey the directives of counsel. The function of advocates is to advocate. The function of the judges is to decide.

Some brief writers are unwise enough to disparage the trial judge or judges of other courts. They should remind themselves that the judges they are writing for will not throw stones at their brother judges, and they are not likely to appreciate it when advocates do so.[13] If the brief writer will imagine that he is speaking directly to the court that had decided against his client, or against his position, and then phrase his comments accordingly, he will instinctively avoid the contemptuous or disrespectful or sarcastic epithet. He will not refer to an adverse decision as "outrageous" or "pernicious" or "irrational."

12. "The aim of the advocate, of course, is to convince the court that he has a good case. Annually, Judge Breitel reminds the students at Columbia Law School, when he sums up moot court practice, that real courts deal with real cases but that in the moot court it is all fake. He tells them that in the moot court the advocate spends his time telling the court how good he is and how poor his case is. In real courts, on the contrary, he says that the lawyer devotes himself to proving how good his case is and to apologizing for how poor a lawyer he is." Pollack, The Civil Appeal, in Counsel on Appeal 29, 40 (Charpentier ed. 1968).

13. "One who criticizes unfairly or hostilely the action of a lower court runs the risk of offending the quite understandable *esprit de corps* of the judicial body." Davis, *supra* note 7, at 103-104.

Instead, he will find a respectful alternative: The court has been "misled" or "led astray" by counsel's argument; it has "failed to appreciate" or has "apparently overlooked" the key facts or the pertinent cases; it has acted under a "mistaken impression" of the evidence or an "outmoded view" of the law; therefore its decision is "out of harmony" with controlling precedent and is, unfortunately, "unsound," "incorrect," "in error," or "erroneous." With phrases like this he says all he needs to say, but he says it with courtesy.

Accusations of impropriety directed at opposing counsel are less of an affront to the court, but judges grow weary of them. They are normally irrelevant to the issues and therefore a waste of the court's time. If they are bitter, they are also unpleasant, as the spectacle of cats fighting in a back alley is unpleasant. Even though they are not so extreme as to violate court rules or rules of ethics, they leave a bad taste in the mouth.

Just as an experienced cross-examiner will approach an attractive witness with courtesy, taking care not to alienate the jury, so will the brief writer approach an opponent's argument. For all he knows the judges or their clerks may find it appealing. Therefore, he will at first describe it in terms that merely imply its weakness: The opponent "attempts" or "suggests" an argument, he "advances" or "urges" or "insists on" a position. There is no suggestion of bad faith; the advocate avoids adjectives like "absurd" or "ridiculous" or "nonsensical." The next step is to point out that the adversary has been "unable" to find facts or law to support his argument, and accordingly "must rely" on inapposite authorities. The implication is that he is doing his competent best, but no such authorities exist. Meanwhile, the brief writer continues, his opponent "seeks to avoid" or is "forced to ignore" the authorities against him; he cannot, however, do so successfully for they are so clearly pertinent. As a result the opponent's argument, while "apparently logical" and "superficially appealing," must fail for it is "without support" and "fatally flawed" and in fact "untenable." Throughout such a passage the opposing counsel himself is accorded respect. He is an able and worthy advocate who cannot help it if the cards are so heavily stacked against him.

Even when opposing counsel is flagrantly inaccurate or misleading, the brief writer will do well to let the facts speak the loudest. Epithets like "deliberately false" or "concealed from the court" are fighting words that ruffle not only the opponent's feathers but the court's. They call for proof of intent, which may be hard to find and which in any case may not be worth the effort. The advocate will usually disrupt his own argument less, and be more persuasive, if he understates his conclusion by writing that his opponent has "misconstrued" or "neglected" or "no doubt overlooked" some obvious fact or case, while citing chapter and verse to the court. The judges will draw their own conclusions without difficulty.[14]

If the advocate avoids wrangling with his opponent, he will earn the respect of the judges. At the same time he will keep their focus on the issues, where it belongs, so that he can proceed with his job of persuasion.

STEP-BY-STEP PROOF

The brief writer must expect that his product will be tested by experts. His opponent will seek to find each flaw or crack, each chink in the armor, and then try to pull his argument

---

14. "Reflections on the adversary throw a shadow on the spokesman's own standards and the strength of his presentation." Godbold, Twenty Pages and Twenty Minutes — Effective Advocacy on Appeal, 30 Southwestern L.J. 801, 817 (1976).

"But courts are not interested in controversies between lawyers, and if counsel wants to accuse his opponent of untruths, he had better be prepared to prove it." Goodrich, A Case on Appeal — A Judge's View, in A Case on Appeal 1, 18 (4th ed. 1967).

"Avoid scandal, impertinence and sarcasm. In pointing out your adversary's misstatements of fact or law, be courteous about it — strive to find a charitable cloak for his improprieties. In other words, it is proper to annihilate your adversary — but do it gracefully." Peters, The Preparation and Filing of Briefs on Appeal, 22 Cal. St. B.J. 175, 183 (1947).

apart. The judge who reads the brief will do much the same, but for a different purpose. He will want to know if the brief presents a reliable basis for decision. He and his clerk will test it section by section against the opponent's brief—first the issues presented, then the statement of facts, then the argument itself—to see which side has the better of each issue.

Knowing that this brief must withstand multiple attacks, the author will try to make it impregnable. He will assert only what he can support or prove as he proceeds, unless his proposition is so obvious as to need no support. If he makes an assertion of fact, he will cite to the relevant evidence and perhaps quote from it; if he states a proposition of law, he will cite or summarize or quote from a pertinent authority. Step by step and point by point, the brief writer will nail down each plank of his argument.

As he writes, the advocate will be careful never to overstate, or to claim more than he can prove, or his opponent will pounce on him in reply. Instead, when he states a conclusion, he will express it conservatively and often with deliberate understatement, so that the judge will be wholly convinced of it as far as it goes. As one carefully documented assertion succeeds another, he will build an impression of reliability that in time will take on a cumulative force of its own. That is to say, the judge will begin to trust him.

The opposite of such careful restraint in argument, of course, is the exaggeration or the careless or perhaps deliberate overstatement. Judges have repeatedly warned in their writings that they are no fools and that they are experienced in sniffing out the sham argument or overblown statement of fact. They know what is mere implication or inference. They know the difference between a dictum and a holding. They resent overstatements when they find them and when they do they cannot help but mistrust the brief as a whole.[15]

15. "Remember the justices are human. If they find counsel making a misstatement of fact they necessarily mistrust him—and mistrust everything else he may state." Peters, *supra* note 14, at 179.

"Nothing, perhaps, so detracts from the force and persuasiveness of an

The real danger for the brief writer is not so much that he will deliberately exaggerate, but that he will let his advocate's zeal get the better of him. He will destort the truth as a child does, saying not what is verifiably true but what he wishes were true and therefore imagines to be true. Anything to the contrary he simply blots from his mind.

The brief writer's safeguard against such temptations is to read and reread each of his assertions skeptically, as the judges and his opponent certainly will. He must test each of his own statements with the questions a judge would ask: Where is the evidence for this? Is this proved? Does the case really stand for that proposition? Does this necessarily follow? If the answers are not clear and positive, he must scale down his assertions until they conform to the supporting facts or authorities. When he does so, he will frequently find that the limited version is not weaker but stronger. It still says all that he needs to say, but now it is beyond attack. For example, the brief writer may find on reading a draft that he has written the following sentence:

On September 13, Oppenheimer advised O'Reilly that the shipment would be delivered not later than the end of the month.

Unfortunately, as he now realizes, the evidence at trial is not clear enough to justify his flat statement. What the evidence shows is a reasonable and probable inference that Oppenheimer so advised O'Reilly. Very well, he decides, let the facts speak for themselves. Accordingly he revises as follows:

On September 13, according to O'Reilly, Oppenheimer advised him that the shipment would be delivered "in about

---

argument as for the lawyer to claim more than he is reasonably entitled to claim." Rutledge, The Appellate Brief, 28 A.B.A.J. 251, 254 (1942).

"Inaccuracy in statement or misleading argument will obviously destroy the court's confidence in the brief." Tate, The Art of Brief Writing: What a Judge Wants to Read, 4 Litigation 11, 12 (Winter 1978).

> two weeks"; O'Reilly therefore marked it in his calendar as probable by the end of the month (Tr. 572). Oppenheimer testified he could not recall any such telephone call (Tr. 849). He conceded, however, that the schedules of his own production and shipping departments (Exs. 143, 144) were, as he put it, "compatible with such a delivery date" (Tr. 894) and that O'Reilly was calling him about the shipment "almost daily" (Tr. 863). Thus the inference is fully justified that Oppenheimer did assure O'Reilly the shipment would arrive about the end of September, and not six weeks later.

This revised statement conforms to the evidence. It is not vulnerable to attack, and it may be stronger in its impact than the original.

Let us now suppose a different case, one in which a brief writer finds, during revising and editing, that he has written the following sentence:

> None of respondent's cases holds that such a determination by the agency is beyond review in this Court.

On reexamining his opponent's cases, however, the brief writer finds that one of them does include a statement to that effect, although it is only dictum, and the facts of the case are distinguishable. On reconsideration he rewrites his assertion as follows:

> Respondent has cited only one case in which a court has stated that such a determination was beyond the review of the courts, but the facts were very different and the statement was dictum. [Discussion] Apart from this case there is no authority to support respondent's position.

The strength of the revised version is that the writer has now dealt with the adverse dictum, rather than seeming to avoid it. Now his assertion cannot be attacked as overbroad, because it has been hand-tailored to fit the authorities themselves.

The brief writer will do well to keep in mind that a case

need not be perfect but only better than the opposition's. Inevitably there will be some evidence or some case authority contrary to one's position. The skilled advocate will seek to overbalance the contrary evidence or show why it is unimportant, but he will not misstate it; he will try to distinguish the contrary cases, but he will not fail to discuss them. An advocate knows that if he asserts unsupportable factual summaries or untenable legal conclusions he puts in jeopardy the trust he is trying to build and hence the persuasiveness of his whole argument. It is better to concede a point where necessary than to risk the integrity of the brief as a whole.

SELECT AND DISCARD

To be persuasive, the brief writer has no choice but to be selective. He has at hand a mass of detailed fact and an almost infinite body of law, but the judge cannot be expected to consider more than a fraction of it. The advocate must choose what is important and discard the rest.

The judges themselves urge lawyers to do so. As Justice Tate of the Louisiana Supreme Court wrote in a recent article,

From the mass of materials available [the advocate] should repeatedly select and discard—*select* essential issues, facts and authors; *discard* and winnow others ruthlessly, along with excess words and repetitious argument. (Emphasis in original.)[16]

Even if judges had more time to read briefs, the able brief writer would use only the best of the available raw materials and discard the remainder. Selectivity is the first principle. It

16. Tate, *supra* note 15.
"When you are the master of the subject, select and discard the material; then select and discard again, and then again." Prettyman, Some Observations Concerning Advocacy, 39 Va. L. Rev. 285, 293-294 (1953).

enables the writer to highlight the essence of the testimony and the exhibits and to pick out the definitive decisions and the clearest and most memorable passages from judicial opinions. What is secondary, repetitious, or cumulative is excluded because it will only detract from the force of an effective presentation.

The principle of selectivity is clear enough, but applying it is more difficult. How does the advocate go about deciding what to include or exclude in the brief? There are no hard and fast answers, for it all depends on the individual case, but there are at least a few questions that may be helpful in testing the value of available points and authorities.

One question the brief writer may keep in mind is whether any part of the presentation is so obvious that it need not be stated at all. Many briefs are padded with propositions of law so simple and assertions of fact so apparent that no one would question them; and yet there they are, complete with accompanying citations to authorities or to the record, as if they needed to be proved in the first place. These should be deleted or at most merely mentioned in passing. The way for the writer to test them is to take them out, and then see if anything of substance is lost. Utility, not relevance, is the criterion: Does the obvious statement add anything to the argument?

Another useful question is whether any part of the writer's brief is unnecessarily repetitive or cumulative. Again, relevance is not the test, but added value or utility is. The writer, let us say, has five sound and relevant cases to support a point of law. The question is: Why use more than one? If he asks the question whenever he is tempted to use string citations, he will usually decide on a less repetitive alternative. For example, he might:

1. use one case, which is complete, up-to-date, and authoritative
2. use an older but leading case, plus a recent holding to bring it up to date
3. use a leading case, plus another that is close on its facts

4. use a leading case, plus another for its apt and telling quotation.[17]

Only when the repetition is itself significant should the writer use the whole group of authorities, as for example when a single principle has been applied to a variety of comparable fact patterns; if so, he should show the significance of such applications with parenthetical phrases after each case, which will flag for the judge the reason each decision is independently significant.

Perhaps the writer has available the testimony of three witnesses and passages from two exhibits, all of which tend to prove the same fact. How much should be quoted, paraphrased, or cited? Here, as in choosing legal authorities, the author should weigh the persuasive value of each source, and then, having picked the best, ask if any further source would add anything. He may decide to quote the witness whose phraseology is sharp and clear, and merely note that the others testified to the same effect, with citations to the record. On the other hand, he may decide that a contemporaneous memorandum is the most convincing, and that the later testimony of witnesses can be attacked as self-serving; if so, he may omit even a reference to the testimony. If one of the witnesses is an adverse party whose testimony is an admission or concession, the writer may weigh it most heavily of all; perhaps he will briefly describe the rest and then, as a climax, triumphantly quote his adversary.

Whenever a quotation is used, it is especially important to be concise. The writer should be attentively selective, but at the same time scrupulously fair. Quotations are often too long. The writer may insert an entire paragraph when the essence of it appears in a single sentence or perhaps even a phrase or a word. Words must not be taken out of context, of course, and sometimes the author may need the full quotation merely to convince the reader that he has not done so. But

17. "Two or three decisions directly in point are worth a dozen which are not, or in most cases, a dozen which are." Goodrich, *supra* note 14, at 17.

whenever he can, the writer should pare the quote down to what makes it distinctive and important. He should also avoid repetition, which often occurs when the writer states the substance of the quotation in a paraphrase and then adds the quote itself. Usually it will be more forceful to omit the paraphrase and to allow the quotation itself to state the thought.

The main point is that in brief writing, as in any art, authors make their points most tellingly with quality, not quantity. In this sense, less is more. A brief that contains nothing but directly relevant points, and nothing but apt authorities and pat quotations, can hold the judge's attention from beginning to end. If so, it has the best chance to persuade.

A persuasive brief is sensitive to its reader's characteristics, needs, and limitations. Its author has realized that his or her job is not to lecture the court or to engage in a battle of dialectics, but to appeal to a human judge.

If a brief is to be appealing, it must deal not only with the precise application of authority to fact, but with the reasons why a line of authority may soundly be applied. It must concern itself not only with the narrowly relevant, but with those broader considerations that bear on ultimate justice in the present case and similar cases.

If a brief is to be trustworthy, it must be accurate and reliable throughout, not only for what it states, but for its completeness. It must meet the important facts and authorities cited by the opposition. From time to time it must make concessions, for the advocate's case is not perfect and need not be.

If a brief is to be emphatic, it must set forth the predigested essence of the facts, the equities, and the law and logic of the case, not only to save the judge's time and energy, but to stress what is important. It must be selective and succinct, or the essentials will be lost.

If a brief is to be finally convincing, it must offer a course of action the judge can follow with confidence. He must be able to rest with it, satisfied in the main with its result. The suggested decision may not be perfect, for seldom is anything perfect, but the judge must believe that it is, in essence, the soundest of the alternatives available to him.

6

DEFINING
THE ISSUES

Functionally a brief consists of three necessary parts.

1. A brief statement of the issues before the court, which in an appellate brief is called Statement of Issues, Questions Presented, or Specification of Errors
2. A statement of the facts relevant to the issues, usually called Statement of the Facts, Statement of the Case, or merely Statement
3. A statement of the relevant law and application of that law to the facts, entitled Argument

In longer briefs it is often helpful to add a short introductory statement at the beginning, sometimes called Introduction, which provides a preview of the entire brief. Also optional is a concluding statement, entitled Conclusion, which may summarize key points or state in detail what the court's decision should be.

Each of the three essential parts of a brief has its own requirements; judges have frequently stated their expectations with respect to each of them. This chapter examines those requirements and expectations relating to the first part of a brief, the questions presented. Chapter 7 examines the statement of facts, and the last essential part, the argument itself, is taken up in Chapter 8.

Of the three essential parts of a brief the shortest, and usually the most difficult to write, is the section or paragraph in which the author defines the issues. Some court rules require that it be stated at the very beginning of the brief; if not, it will be set forth somewhere near the outset. In a brief filed with the trial court it may have no designation, but the brief writer will nevertheless set forth in some form, with or without a title, the questions the court is asked to decide.

For the judges a clear definition of the questions presented is a necessity, because without it they cannot intelligently read the briefs. First they must learn what the dispute is about. After they understand the issues, and only then, can they grasp the significance of each fact and each point of law as it makes its appearance. Now they have a focus.[1]

Advocates, however, frequently fail to give the judges the focus they need. As Judge Prettyman of the District of Columbia Circuit observed in a law review article,

> Believe it or not, this phase of appellate advocacy is one which calls for the greatest degree of skill and is the one most usually botched by counsel. . . . By and large—not universally, but more frequently than not—the appellate court has to read the whole of both briefs and match them one against the other to ascertain where they conflict, in order to find out what the disputed question is. A primary task of appellate counsel is to state the question he wants the court to decide; describe the error the trial tribunal is alleged to have made. The task requires consummate skill, and it also requires careful, painstaking labor.[2]

For the advocate the statement of issues is of crucial importance, for with it he stakes out his battleground. If he can fight on friendly terrain he may win; if he has to do battle on his adversary's turf, he may lose. Accordingly he chooses his own

1. "In most jurisdictions a succinct statement of the question or questions to be argued is the first element of a brief. This is to aid the court in reading the statement of facts that follows intelligently in light of the issues. . . . [Judges] will read first of all the appellant's statement of the questions to be argued and then the respondent's. They do this because they want to see whether counsel agree on the issues, and if they disagree, in what respects." Vanderbilt, Forensic Persuasion, 7 Wash. & Lee L. Rev. 1, 20 (1950).

A good summary of what judges wish to see in a statement of issues, based on considerable correspondence and research on the subject, is contained in Cooper, Stating the Issues in Appellate Briefs, 40 A.B.A.J. 180 (1960).

2. Prettyman, Some Observations Concerning Appellate Advocacy, 39 Va. L. Rev. 285, 288 (1953).

issues when he can. If he cannot choose the issues, he at least adopts a viewpoint on each, and does not uncritically accept the description of his adversary. So far as he can, he tries to shape each issue to emphasize his strong points.

In stating the issues, however, the advocate is strictly limited by the requirements of intellectual honesty. Judges not only expect the statement of issues to be clear so that they will understand it, they also expect it to be essentially nonpartisan so that they can trust it. Therefore, the advocate should not leap prematurely into argument without providing the judges a reliable and trustworthy definition of the issues. It is no more than effective writing, and it is certainly effective advocacy, to give judges the focus they need.

CHOOSING THE ISSUES TO PRESENT

Before he writes his statement the advocate must decide what the issues are, and here he may have a choice. If he represents the moving party in the trial court, or the appellant or petitioner in a court of appeal, he may have a variety of grounds for the relief he asks—some fundamental, some technical, some weak, some strong—but the question is how many he should use. Assuming all of his grounds are at least tenable, should he be selective and, if so, when and why?

The natural tendency of the careful lawyer is to include every issue and every argument. Consciously or subconsciously, he is thinking that any relevant and tenable argument might possibly win; therefore it must be assigned some value. As a lawyer he must not abandon anything of value to his client; therefore he must include each issue and an argument to accompany it. If he would not discard a tenable claim or defense in a pleading, why should he abandon an available and tenable argument?

The answer is that in a brief, unlike a pleading, no points are awarded for the articulation of all possible issues. The purpose of a brief is to persuade, and in the art of persuasion quality is what counts, not quantity. Selection enhances quality; less becomes more. As judges have repeatedly emphasized, they are not impressed with a collection of miscellaneous points on appeal, or in any argument. The weak points do not add to the strong, but detract. Because they are weak they suggest, by association, that the other points are weak as well.[3]

This is not to say that the advocate should push the principle of selectivity to its logical extreme, and therefore discard all issues and arguments other than his best. Often it is too risky to do this, for a variety of tactical reasons.

One reason, and the most obvious, is that the advocate cannot see with the minds of the judges, and therefore can predict only imperfectly what arguments will be persuasive. If he has one argument he rates as very strong, and two he rates as moderately strong, and two he rates as weak, he will probably settle on the first three. He cannot afford to abandon points on which he has a serious chance of success, and that are not so weak as to detract from his best.

The advocate may also be justified in retaining a point that, although limited in scope, is related to and supports another argument. Perhaps it is a logical subsidiary to another point; it might not be important on its own, but it adds strength to another. Perhaps it can logically be grouped with other smaller points to make one large and persuasive one, as when a group of related errors in jury instructions or in evidentiary rulings together may constitute prejudicial error.

3. "Appellate advocacy on civil appeals calls for courage in the lawyer: the courage to forgo, the willingness to pass, alluring grounds that may exist in the record. The lawyer must make difficult choices. He must make calculated judgments in abandoning points for appeal. The compendious effort that throws everything erroneous or even everything reversible at the court runs the risk of pegging the strength of the appeal to the weakest link. Selectivity then is the key." Pollack, The Civil Appeal, in Counsel on Appeal 29, 39 (Charpentier ed. 1968).

"I have never been able to understand the motives of counsel who raise a great number of issues they must understand the court will decide adversely to them; the few arguable issues raised by them tend to be regarded as nonmeritorious by association." Tate, The Art of Brief Writing: What a Judge Wants to Read, 4 Litigation 11, 13 (Winter 1978).

Defining the Issues

The advocate will also be sensitive to the possibility that the judges may need a choice of issues. They may not want to decide what he sees as the major issue, either because they cannot agree on its disposition or because they would prefer some different case as a vehicle for announcing their rule of law. In such cases they may be grateful for a limited alternative, perhaps a statutory interpretation in lieu of a constitutional adjudication or a technical defense in lieu of a defense on the merits. Whenever his principal issue on the merits is controversial or may not be ripe for decision, the advocate will try to offer the judges a way in which they can avoid it, if they feel they must, and still decide in his favor.

If, on the other hand, his strongest point is a technical one and his position on the merits is weaker, the brief writer may include both issues for a different reason. The wise advocate knows that a case resting solely on a technicality is unappealing and sometimes unpalatable to judges interested in doing equity. Accordingly he will always be loath to let the merits go by default. If he can tenably argue some other ground reaching to the merits of the case, the judges will more comfortably accept his technical point, and less diligently look for ways and means to avoid it.[4]

With these considerations in mind the advocate will choose what he thinks is his strongest combination of issues, those that collectively have the most appeal and are the least vulnerable to attack. He will weed out issues on which his position

4. "Strive to make it easy for the court to decide in your client's favor, and difficult to decide against your client, by presenting more than one reason, if more than one is available, why your client should prevail." Peters, The Preparation and Writing of Briefs on Appeal, 22 Cal. St. B.J. 175, 183 (1947).

"[Y]ou must show that the procedural rules—*and* the substantive rule of law you espouse—are appropriate in the particular case and that, fairly applied to the facts, they dictate a favorable outcome. You cannot rely entirely upon procedural devices in responding to a troublesome, meritorious argument. You should meet your opponent's points in such a way that it will not appear your case is devoid of merit and all that remains is a rule of procedure to save you." Kaufman, Appellate Advocacy in the Federal Courts, 79 F.R.D. 165, 168-169 (1978).

is unavoidably weak, and that serve no supportive purpose. As always, he will bear in mind the identity and position of his readers, and try to answer the question: If I were in their shoes, what points would be most persuasive?

THE CLEAR, CONCISE STATEMENT

The drafting of a statement of issues or questions presented is typically difficult because much is expected of it. The judges want the legal issues stated fairly and accurately, and keyed adequately to the factual setting; yet they want the statement concise, and at the same time understandable and clear. The advocate wants to satisfy the judges in these respects, but at the same time hopes to phrase the questions presented so that they suggest favorable answers.

The questions or issues should be expressed, as stated in Rule 21.1 (a) of the U.S. Supreme Court Rules, "in the terms and circumstances of the case but without unnecessary detail." It is inadequate merely to state the legal issue without any reference to the factual setting in which it arises (*e.g.,* "Whether the defendant is entitled to judgment notwithstanding the verdict" or "Whether the trial court's instructions were erroneous and prejudicial"). It is premature, however, to include in a statement of issues the detailed evidence that normally appears in the statement of the case or the statement of facts. Judges expect to be apprised initially of the factual nature of the case so that they will see not only the legal issue but the setting in which it is to be applied. In a simple case, for example, the issue may be stated in a sentence like the following:

Where the purchaser's building was worth more at trial than the price paid, was it prejudicially erroneous to instruct the jury that his damages were limited to his out-of-pocket loss?

Such a formulation is a sufficient preview. The judges do not yet know all of the relevant details, but they know what their assignment is, and they can now read the briefs with a purpose.

The format for the statement of each question depends primarily on what will make the issue clear to the judges. There is ordinarily no reason for long and involved sentences that read like the headnote to an opinion or the preamble of a contract. For example

> Whether, where plaintiff [description of facts relating to the plaintiff] and defendant [description of facts relating to the defendant] and [description of additional and further facts], it is prejudicially erroneous to exclude evidence relating to [description of evidence excluded].

Here the reader does not even know what the question is until he has worked his way through a series of qualifying clauses. It is at least somewhat better to state the question itself first, and then add the qualifiers.

> Whether there was sufficient evidence in a negligence case to support a verdict for plaintiff where [circumstances of accident] and where there was testimony that [description of testimony] and tests conducted after the accident showed that [description of test results] and defendants admitted that [description of defendants' admissions].

Better yet, the brief writer will try to break up the long sentence and write something more readable. For example, in an environmental case,

> This case involves the diversions of water from the Three Pines Wilderness Area. Plaintiff American Environmental Association was formed for the purpose of preserving wilderness areas like Three Pines. Some of its members who live nearby use Three Pines for weekend recreation, while others visit it on annual camping trips. Like other visitors they depend on a plentiful supply of water within the

wilderness area. The issue on this appeal is whether the Association has standing to sue to enjoin the existing and threatened diversions.

Such a formulation has the advantage of being readable. It is just as concise as the one-sentence format and is much clearer.

Where there is more than one issue, the same simple statement of fact can often serve as the background for all of them. For example, in a contract case,

Plaintiff Brewer & Company signed a written contract with defendant Hi-Tech, Inc., to purchase a computer and associated software designed specifically for Brewer's business. One condition in the contract was that the system reach certain performance levels within six months of installation. After the six months' period had expired, Brewer notified Hi-Tech by letter that the equipment did not perform as promised and tendered it back to Hi-Tech. Hi-Tech claimed the contrary and sued for the contract price. The issues on this appeal are

1. Was the condition in the sales contract relating to performance levels ambiguous, so as to permit parol evidence as to its meaning?
2. Was evidence of Hi-Tech's representations in its sales brochures properly excluded, as inconsistent with the contract conditions?
3. Was evidence of the unsuitability of the equipment for Brewer's purposes properly excluded, as inconsistent with the sales contract conditions?

In this example the brief background setting avoids repetition and permits each issue to be stated succinctly.

The issues should be stated so simply and so clearly that the judges will grasp them at once. Nowhere in the brief is clarity more important. Because the judges will normally examine both statements of the issues first, reading one after the other and comparing them, it is here that the brief writer makes an invaluable first impression. If the questions are presented simply and clearly, judges will begin to respect the brief writer, and will await the suggested answers with interest.

THE FAIR STATEMENT

The statement of issues or questions presented is the worst place for any kind of conclusion or argument. At the beginning of a brief the judges are looking for a fair and reliable guide to the issues, and no more. If they are to draw conclusions for one side or the other they must first be introduced to the facts and then led step by step through the argument. They cannot be force-fed at the outset, and the brief writer who tries to do so will merely cause them to turn to the statement supplied by his adversary.

Brief writers are sometimes counseled to phrase the questions presented in such a way that there can only be one answer, if this can fairly be done. But this is a tricky and dangerous game for the advocate who must persuade professionals. If the right answer can be forced only by loading the question with a one-sided recitation of facts, or by eliminating key elements and so oversimplifying the issue, the attempt is likely to boomerang. The judge who reads a statement packed with evidence favorable to one side will naturally wonder why all the detail is necessary: Is counsel afraid of the issue itself? The judge who reads an oversimplified statement will ask himself the obvious questions: If the case is that simple, why does counsel find it necessary to write a lengthy brief in support of it? Why does his table of contents show on its face that the issue is far more complicated than his description? The fact is that issues presented to the courts for decision are rarely so one-sided or so simple that they can fairly be phrased by a question that answers itself.[5]

5. Frederick Bernays Weiner suggests that in formulating an issue beginning with the word *whether* the essential technique is "so to load the question

Accordingly wise advocates will be patient in their exposition. They will understand that judges need, first of all, to understand the issues. After this they will be happy to turn to the facts and then grapple with the arguments. But they do not wish to be crowded. The aggressive advocate who insists on an argumentative statement of the issues not only fails to persuade with it; he risks losing his audience right at the start and before he even begins his argument.

The most that brief writers can safely do as advocates is to emphasize and highlight their perceptions of the issues, while at the same time stating them accurately. An advocate's choice of words to describe the question presented may be subtly different from his adversary's. He also may legitimately differ from his opponent in his portrayal of the factual setting in which the issue arises. One advocate might stress fact X as being decisive, whereas the adversary might highlight fact Y, which underlies the opposing theory of the case. Although the resulting statements will differ in emphasis, the issue itself will be recognizable in each.

Good examples of such statements appear in the briefs filed in the reverse discrimination case of *Steelworkers v. Weber*.[6] The employer and the union had agreed to reserve for black em-

---

with the facts of the particular case or with the relevant quotations from the statute involved, *fairly stated,* that you can almost win the case on the mere question presented." (Emphasis in original.) Weiner, Briefing and Arguing Federal Appeals 73 (1961).

Various judges, however, have cautioned against unduly loading the questions: "I have read advice that questions be stated so as to produce a satisfactory answer. . . . Appellate judges are, at the very least, professionals at dissecting argument and at exploring propositions hurled at them. To suggest that they may be tricked by inaccurate phrasings of such questions as the questions presented and the facts is an unbelievable arrogance. The advocate who follows that course will, I assure you, soon be trying to figure out why he is never on the successful side of an appellate proceeding." Prettyman, *supra* note 2, at 297-298.

Judge Godbold, citing Weiner, states, "No one gains any advantage, tactical, personal or otherwise from these semantical ploys." Godbold, Twenty Pages and Twenty Minutes — Effective Advocacy on Appeal, 30 Southwestern L.J. 801, 810 (1976). To the same effect *see* Tate, *supra* note 3.

6. *Steelworkers v. Weber,* U.S. Supreme Court Nos. 78-432, 78-435, and 78-436, October Term 1978.

ployees 50 percent of the openings in a craft training program in order to correct a racial imbalance. Weber, a white employee, had sued under Title VII of the Civil Rights Act and won in the courts below, but the Supreme Court granted certiorari and later reversed.

In their briefs on the merits the petitioners (the employer, the union, and the Equal Employment Opportunity Commission), naturally emphasized what they regarded as the remedial and beneficent characteristics of the affirmative action program. The steelworkers union, deeming it to be important that the program was adopted through collective bargaining, phrased the question presented as follows:

> Does Title VII of the Civil Rights Act of 1964 make unlawful a program, adopted by an employer and union in collective bargaining, which reserved for black bidders 50% of the openings in an in-plant craft training program in order to eliminate a racial imbalance in the skilled craft workforce?

The employer, Kaiser Aluminum & Chemical Corporation, emphasized that the program was in fact a remedy for past exclusion of blacks from craft unions, and accordingly so phrased its statement of the issue.

> May an employer and a union lawfully consider race in the selection of employees for participation in a new craft training program established in part to remedy the past exclusion of blacks from craft employment?

The EEOC, arguing that an employer vulnerable to a charge of discrimination should be encouraged to take voluntary steps to avert such a charge, described the issue as follows:

> Whether, in the absence of an admission or proof of past discrimination, an employer and a union may adopt a training program based in part upon a racial criterion to remedy apparent discrimination in hiring for skilled craft jobs at one of the employer's plants.

Weber, the white employee excluded from the training program, of course saw the case very differently. In his view, the company and the union had established a racial quota and so were discriminating against white workers in violation of Title VII. As he understood it, there was no occasion for remedial action because the existing black employees had suffered no discrimination. Accordingly his counsel phrased the question presented as follows:

> May an employer and labor union, solely in order to achieve a desired ratio of minority workers in craft positions at a manufacturing plant and in the absence of any prior discrimination against the minority workers at that plant, institute a racial quota for admission to craft training programs that is preferential to members of minority groups and discriminates against whites, where job seniority would ordinarily determine entry into the training programs?

Thus each of the statements of the questions presented in the *Weber* briefs was legitimately different. None was distorted, but each stated the same issue in terms of the factual setting the litigant regarded as significant.

Suppose, however, that an opponent does misstate the issues before the court. How should the advocate deal with it? In such cases, the distortion should be pointed out in the responding brief or the reply brief, sharply and concisely. For example

The issue is not as stated by appellant. There was no evidence at trial that Blake & Co. ever accepted the change in specifications which General Industries sought to impose upon it, nor any evidence from which such an acceptance could be inferred. In the absence of such evidence appellant's phrase "following Blake's acceptance of the change" misstates the issue before the Court. Correctly stated, the issue is as follows: [Appellee's statement of the issue].

Defining the Issues

In this example the appellee's statement is not premature argument but a notification to the court that there has been a clear-cut misstatement that requires correction. Assuming the appellee is right on the evidence, the judges will appreciate the correction. They will not appreciate the misstatement that occasioned it.

7

FACTUAL
STATEMENTS

A good brief can often win a case on its factual statement alone. If the statement is clear and compelling the legal argument to follow approaches the superfluous. As the judges absorb the facts, they will call to mind, without prompting, the principles that should decide the case; all they need is a confirmation in the form of suitable authorities. The facts point directly to the applicable rules of law, and the rules of law decide the case.

John W. Davis, the celebrated advocate, stressed this point many years ago in an often-quoted address before the Association of the Bar of the City of New York.

> For it cannot be too often emphasized that in an appellate court the statement of the facts is not merely a part of the argument, it is more often than not the argument itself. A case well stated is a case far more than half argued. Yet how many advocates fail to realize that the ignorance of the court concerning the facts in the case is complete, even where its knowledge of the law may adequately satisfy the proverbial presumption. The court wants above all things to learn what are the facts which give rise to the call upon its energies; for in many, probably in most, cases when the facts are clear there is no great trouble about the law. *Ex facto oritur jus,* and no court ever forgets it.[1]

Today these remarks apply with special force to briefs. In appellate cases the judges first learn of the facts from the briefs, and so form their first impressions of the case. In the trial court the sequence may be different; but even when the

1. Davis, The Argument of an Appeal, in A Case on Appeal 98, 99 (4th ed. 1967).

judge has heard evidence before he reads the brief on an issue, he will look to the briefs to provide a summary of the pertinent facts. In all cases, unless there is a pure question of law to be decided, the advocate's written statement of the facts will be of prime importance.

The more complex the case, the greater the advocate's opportunity, for he is the master of the facts, and the judges do not have the time to be. Here, especially, the judges must rely on counsel. As Chief Judge Kaufman of the Second Circuit recently stated,

> Particularly in complex situations it is vital to make the facts sing out as clearly and simply as possible. Many cases involving alleged violation of the securities laws, for example, are extremely involved and technical. The plaintiff's advocate must breathe life into each of the significant underlying transactions, so that the mere recital of events lays bare the chicanery. And, of course, the defendant will usually attempt to portray the transaction as a perfectly sensible business arrangement.[2]

To achieve clarity and simplicity where the underlying facts are involved and technical, to breathe life into them, to make them sing out—these are certainly the goals of the brief writer. But merely to state these goals is to reveal the nature of the challenge. In complex cases the advocate will often spend more time and energy on stating the facts than in arguing the case, for it is in the factual statement that the battle is often won or lost.

CHOOSING AND ARRANGING THE FACTS

A good statement of fact is highly selective because the issues before the court are limited and the principal authorities even more so. The advocate's purpose is to fit the facts, if he fairly

2. Kaufman, Appellate Advocacy in the Federal Courts, 79 F.R.D. 165, 166-167 (1978).

can, to the specific statutes and cases that will win. At the same time he must deal with adverse or awkward facts, for it is neither candid nor wise to ignore them. As Judge Friedman of the Federal Circuit put it in a recent article,

> If there are adverse facts that the other side will stress, bring them out yourself and explain them away or minimize their significance. That is better than to permit the other side to present them first and then accuse you of ignoring them. It also creates a good impression with the court, since the judges see before them a candid and forthright advocate.[3]

Nevertheless if the advocate's best case requires elements A, B, and C, his first job is to round up each and every fact tending to prove elements A, B, and C. His next job is to highlight them in his statement. In short, he keys his selection of facts to his intended argument.[4] As Judge Kaufman of the Second Circuit stated in the course of a series of lectures,

> The consummate advocate will inspire his narrative with meaning so that only the legal doctrines that favor his client seem relevant and appropriate. In this sense, the story serves as a prelude to your legal argument. And, if the facts are written compellingly, your discussion of the law need only articulate and confirm the decision your tale demands. Indeed, the standard to strive for was that set by William Murray, who later became Lord Mansfield, one of the greatest English judges. It was said that when he finished his statement of facts, the argument of the law seemed superfluous.[5]

At the same time the advocate will collect and stress those facts that show his client's position to be fair and equitable, and his opponent's position to be unfair or overreaching or dishonest. If his opponent has lied, or omitted or concealed

3. Friedman, Winning on Appeal, 9 Litigation 15, 16 (Spring 1983).

4. "The statement should contain all the material facts. I would emphasize 'material' rather than 'all' in that sentence. Do not bury the point of the case in a sand of minutiae." Prettyman, Some Observations Concerning Appellate Advocacy, 39 Va. L. Rev. 285, 291-292 (1953).

5. Kaufman, *supra* note 2, at 167.

material facts in court, he will see to it that the judges grasp that point and do not forget it. Such facts may not be wholly relevant to the issues, they may not form the basis for an argument, but they will be directly pertinent to the court's overall assessment of the case. The judges are rightly concerned with where the equities lie. Furthermore the equitable facts are interesting. They show the characters, the plot, and the outcome of the story in concrete terms, which are easy to follow and to remember. Accordingly the advocate will find ways to weave facts of equitable significance into the fabric of his statement.[6]

If the brief writer is to key his facts to the relevant authorities and also to considerations of equity, he has no choice but to approach the case as a whole—before he drafts his statement, and while he is redrafting and editing it. He must consider the facts, the law, and the equities all at once. He cannot finally choose his facts, and then organize them, without a detailed knowledge of the authorities, including the exact wording of statutes and regulations and the specific reasoning of the cases, and without a developed theory of the equities. But he also cannot finally select the authorities he will use, or settle on his equitable approach, unless he has a detailed knowledge of the facts that will support them. Each depends on the other.

Accordingly the brief writer will solve his puzzle the only way he can, which is by trial and error. After he has read and summarized what he thinks are the applicable authorities, he will comb transcripts, exhibits, and any other sources for what he thinks will be the legally and equitably relevant facts. Then, as he organizes what facts he has, they will suggest the need for more authorities. He has found evidence that seems favorable and persuasive: Has it been a basis for decision in any

6. "Remember that the appellate courts are very busy, and an interesting statement will necessarily make a better and stronger impression than a purely factual discussion. If your client's cause is just and equitable, bring the justice of the cause to the court's attention, and thus take full advantage of the judges' human desire to see that justice prevails." Peters, The Preparation and Writing of Briefs on Appeal, 22 Cal. St. B.J. 175, 179 (1947).

prior cases? Back he goes to the law. Later, as he reexamines the authorities, a new factual question will come to his mind. He has found a case that depends for its holding on the existence of a given fact: Is there any evidence like this in his record? Back he goes to his sources of fact. The process is painstaking, but there is no other way to build a coherent brief in a complex case, so that the facts will be integrated with the applicable authorities, and at the same time will persuasively show where the equities are.

The process of integrating facts and law is enough of a puzzle, but to this often must be added a related problem: Should the brief writer put together one complete statement of fact, or several of them? He will, of course, state the generally useful facts near the beginning of his brief, but if there are different issues for decision, should he state all the facts at once, or place the facts relating to issue A before the argument on issue A and the facts relating to issue B before the argument on issue B, and so on?

Logically the answer should be that if the facts and the law on different issues are interrelated the brief writer should prepare one unified statement of fact, whereas if they were readily separable he should draft separate statements before each argument, with no more than a limited and generalized statement at the beginning. There is, however, another very practical reality to be considered, which is that judges, like other people, have limited memories. A short brief in a simple case is one thing, but if judges are asked to read a complex statement of facts and then to recall the evidence relevant to one specific issue 40 pages later they may, quite understandably, have only a dim recollection of it.

Accordingly whenever a brief is long and complex it is a practical necessity to supply a relevant statement of fact before each legal argument. The brief writer has two choices: (1) a complete factual statement at the beginning, followed by summaries or reminders of the relevant evidence before or during the course of each argument, or (2) a generalized summary at the beginning, followed by detailed statements before or during the course of each argument. But he must do one or the other, unless he expects the judges to demonstrate total and selective recall. Even at the cost of some repetition he must be sure that the facts and the legal issues are keyed to each other in the judges' minds as well as his own.

NARRATIVE STATEMENT

When the brief writer has marshaled his facts so that they will key into the argument, he is ready to state them in clear narrative form. He has an audience ready, even eager, to learn the facts of the case, for to the judges these are of primary interest. He has at hand all the raw materials for an absorbing narrative. The subject may be a crime and its prosecution, or a disaster and its resulting injuries, or an argument made and then broken, but something of interest has happened. Because of it the participants now confront each other in court. The brief writer has the story at his fingertips, and he has only to write it.

If, despite all this, the statement of facts is confusing, or dry as dust, the brief writer has missed his best chance to appeal to his audience by means of the written word. His argument, perhaps, must be technical and disputatious, but not his statement of facts. The statement should be as simple, clear, and memorable as a narrative in any well-written book of nonfiction. It should keep the judges' interest from beginning to end.

Simple writing is a major part of the technique. In this, as in many other skills, Justice Cardozo was a master. Consider, for example, his one-paragraph statement of the facts in the celebrated negligence case of *Palsgraf v. Long Island R. Co.*

> Plaintiff was standing on a platform of defendant's railroad after buying a ticket to go to Rockaway Beach. A train stopped at the station, bound for another place. Two men ran forward to catch it. One of the men reached the platform of the car

without mishap, though the train was already moving. The other man, carrying a package, jumped aboard the car, but seemed unsteady as if about to fall. A guard on the car, who had held the door open, reached forward to help him in, and another guard on the platform pushed him from behind. In this act, the package was dislodged, and fell upon the rails. It was a package of small size, about fifteen inches long, and was covered by a newspaper. In fact it contained fireworks, but there was nothing in its appearance to give notice of its contents. The fireworks when they fell exploded. The shock of the explosion threw down some scales at the other end of the platform many feet away. The scales struck the plaintiff causing injuries for which she sues.[7]

Here in a few words, all of them simple, and in a chronological format, the story is concisely told. We read the statement with ease, and we learn the essential facts.

When the facts are complex or technical, they must be divided into bite-sized pieces, and then set forth and explained and summarized one after the other, like lessons in a textbook. Step by step the judges will learn, like any students, but they cannot be expected to understand if the whole body of the evidence is thrown at them in an undifferentiated mass. Usually it is helpful to begin with the fundamentals—in a commercial case, say, the nature of the industry, the meaning of technical terms, the background of the parties, and their roles—and then proceed with the narrative of who did what to whom. Throughout, the statement should be carefully subdivided into topics, and then each topic separately introduced, detailed, and summarized.

Often a brief introductory statement will be helpful. As Justice Peters of California wrote,

> If your case is complicated on its facts I think it is an excellent practice to start your statement of facts with a short four- or five-page general statement. This should be carefully worded with only the basic facts mentioned. It, as well as the detailed statement that follows, should be clear, concise, interesting and

7. *Palsgraf v. Long Island R. Co.*, 248 N.Y. 339, 162 N.E. 99 (1928).

readable. Then follow the general statement of the facts with a detailed statement in which transcript references are given.[8]

Whenever the narrative can be stated in chronological order it should be, for this is the natural way to tell any story, and the easiest to understand. In a complex case, however, the facts must usually be arranged topically as well, if they are to be understandable. The writer may proceed from topic to topic, narrating each one in chronological order, or he may go from time period to time period, writing about one topic after another within the period. He will choose his format for maximum readability, and then make sure to help his readers with subheads, transitions, and summaries as he moves from segment to segment.

Interim explanations and summaries are most important. The judges should be told not only what the evidence is but what it means, and this at frequent intervals. It is impossible to give them periodic quizzes, as at the end of a chapter in a schoolbook, but it is entirely feasible to write so that they could pass such tests if they had to. In fact, summaries of the evidence, with interim factual conclusions, are essential to an understanding of a complex case. As Justice Cardozo explained it, when providing an interim summary in his opinion in the stock fraud case of *McCandless v. Furlaud,*

> Checks and credits have now been traced through their bewildering entanglements. None the less when the process of analysis is over, it is legitimate to forget the details, and fix our minds on the results. The situation can be simplified without obscuring its essential features. Indeed only in that way will the realities of what was done be manifest.[9]

8. Peters, *supra* note 6. In Goldfarb and Raymond, Clear Understandings: A Guide to Legal Writing (1982) at pages 70-71, the authors suggest that in every brief the beginning portion should include a statement of "who did what to whom." The brief writer, however, should use his own judgment in each case. The brief may concern purely technical issues, in which case the human story behind the dispute may not be relevant for either side. In some cases a narrative of the underlying human conflict might be helpful to one side, but decidedly unhelpful for the other; one advocate will emphasize the story, but the other will be well advised to leave it alone.

9. *McCandless v. Furlaud,* 296 U.S. 149, 154 (1935).

The use of separate segments makes possible a series of clear statements, but it should not be permitted to isolate each part from the whole. If the relationship of each to the entire narrative is not readily apparent it should be stated. For example

> The trial court's ruling admitting such evidence represented its final decision on the issues. Already the Carson Report (Ex. 44) and the McNamara testimony on the same subject (Tr. 893-912) had been admitted over objection, as discussed above (pp. 28-31). From then on, all of the appellee's evidence on the point was allowed (Ex. 45, 46, 47, 48; Tr. 971-82).

For another example

> While General Industries was concluding the first full year of production at its Dublin plant it was also exploring the possibilities of a joint venture with S. A. de Chimie de Bruxelles, the largest chemical company in Belgium (Tr. 478-491). These talks continued sporadically from March, 1979, to September, 1980, when, as Harold Johnson testified, "The Kuhlmann people asked us to meet with them in Frankfurt" (Tr. 1159).

Explanations like these cross-reference one segment to another, in subject and in time, so that the facts can be seen as a whole.

PERSUASIVE STATEMENT

Any good advocate tries to make the facts speak for him. If he can do this he is at his most convincing; although his words can be contradicted, the facts themselves cannot. So Mark Antony harangued the citizens in Shakespeare's *Julius Caesar* as he gathered them around the bloody corpse:

For I have neither writ, nor words, nor worth,
Action, nor utterance, nor the power of speech,
To stir men's blood: I only speak right on.
I tell you that which you yourselves do know;
Show you sweet Caesar's wounds, poor poor
    dumb mouths,
And bid them speak for me.[10]

In a brief the advocate must not distort or misstate the facts, but he can, like Antony, highlight the ones most persuasive to his cause. This he does by stating them in all relevant detail, making them stand out as sharply and memorably as possible. He centers on hard figures, illuminating quotations, telling admissions, startling contradictions, and all that reaches to the emotions. He groups his facts; he introduces them and summarizes them to show their meaning and their relationships; he characterizes them in his choice of words when he can aptly do so; but most importantly he lets them speak for themselves.[11]

The technique of focusing on illuminating detail is particularly effective when the facts are complex, because it shows the judges what is clear and concrete in the mass of evidence. Consider, for example, the following paragraphs from the government brief in the price-fixing case of *United States v. United States Gypsum Company:*

> In 1962 Graham Morgan, chairman of the board of United States Gypsum (USG), authorized in writing a select group of pricing officials to participate in the discussion and exchange of prices and terms and conditions of sale with USG's competitors

10. Act III, Scene II.
11. As Justice Rutledge put it in an article, Rutledge, The Appellate Brief, 28 A.B.A.J. 252 (1942), "[T]his phase of the brief [the statement of fact] gives opportunity for placing emphasis ... where the writer thinks it should be. . . .
"Finally, and this is related to all the foregoing, what color shall be given to the facts? There are times when color, which is more than emphasis, more than truth, more than the bare fact itself in proof, gives meaning concealed or dimmed without it. In what light is this or that fact to be regarded? How is it affected by this or that other one or by the general complex? The brief gives the legal painter his chance. But it is a dangerous one if he attempts to apply color which is not on the palette of the case."

(II A. 987-988; V A. 2654). He allowed inquiry into the entire "competitive situation in a market" (V A. 2654). Morgan recognized that such exchanges would have to be reciprocal (*ibid.*):

> It is often advisable to answer such inquiries [from competitors], because otherwise the competitor may be misinformed as to our prices and policies and answering the inquiry may avoid consequences unfavorable to the Company.

The "unfavorable" consequences that the defendants sought to avoid were lower prices and nonadherence to published terms and conditions of sale (I A. 159-160, 339-340, 501; II A. 588-589, 659-660). Deviations often were reported on forms used by the defendants' field sales forces to request authority to meet competition (I A. 150). If a "deviation"—whether or not it actually existed—led to lower prices or better conditions of sale by any major competitor, the "deviation" would spread (I A. 247-248, 340-341; II A. 588-589, 659; IV A. 2251; V A. 2410).

To guard against this, the defendants checked "significant" deviations with one another. They concentrated on, for example, the first changes reported in a market (*see, e.g.,* II A. 694, 909-910, 1104-1105): those allegedly granted to large customers (*see, e.g.,* I A. 232): and those involving "excessive situations" affecting market stability (*see, e.g.,* II A. 542, 552; IV A. 2298-2299). The more competitive activity there was in a market, the more the defendants exchanged information in an attempt to abate that competition (*see, e.g.,* I A. 213, 331, 627; C.A. App. 1722a).[12]

In this example the brief writer has focused attention on a memorandum, the importance of which is evident from its subject matter and from the elevated position of its author. The writer has then used telling quotations ("unfavorable," "deviation," and so on) and phrases of his own ("to guard against this," "to abate that competition") to characterize the resulting arrangement among competitors, leading to an argument that their purpose was to fix prices in violation of the Sherman Act.

12. U.S. Supreme Court No. 75-1560, October Term 1977.

When the brief writer is limited to facts that his adversary has proved or offered to prove, as when he is attempting to uphold a dismissal, summary judgment, or direct verdict, he may be able to state those facts in a way that emphasizes their crucial gaps and limitations, and so leave the reader convinced the judgement was right.

An example of this technique is furnished by the case of *Niemi v. National Broadcasting Co.* Defendants had telecast a fictional drama in which a girl was sexually assaulted; shortly afterwards, in real life, a girl was brutally attacked in a similar manner. She sued the television network for negligence, claiming that the show had inspired the real-life crime. The trial court held that the telecast was protected by the First Amendment, because it merely depicted a crime and concededly was not intended to incite members of the audience to commit a similar crime. The case was dismissed before trial. On appeal, however, plaintiff contended that she need not show incitement: If the show caused the later crime, even if not so intended, the First Amendment did not apply.

In their brief on appeal, defendants' counsel were not in a position to dispute the facts that plaintiff offered to prove. They could and did, however, describe those facts in such a way as to suggest that the evidence of proximate cause was vague and uncertain, and that no one could accurately foresee the effects of a crime show on a viewing audience. The factual summary led directly to the later argument that if First Amendment protection were denied in a case of this kind then almost any dramatic show depicting violence could give rise to a broadcaster's liability. Relevant excerpts (with footnotes omitted) are quoted below.

Although appellant's counsel acknowledged that contradictory testimony existed (R.T. 730-33; 742:2), he asserted that some members of the Smith group saw the shower scene from "Born Innocent." (R.T. 734:1-25; 740:4-5) Appellant also contended that, in any event, each of the four, including Sharon Smith, (who alone admitted wielding the bottle used in the assault) had *heard* about the scene in "Born Innocent" prior to the Baker Beach incident. (R.T. 730-33)

Factual Statements

Appellant offered to introduce expert testimony that the attack upon appellant was proximately caused by the influence of the film "Born Innocent" on these assailants because they either saw or at least heard about the assault scene in that film. (R.T. 752:4-12) It was also argued that it was foreseeable that third parties would commit a criminal act in imitation of such a scene and hence that the film's broadcast was negligent and reckless. Such allegations were premised primarily on studies and proposed expert testimony which appellant argues would have proved that viewing televised violence may increase aggression among children. (R.T. 681-85; 745:25-749; 751:17-753:10) . . .

It was alleged to be particularly negligent to broadcast the film at the time it was shown. (See generally R.T. 675:3-8; 701:14-16; 704: 24-705:7) In addition, appellant argued that it was negligent to precede the broadcast with an audience advisory suggesting parental discretion since "an advisory to a child is like a red flag to a bull." (R.T. 706) Paradoxically, appellant also asserted that respondents were negligent in *not* using an audio, as well as a visual advisory. (R.T. 705:26-27)[13]

Throughout this summary of the adversary's evidence the reader is made aware of the uncertainties inherent in a proximate cause standard, as compared to a required element of actual incitement. The stage is set for an argument based on law and social policy.

It is often a matter of opinion which facts are important, and it is therefore quite legitimate for opponents in any controversy to highlight different sets of facts as being crucial for purposes of the decision. Judges themselves differ sharply in the facts they pick to emphasize. In *Saia v. New York,* for example, which tested the validity of a local ordinance forbidding sound amplification devices without permission, the majority of the Supreme Court held that the ordinance violated the First Amendment. Accordingly their statement of fact emphasized the serious nature of the prior restraint on the appellant's rights of free speech.

13. *Niemi v. National Broadcasting Co.*, Cal. Ct. App. (1st Dist., Div. Four) No. 1 Civil 46981

Appellant is a minister of the religious sect known as Jehovah's Witnesses. He obtained from the Chief of Police permission to use sound equipment, mounted atop his car, to amplify lectures on religious subjects. The lectures were given at a fixed place in a public park on designated Sundays. When this permit expired, he applied for another one but was refused on the ground that complaints had been made. Appellant nevertheless used his equipment as planned on four occasions, but without a permit. He was tried in Police Court for violations of the ordinance. It was undisputed that he used his equipment to amplify speeches in the park and that they were on religious subjects. Some witnesses testified that they were annoyed by the sound, though not by the content of the addresses; others were not disturbed by either.[14]

The dissenters, however, emphasized the facts showing that appellant's loudspeakers were obtrusive and annoying.

The appellant's loud-speakers blared forth in a small park in a small city. The park was about 1,600 feet long and from 250 to 400 feet wide. It was used primarily for recreation, containing benches, picnic and athletic facilities, and a children's wading pool and playground. Estimates of the range of the sound equipment varied from about 200 to 600 feet. The attention of a large fraction of the area of the park was thus commanded.[15]

Just as judges do in their opinions, advocates in their briefs may legitimately choose different sets of facts to emphasize. They should not omit key facts against them, but the facts they highlight will certainly be different. For example, in the recent case of *Upjohn Co. v. United States* the question was whether files relating to an internal investigation conducted by the company's general counsel were privileged, when many of the participants were not part of the company's "control group." The company argued, in effect, that their counsel's investigation had been conducted as confidentially as possible, given the circumstances, and that application of the control group test

14. *Saia v. New York,* 334 U.S. 558, 559 (1948) (majority opinion).
15. *Ibid.* 562-563 (dissenting opinion).

would effectively destroy the privilege. The government replied, in substance, that the investigation was far broader than a mere inquiry by counsel, and that the control group test should be followed. Accordingly the factual statement for Upjohn stressed the point that the investigation was conducted by Gerard Thomas, as general counsel, and through members of "senior management."

> During their investigation, Mr. Thomas and outside counsel interviewed approximately 86 officers or employees of Upjohn or its affiliates. Those interviewed were selected from among the members of Upjohn's senior management because they exercised supervisory authority over the expenditures of an operating unit of the Company. . . .
>
> As part of the investigation, the attorneys also prepared a questionnaire, which was sent to the members of senior management responsible for the activities of Upjohn's foreign affiliates. They were instructed to answer the questionnaire fully and accurately, and to submit responses directly to "Gerard Thomas, the Company's General Counsel."[16]

On the other hand the United States in its statement of facts emphasized that R.T. Parfet, Jr., the Chairman of the Board, was in overall charge of the investigation, and that all foreign employees of the company were asked to provide information.

> In his capacity as chairman of the board and chief executive officer, Parfet stated to the employees that he felt that "the subject must be thoroughly reviewed and [had] charged Gerard Thomas with that responsibility" (J.A. 39a; *see also id.* at 28a). . . .
>
> In a letter dated March 8, 1976, accompanying the questionnaires, Parfet stated to the Company employees that he had decided that "it is imperative that the management of this company [have] full knowledge of any [improper] payments . . . made by The Upjohn Company or any of its subsidiaries" (J.A. 40a). He encouraged Upjohn's employees "to discuss these

---

16. *Upjohn v. United States*, U.S. Supreme Court No. 79-886, October Term 1979.

questions with anyone in your subsidiary who you believe would be able to provide useful information" (J.A. 42a). If the employee had any questions, Parfet advised that he "should feel free to communicate directly with your management and with Gerard Thomas who has general responsibility for this investigation" (J.A. 43a).[17]

Thus the government statement does not directly contradict the company's, but it brings out and emphasizes the breadth of the inquiry and the numbers of employees actually and potentially involved.

When specific facts like these are stated it is usually desirable to point directly at their significance by summarizing them or characterizing them in a sentence or a paragraph. The brief writer should make sure that his readers do not fail to draw the connection between his facts and the authorities he will shortly argue. A clear-cut example is afforded by one of the amicus briefs in *Steelworkers v. Weber.*

The relevant facts are clear. Respondent Weber is a white employee at Petitioner Kaiser Aluminum & Chemical Corp.'s ("Kaiser") Gramercy Works in Louisiana. He was an applicant for an on-the-job training program which used plant seniority as its preeminent nonracial qualifying factor. But, pursuant to a 1974 agreement between Petitioner Kaiser and Petitioner United Steelworkers of America ("Steelworkers"), separate racially segregated seniority lists were used for this purpose and only this purpose. An "entrance ratio" of one minority worker to one white worker was established for the program and was to continue until there was 39% minority representation in each craft. This figure was chosen because of its relation to the number of blacks in the area surrounding the plant. *As a result of this 50% quota, Weber's admission was denied. A black employee with less seniority was admitted to the program from which Weber was excluded solely because of his race.* (Emphasis added.)[18]

17. *Ibid.*
18. Brief Amici Curiae of Anti-Defamation League of B'nai Brith, *et al.,* *Steelworkers v. Weber,* U.S. Supreme Court Nos. 78-432, 78-435, and 78-436, October Term 1978.

Here the brief writer first states the facts in a relatively neutral fashion, and then characterizes the program as a "quota" that resulted in the white employee's being "excluded solely because of his race." These factual conclusions from the bridge between the evidence and the legal argument to follow.

DECISIONS AND FINDINGS BELOW

When a case is on appeal the brief writers must tell the court what happened in the court or agency below, as well as describe the relevant evidence. The two factual statements may be presented under a single heading (usually "Statement of the Case" or "Statement") or set forth under separate headings, one for the facts ("Statement of Facts," "The Evidence," etc.) and one for the proceedings of the lower court or agency ("Proceedings Below," "Decision(s) Below," etc.). Rule 28(a)(3) of the Federal Rules of Appellate Procedure requires a "statement of the case" that "shall first indicate briefly the nature of the case, the course of proceedings, and its disposition in the court below," to be followed by a statement of the facts. Many rules of court do not specify any particular order.

A statement of proceedings below should be reliable and fair, not only because it is a recital of fact but because judges resent distorted descriptions of the work of other judges. The lawyer for appellant or petitioner who will not even state the adverse ruling accurately or who cannot bring himself to state it without in the same breath arguing that it is without basis in law or fact, is certain to annoy his readers. First judges want to know what the decision was. After that they will be ready to hear why it was erroneous.

Thus many statements of the proceedings below are confined to a strictly impartial statement of the results reached in the prior proceedings. For example, in the case of *National Labor Relations Board v. Allis-Chalmers Mfg. Co.*, where a prior NLRB order had been set aside by a court of appeals, the

NLRB in its Supreme Court brief reviewed the prior proceedings in entirely neutral language.

> The Company filed charges with the Board alleging that the Union's assessment and attempted collection of the fines constituted restraint and coercion of the employees in the exercise of their right to refrain from participation in union activities, in violation of Section 8(b)(1)(A) of the National Labor Relations Act (R. 3-4). The Board (with Member Leedom dissenting) held that the conduct complained of did not violate that Section, and dismissed the complaint issued by the General Counsel (R. 13-24).
>
> The Company petitioned the court below to review the Board's dismissal order. A panel of the court (Judges Kiley, Knoch and Castle) upheld the Board's decision (R. 84-93). Following a rehearing *en banc,* the court (with Chief Judge Hastings, and Judges Kiley and Swygert dissenting) withdrew its earlier opinion and held that the Union's action violated Section 8 (b)(1)(A) of the Act (R. 96-123). The court accordingly set aside the Board's order dismissing the complaint, and remanded the case to the Board for further proceedings (R. 103).[19]

There is no reason, however, why the brief writer cannot emphasize whatever aspects of the decision below he thinks will help his case, provided he does not distort the decision itself. As with the evidence, he can key his statement to his argument to follow.

If there is one decision below, the brief for the appellee or respondent will usually set forth at some length, with a liberal use of quotations, to show that it is well considered and sound. The opposing brief will state the same holding, but will focus on questionable points in the court's reasoning, and on conclusions that may be erroneous, with quotations designed to pinpoint these portions for later argument.

If there are two decisions below, and they reached opposite conclusions, each side will stress the one favorable to it and minimize the other—again, without misstating it. Thus in the

19. *National Labor Relations Board v. Allis Chalmers Manufacturing Co.,* U.S. Supreme Court No. 216, October Term 1966.

Gypsum case, for example, the government's statement in its Supreme Court brief on the merits begins with the result at trial, so emphasizing the jury verdict convicting the company.

> After a 19-week trial, respondents were convicted of conspiring to fix the prices and terms of sale of gypsum board, in violation of Section 1 of the Sherman Act. The statement of the evidence that follows is presented, as it must be, in the light most favorable to the prosecution. *See Glasser v. United States*, 315 U.S. 60, 80.[20]

In the company's counterstatement of the case, however, the Court of Appeals decision is placed first so that the claimed errors at trial can be stressed from the beginning.

> The Court of Appeals *reversed* respondents' convictions under Section 1 of the Sherman Act, 15 U.S.C. § (1973), and remanded for a new trial. Judges Hunter and Adams *joined in ordering reversal* because the trial court refused to permit the jury to consider respondents' lawful purpose to comply with the Robinson-Patman Act in determining whether their limited exchanges of competitive information violated the Sherman Act (Pet. App. 12a-29a; 550 F.2d at 120-27). Judge Hunter also believed that the trial judge's incorrect instructions on key aspects of conspiracy law constituted *additional grounds for reversal*. (Pet. App. 29a-39a; 550 F.2d at 127-30). Judge Adams *reinforced the judgment of reversal* in a concurring opinion which detailed the facts supporting his conclusion that the trial court coerced verdicts from a deadlocked jury by conveying to the jury foreman, in a private meeting held on the seventh day of sequestered deliberations, the clear impression that the court wanted a verdict "one way or the other." (Emphasis added.)[21]

Findings of fact deserve special emphasis in the statement. Ordinarily such findings are entitled to deference at least; if supported by evidence they may be conclusive. Accordingly, the brief writer will hammer them home whenever they are in his favor. Often it is most effective to state the relevant facts

---

20. *United States v. United States Gypsum Co.*, U.S. Supreme Court No. 76-1560, October Term 1977.
21. *Ibid.*

and then the relevant finding, then another set of facts with its relevant finding, and so on, topic by topic, through one unified statement. If carefully done, such a statement can build a virtually impregnable wall of facts.

For example, in *Great Atlantic & Pacific Tea Company v. F.T.C.*, the Federal Trade Commission brought action against A & P for inducing price discrimination. When the case reached the Supreme Court the Commission had the benefit of favorable findings by an administrative law judge and by the Commission itself, as approved by the Court of Appeals. These the Commission interspersed with references to the evidence throughout a single "Statement." The following are two illustrative paragraphs.

> A & P itself determined that Borden's offer was "substantially better" and "considerably more attractive" than Bowman's (A. 214a-215a, 304a-305a, 772a-779a, 841a-880a, 1089a, 1121a-1122a). Borden's final bid offered A & P nearly $83,000 in additional annual savings. Borden thus offered annual savings approximately 11 percent greater than those offered by Bowman. The administrative law judge, the Commission, and the court of appeals all rejected A & P's contention that Bowman's offer was as good as or better than Borden's (A. 1112a, 1199a, 1210a & n.16; Pet. Ap. 4a-5a, 6a, 17a, 19a). . . .
>
> The Borden–A & P agreement entailed some reduction of services to A & P. Two months after the beginning of the private label service to A & P, Borden extended to other retail customers in the Chicago area the same limited service option. (A. 1105a-1106a). The discounts offered to other customers electing reduced services were not as large as those given to A & P (A. 1097a, 1105a-1106a). The administrative law judge found that the discriminatory prices received by A & P were between 6 percent and 22.5 percent lower than the prices paid by A & P's competitors (A. 1093a-1099a, 1183a-1192a).[22]

Faced with this kind of a statement, the opposing advocate can argue that the findings are incorrect or incomplete or inconclusive, as the A & P brief writers did, but the battle is uphill.

---

22. *Great Atlantic & Pacific Tea Co., v. F.T.C.*, U.S. Supreme Court No. 77-654, October Term 1978.

8
THE
ARGUMENT

When the judge reaches the argument in a brief he already has a grasp of the questions presented, and he has been at least introduced to the principal facts. He may already have a tentative decision in mind, but it is not firm until he (a) reviews the authorities and (b) learns how the opposing advocates argue the facts and the law. Both the authorities and the argument are traditionally included in the part of the brief entitled "Argument," and both are essential to the judge's understanding of the case.

To the extent that the argument states existing law it, like the statement of facts, must be accurate. Lawyers are under a duty not to distort the authorities they cite. They are also ethically required to bring to the court's attention "legal authority in the controlling jurisdiction directly adverse to the position of his client" unless his adversary has already done so.[1]

The same Canon of the ABA Code of Professional Responsibility just quoted, however, reminds the advocate to "argue the existing law in the light most favorable to his client," and related rules remind the bar that "adverse presentation" of the evidence and the issues is an essential element of the adversary system.[2] In the argument, accordingly, the brief writer should comment on the facts, not just describe them; comment on the authorities, not just summarize them; analyze the options, not just state what they are. He should tell the judges unhesitatingly why he is right and his opponent is wrong.

The court's ultimate question to counsel is: What should be

1. Canon 7, E.C. 7.23, ABA Code of Professional Responsibility, as amended 1980.
2. *Ibid.*, E.C. 719, E.C. 720.

done with this case, and why? To this question the advocate should provide a direct answer. In his mind's eye he sits at the judge's right hand and advises him, as an expert with a partisan point of view. His opponent sits on the other hand of the judge, and gives him different advice, but both advocates are counselors in the broad sense of the word. Both are saying: If I were in your shoes, here is what I would do, and why I would do it, and how I would justify my decision.

Because he is fundamentally a counselor, though partisan, the brief writer should avoid the verbal brawl. He is not being asked to put on an exhibition fight with his adversary, while the judge sits by as a spectator, but to assist the judge in reaching a just and reasoned decision. Let his opponent kick and scream; the effective advocate will avoid the temptation. He will not get down into the pit, but will sit where he belongs, right by the judge's side, and advise him.

ORDER OF ARGUMENT

Ordinarily counsel for the appellant or petitioner or moving party will place his strongest point first, because he wants to make a powerful impression on the judges from the outset.[3] He has the burden of persuading them and he must get their attention; if he saves his best for the last, their minds may be set against him before they ever reach it. As Judge Goodrich of the Third Circuit expressed it,

> For the appellant the best rule is to bring up the strongest point first and hit it as hard as it can be hit. It is the first point which necessarily assumes primary importance in the minds of

3. "Generally, a point that goes to the very heart of the case should be argued first. An experienced judge will usually select the strongest issue for study first. But the Judge initially may not know what is counsel's strongest issue, unless counsel, based on his knowledge of the facts and his legal research, directs him." Tate, The Art of Brief Writing: What a Judge Wants to Read, 4 Litigation 11, 14 (Winter 1978).

the men in the black robes while their attention is at its highest. If unimpressive and smaller points are discussed before the biggest ones are taken up, the impression will be that this case does not amount to much. But if a good strong point is effectively presented, the smaller ones may fall into place as clinching arguments to support the conclusion already indicated by the strong first point.[4]

There are, however, exceptions to this rule. If, for example, the petitioner in a court of last resort has won at trial only to lose in a court of appeal because of a technicality, Counsel may have to place a technical point first to convince the court that it need listen to the merits at all.

Counsel for the responding party should not unthinkingly follow his adversary's sequence, but should not automatically reject it, either.[5] It may possibly be the order in which his own argument can best be developed, or it may be as good as any other; if so, it will make for clarity and convenience if he follows his opponent point for point. But the advocate for the responding party should also have the right to emphasize what is important from his own point of view. If he has what he thinks is a winning argument on an issue his adversary ignores, he should not hesitate to place it first, and to state why he thinks it is decisive. He should establish his own issues in the minds of the judges.

Whatever order he chooses, the brief writer will do well to explain it at the outset. Just a sentence or two will tell the court how the issues interrelate, and why he has chosen a given sequence. In an appellant's brief, for example, the author might state,

In this brief appellants will first argue the challenged instructions and evidentiary rulings respecting the appellees' Canadian venture, because these are logically interrelated. Taken together, these were so prejudicial as to require reversal.

4. Goodrich, A Case on Appeal—A Judge's View, in A Case on Appeal (4th ed. 1967).
5. *See* Stern and Gressman, Supreme Court Practice 718 (5th ed. 1978).

In a brief for appellees the advocate might explain why he has chosen to follow a different order than the appellant has chosen. For example

Appellees will present first their contention that the statute of frauds requires an affirmance, regardless of the court's disposition of the other issues on this appeal. Secondly appellees will deal with the asserted errors at trial, in the sequence used in appellant's opening brief.

As the brief writer proceeds from issue to issue and argument to argument he will help the court if he continues to explain the logical interrelationships. For example

Such wholesale exclusion of relevant evidence, as described above in detail, in itself warrants reversal. But these errors were compounded by remarks of the trial judge referring to the offered evidence that could not have failed to prejudice the jury. We now consider these remarks, and the context in which the jury heard them.

Here the two interrelated arguments are linked together so that one builds upon the other.

Some brief writers have the unfortunate habit of insisting that each argument is independently decisive, and then stating in the next breath that if it fails another argument is independently decisive, but if the second argument loses, there is a third argument, and so on. Thus they proceed, in what might be called a trench-by-trench retreat. For example

As argued above, the claim is barred by limitations. If the court rejects that contention plaintiff is nevertheless barred by laches and estoppel, and even if plaintiff is not so barred, the evidence nevertheless shows that plaintiff knowingly waived any claim he might have had.

The difficulty with such formulations is that they are defensive. To write "even if" clauses is to suggest that the advocate will lose at each successive step. Psychologically it is more persuasive to take a positive approach like the following:

> Not only is the claim barred by limitations, as previously demonstrated, but plaintiff's own conduct bars his claim on established principles of laches, estoppel, and waiver.

This formulation avoids suggesting that the court may reject the brief writer's arguments one after another. Instead the court is confidently invited to consider and accept each argument.

ESTABLISHING THE ARGUMENT

Establishing one's own argument is essentially a job of clear exposition, tailored to an adversary setting. Three important persuasive techniques, previously discussed in Chapter 5, are worth repeating at this point:

1. *Select and discard.* The brief writer should choose authorities that are binding, factually pertinent, and well reasoned, well written, and thus illuminating. Other authorities should be discarded because they merely detract from the best. Less is more.

2. *Argue step by step.* The brief writer should take only such forward steps as his readers can follow with conviction. The argument should be broken down into as many portions as necessary to permit an easy progression. Each point should be demonstrated before the next one is tried.

3. *Shrink conclusions to fit the authorities and the facts.* Overstatements are vulnerable, but assertions tailored to what the cases hold or to what the evidence warrants cannot be successfully attacked. Often conclusions are best set forth by quoting the authority itself.

As the relevant case authorities are set forth, their facts should be continuously compared to the facts in the case at hand, so that each cited decision will be recognized as directly pertinent and therefore persuasive. A good example of this technique is afforded by the defendant's brief in *People v. Massey*, a burglary case, on a typical motion to suppress evidence seized by police incident to the warrantless search of an automobile. Excerpts, without accompanying footnotes, are given below.

When the officers first observed the vehicle in which defendant was riding, there was nothing to suggest any illegality except that, apparently, the vehicle did not have its headlights on. Even if the police officers had made a routine traffic stop, such a stop, even to issue a traffic citation, would not have justified a search of the vehicle as an "incident" to the traffic stop. *People v. Superior Court (Kiefer)*, 3 Cal. 3d 807, 812, 478 P.2d 449, 91 Cal. Rptr. 729 (1970) (Evidence suppressed where police opened car door after stop for speeding and found marijuana on floor of car); *People v. Cassell*, 23 Cal. App. 3d 715, 100 Cal. Rptr. 520 (1972) (Police cannot make routine search for weapons after a traffic stop; furtive gesture did not provide probable cause for such a search after stop for a taillight violation); *People v. Moray*, 222 Cal. App. 2d 743, 35 Cal. Rptr. 432 (1963). . . .

Here, the police report indicates that, as the police car pulled alongside the vehicle, one of the officers observed a black male sitting in the front passenger seat wearing a blue jacket and a white shirt, which was part of the dispatched description of the burglary suspect at 1763 Union Street. But that observation did not provide sufficient justification even for a temporary detention. . . .

The circumstances here fall far short of circumstances justifying a detention illustrated in the cases. *See, e.g., People v. Flores*, 12 Cal. 3d 85, 91, 524 P.2d 353, 115 Cal. Rptr. 225 (1974) (police detained car and its occupants due to fact that their descriptions matched that of *a vehicle and persons* suspected of specific criminal activity); *People v. Peterson*, 85 Cal. App. 3d 163, 149 Cal. Rptr. 198 (1978) (co-defendant seen in a dark parking area, in unlit car in known high crime area, and defendant was seen running from behind a building to his car).

Here, the police observation indicated only a black male riding in an automobile wearing a blue jacket and a white shirt. Although the police had a report that a burglary had been committed recently, there were insufficient "specific and articulable facts" which, objectively viewed, would lead one to suspect that the person he intended to detain was involved in the burglary. For one thing, the police had no information that the reported burglar had an automobile or a companion. Furthermore, there must be numerous black males who, on any given day, wear white shirts and blue jackets.[6]

Quotations from relevant sections of statutes and regulations are essential; the judges quite naturally want to see the text of any such governing language set forth verbatim. Any attempt to summarize them, or to quote selected words and phrases, is immediately suspect. In order to consider the content, the judges must, of course, examine the full text of each relevant section.

Quotations from opinions, however, are discretionary. If they are brief, and apt in their language, they can be highly effective. But the writer should avoid numerous and lengthy quotations from opinions following one after another. Collectively such strung-together quotations are dull. They are also no substitute for the well-constructed argument that carefully explains how each authority fits with the central reasoning of the brief. Each quotation means little or nothing unless the facts and holding of the decision are indicated at the same time. As Judge Prettyman of the District of Columbia Circuit warned,

I would speak one emphatic, although trite, negative word. Never rely upon a quoted extract from an opinion, unless it accurately sums up the decision upon the point. Sentences out of context rarely mean what they seem to say, and nobody in the whole world knows that better than the appellate judge. He

6. *People v. Massey*, Cal. Sup. Ct., County of San Francisco No. 101712.

has learned it by the torturing experience of hearing his own sentences read back to him.[7]

In addition to setting forth the authorities, and linking them with the facts of his or her own case, the brief writer should explain the reasons behind each rule of law. The judges want not only an explication of the rule advanced by the advocate, but an explanation of why it is sound, equitable, and consistent with common sense, and therefore should be applied in preference to the competing rule advanced by the other side. As Justice Rutledge wrote many years ago,

> Perhaps my own major criticism of briefs, apart from that relating to analysis, would be the lack of discussion on principle. . . .
> . . . What judges want to know is why this case, or line of cases, should apply to these facts rather than that other line on which the opponent relies with equal certitude, if not certainty. Too often the *why* is left out.[8]

A good example of an argument that logically supports the desired construction of a statute is afforded by the petitioner's brief in *Teamsters v. Daniel.* The issue was whether the federal securities laws were intended to regulate employee participation in a compulsory and noncontributory pension plan. In arguing that Congress intended no such regulation, the Teamsters' brief first cites and quotes its best authority and then proceeds immediately to set forth the essence of the argument from a practical viewpoint.

> The heart of the matter is that when an individual becomes a participant in an involuntary non-contributory pension plan he is not in the capital market; he is in the labor market. In his capacity as wage earner and potential pension beneficiary, the employee is not an "investor" in any sense understood by Congress when it was protecting investors in the securities markets, and he does not acquire anything which can reasonably be

7. Prettyman, Some Observations Concerning Appellate Advocacy, 39 Va. L. Rev. 285, 295 (1953).
8. Rutledge, The Appellate Brief, 28 A.B.A.J. 251, 283 (1942).

assimilated to any of "the many types of instruments that in our commercial world fall within the ordinary concept of a security" H.R. Rep. No. 85, 73d Cong., 1st Ses$., 11 (1933), quoted in *Forman*, 421 U.S. at 847-848.[9]

Analogies often help illuminate an argument. Indeed, if it is not farfetched, an analogy may be the most effective way to drive the point of an argument home. Thus in the recent case of *American Society of Composers, Authors & Publishers v. Columbia Broadcasting System, Inc.* it was argued in one of the amicus curiae briefs that ASCAP was in effect an economic unit and that an agreement among its members on royalty rates was not an illegal restraint. The author suggested the following analogy:

> In this inability to function and simultaneously provide a fully competitive market internally, ASCAP precisely resembles a major law firm. When clients come to a law firm with complex pieces of work, the firm assembles the talents of the lawyers at its call and determines the rewards of each. The panel majority's rationale would call that a combination that tampers with price structure and illegal *per se* under *Socony-Vacuum*. Presumably, in order to comply with the Sherman Act, the individual lawyers in the firm must bid against one another to work on every client's case.[10]

During the exposition of the argument, the writer should pause from time to time to provide an interim summary. The judges need to understand and to be convinced of each step, and for this they may need a pointed conclusion in direct and simple terms. A good example derives from the case of *Kahn v. Shevin,* in which a widower claimed that a Florida statute limiting a tax exemption to widows unfairly discriminated against him as a male. At the conclusion of a major section of his argument the plaintiff, as petitioner in the Supreme Court, summed up as follows:

9. U.S. Supreme Court No. 77-753, October Term 1971.
10. Brief for Aaron Copland, *et al.*, as Amici Curiae, U.S. Supreme Court No. 77-1583, October Term 1978.

In sum, the *noblesse oblige* to "the weaker sex" exhibited by the court below does not aid women to achieve equality and discriminates unfairly against men. In particular, Fla. Stat. §196.191(1) perpetuates the myth that widows cannot, without assistance, make financial ends meet, but widowers can. Far from having any substantial relationship to a legitimate state interest, the classification at issue reflects stereotypical attitudes toward the roles of married men and women, hence, the financial status of widowers and widows. One-eyed sex-role thinking of this kind no longer accords with reality for a substantial and growing portion of the population.[11]

DEALING WITH OPPOSING ARGUMENTS

In dealing with his adversary's authorities and arguments the brief writer will weigh their relative importance and decide whether they must be dealt with at length, or briefly, or not at all.

If an opposing brief states an entirely obvious proposition, with or without citations, there is usually no reason to comment at all. If a major case is followed by a group of string citations, perhaps the excess authorities can be ignored. If the opposing authorities state a rule of law based on clearly distinguishable facts, the argument often can be brushed aside in a short paragraph. For example

Galloway cites six cases for the proposition that Transnational owed it a fiduciary duty to seek a fair price for the property (A.O.B. 37). Transnational does not question the principle underlying these decisions, but they do not bear on the issue here, which is whether a fiduciary is duty bound to speculate that property values will rise.

When, however, the opposing brief cites an apparently relevant case, or asserts a superficially appealing argument, the

11. U.S. Supreme Court No. 73-78, October Term 1973.

last thing the advocate should do is ignore it. If he can, he will distinguish a case on its facts or its reasoning; if not, he will minimize it and suggest better authorities or a better analysis; if pressed to the wall, he will argue that it is wrongly decided; but he will not allow it to go unanswered. Nor will he ignore an opposing argument that might appeal to a judge. He will show it to be unsound or illogical or irrelevant, but he will deal with it. The judge is waiting to hear his response, and he must give it.

When a case is to be distinguished on its facts, the brief writer will be most persuasive if he ignores immaterial differences and selects only those on which the decision should turn. The following, from Justice Brandeis's dissent in the wiretapping case of *Olmstead v. United States,* provides a clear-cut example.

> The situation in the case at bar differs widely from that presented in *Burdeau v. McDowell,* 256 U.S. 465. There, only a single lot of papers was involved. They had been obtained by a private detective while acting on behalf of a private party; without the knowledge of any federal official; long before anyone had thought of instituting a federal prosecution. Here, the evidence obtained by crime was obtained at the Government's expense, by its officers, while acting on its behalf; the officers who commited these crimes are the same officers who were charged with the enforcement of the Prohibition Act; the crimes of these officers were committed for the purpose of securing evidence with which to obtain an indictment and to secure a conviction. The evidence so obtained constitutes the warp and woof of the Government's case.[12]

Often what is needed is an analysis of the way the brief writer's adversary has keyed facts to authorities. Do the facts really fit the cases, or are they stretched to fit by a clever play on words? In *Rizzo v. Goode,* the Supreme Court dealt with alleged police violations of the Civil Rights Act in Philadelphia. In his opinion for the majority Justice Rehnquist pointed

12. *Olmstead v. United States,* 277 U.S. 438, 481-482 (1928).

out that in the prior *Hague* and *Medrano* cases there was evidence that named officers engaged in deliberate and persistent attacks on specified groups, whereas in the present case the charge was essentially of a failure to act. As he put it,

> Thus, invocation of the word "pattern" in a case where, unlike *Hague* and *Medrano*, the defendants are not causally linked to it, is but a distant echo of the findings in those cases. . . .
>
> . . . Respondents posit a constitutional "duty" on the part of petitioners (and a corresponding "right" of the citizens of Philadelphia) to "eliminate" future police misconduct; a "default" of that affirmative duty being shown by the statistical pattern, the District Court is empowered to act in petitioners' stead and take whatever preventive measures are necessary, within its discretion, to secure the "right" at issue. Such reasoning, however, blurs accepted usages and meanings in the English language in a way which would be quite inconsistent with the words Congress chose in §1983.[13]

Such analysis is especially effective when it attacks the structure of an entire argument. In *Friedman v. Rogers* the district court had invalidated a Texas statute forbidding the use of trade names by optometrists, holding that such information was commercial speech protected under the First Amendment. On appeal the argument was advanced that the statute was a permissible regulation of business conduct, intended to maintain high professional standards. In response the appellees first summarized such arguments and then leveled their guns:

> These arguments, however, are fatally flawed, for the "form of business organization and conduct" that appellants and AOA find offensive is in no way prohibited by the provision at issue here, nor, indeed, by any other provision of Texas law. Section 5.13(d) prohibits trade name use — nothing more and nothing less. Neither it nor any other provision of the Texas Optometry Act sets a limit on the number of offices that an optometrist may own. Neither it nor any other provision sets a limit on the number of optometrists that may be employed.

13. *Rizzo v. Goode*, 423 U.S. 362, 375-376 (1976).

Neither it nor any other provision sets a limit on the number of
patients that an optometrist may treat. The standards of care
that must be provided by optometrists are regulated by the Act
in specific provisions not here challenged or in issue. Section
5.13(d) has nothing to do with these other provisions.

The brief went on to show by hypothetical examples that an
optometrist with a hundred offices and a thousand employees
spending ten minutes per patient would not for those reasons
violate the act, whereas a sole practitioner spending two hours
per patient would violate it if he used a trade name. Thus the
purpose was to reduce the appellant's interpretation of the
statute to an absurdity, and also to lead directly to the appellee's key conclusion:

What Section 5.13(d) actually and directly proscribes is pure
communication, not conduct, nor even some combination of
the two.[14]

The *Friedman* brief thus illustrates a key technique in dealing with an opponent's argument. First, find a fatal flaw in the
reasoning, the facts, or the law relied on and point it out to
the court. Then show how the flaw is so fundamental as to
make the entire argument irrational or absurd.

To this technique may be added another of great importance, which is to show that the argument under attack is inconsistent with another position taken by the same adversary,
either previously or in the same brief. It is rare that any party's
statements or assertions in public and private over the course of
years are so consistent that such an attack cannot be made.
Often opposing brief writers will advance their various arguments so enthusiastically that they will fail to realize they have
advanced diametrically opposite positions in the same brief.

A good example of this technique appears in the government
brief filed in *National Society of Professional Engineers v. United
States,* in which the Society [NSPE] claimed that its rule against
competitive bidding by its members was justified by the need to

14. U.S. Supreme Court Nos. 77-1163, 77-486, October Term 1978.

protect the public safety. The government cut the ground out from under the argument by pointing out that the Society did not follow its own "safety" rule with any consistency.

> NSPE claims that price competition would force engineers to make unreasonably low bids, to cut corners, and thus to endanger the safety of the public. The work of an engineer, it asserts, "affects a population—and usually a large population—rather than an individual" and therefore "the consequences of error . . . are generally greater than in medicine or law" (Pet. Br. 7).
>
> Curiously, however, NSPE now argues that there is little risk of this kind associated with research and development contracts (Pet. Br. 16), although prior to 1972, it applied its ban against disclosing price information to such work. Similarly, safety apparently was not a problem under former Rule 50 of NSPE's Rules of Professional Conduct, which for many years provided that an engineer could ethically inform a client of the cost of services he proposed to provide, although the NSPE discouraged the giving of such information (see J.A. 7182). Moreover, despite the claimed concern for safety, for two years between 1966 and 1968, NSPE's "When-in-Rome" clause expressly allowed fee bidding in foreign countries (J.A. 6487). Nor does NSPE seem concerned for safety in recommending state fee schedules.[15]

If the opposing authorities and arguments are in point and solidly based, then their force must be conceded to the extent necessary. To admit nothing and concede nothing may satisfy one's aggressive instincts, but it is not a persuasive posture for an advocate. However, the brief writer should immediately indicate the limits of the concession and why it will not affect his own central argument. The emphasis should not be on the concession, but on its limited scope. For example

> It is, of course, true that there is no such express exception in the statute. Appellant has never suggested otherwise, but has always argued that the Act was not intended to apply to

15. U.S. Supreme Court No. 76-1767, October Term 1977.

> individuals in his category, and that any such application would produce an absurd result.

As another example

> Plaintiff argues that her alleged emotional distress will be uncompensated if her claim is here denied. True, but not all emotional distress is compensable. The question here is whether plaintiff has made out any cause of action for money damages for the distress she claims to have suffered.

In short, the concession of a point to an opponent should show that nothing significant is involved and should lead the judge back to what is material and decisive.

THE LANGUAGE OF ARGUMENT

As already pointed out in Chapter 5, the argument is no more the occasion for insult and epithet than is the remainder of the brief. Here, as elsewhere in the presentation, words are chosen to persuade judges rather than to illustrate the advocate's hard-hitting zeal or to release pent-up emotions. The name of the game is not to fight but to sell, and for this purpose alone should words be selected.

Partisan language, however, should be used. The argument is the place for comment and characterization, for demonstration of strengths and weaknesses, for appeals to principle and equity. The advocate should not hesitate to make judgments and to use judgmental language where it fits. Now in the argument itself, it is the time to do so. The following example is from the brief for defendants and appellees in a private antitrust case:

> The appellants failed to offer any evidence showing their actual net profits or losses in the sale of vanadium products — the figure which should have been the point of departure for

their entire proof of damage. They failed to produce any evidence from their customers to show how much they could actually have sold. They failed to produce any evidence to show how their costs of doing business in vanadium would have changed through the years. Instead, they deliberately picked figures from an unrelated business in which they had had some success and supplemented this with equally irrelevant figures from the books of the appellees.[16]

The brief writer can and should use words that convey the desired partisan connotations.[17] Such words can be highly persuasive in themselves if they reflect the facts. If, for example, a witness's testimony is superficially believable, but will be shown up as false, the writer can suggest this by a careful choice of words. For example

Smith's carefully crafted testimony on direct examination was that he "would not have been aware of" the $2 million payment when it was made (Tr. 723). Under the guidance of his counsel he recited the list of his many responsibilities as Chief Executive Officer (Tr. 715-17), and plausibly remarked that as a matter of "routine" he left "smaller transactions" in the hands of his subordinates (Tr. 719). He failed to mention, however, that he alone controlled the Special Fund, and that the payment in question was made from an agent of the Special Fund to an agent of the Ministry of Defense.

The brief writer should choose vivid and concrete words when he wants emphasis and bland or neutral words when he does not. In an intersection accident case, for example, defense counsel will pick dry and generalized terms to describe the accident and the resulting injury, but such words will certainly be too bland for his adversary. Plaintiff's lawyer will

16. Brief for Appellees Union Carbide Corporation and United States Vanadium Corporation, No. 16,149, U.S. Court of Appeals, 9th Cir.

17. For examples, *see* Philbrick, Language and the Law: The Semantics of Forensic English 84-92 (1949); Purver and Taylor, Writing the Brief: The Realities of a Criminal Appeal, 15 U.S.F.L. Rev. 31, 50-51 (1980-81).

describe the facts and the issues in concrete words: Defendant ran a red light and smashed into Betty Smith's car; she suffered multiple lacerations and plastic surgery; her face is permanently disfigured; emotionally she may never recover. This is the language of a person who wants a wrong redressed.

In a business regulation case, counsel for the company might describe their client as an "established" and "successful enterprise" that for years has produced a "popular" soft drink made of a "pleasing blend" of "inexpensive ingredients;" now the company is faced with "cumbersome restrictions" and "red tape" for which appropriate "relief" is urgently necessary. Counsel for the agency might describe the company as an "entrenched" and "highly profitable" corporation that for years has "advertised and promoted" a "mixture of water and cheap artificial flavors;" now the company is seeking a non-existent "loophole" or a "special privilege" in an effort to "avoid reasonable regulations" that have been "carefully devised for the benefit of the consuming public."

Brief writers' comments on the law will similarly be expressed in words with contrasting connotations. On one side the broad interprettion of a statute will be described as "liberal," on the other side as "expansive." On one side an older decision will be described as a "leading case" that states the "established, time-tested rule"; on the other side it will be described as an "early decision" from a "simpler era," the reasoning of which is "outmoded today."

Each side will use different vocabularies to characterize their own arguments, on the one hand, and their opponents' arguments on the other. One's own argument, of course, is hardly an argument at all, but rather the simple and inevitable result of the application of undoubted law to clear-cut fact. Happily, such an outcome provides each party with what he equitably deserves. The adversary's argument to the contrary is quite naturally mistaken and confused, because he has the wrong side of the case. For example

‖ Appellant's argument appears to be based on a mistaken
‖ reading of *Green v. Black Motor Co.*

If that is respondent's conclusion, she has been unable to find a single authority to support it. In fact, the law is clearly to the contrary.

Appellees struggle to fit the facts of this case within the mold of the *White* doctrine, but the factual elements of this case are fundamentally different.

That, unless we misunderstand it, is petitioner's position. If so, it confuses common law principles with the standards specified in the statute.

SECTION HEADINGS AND SUMMARY OF ARGUMENT

A brief is, among other things, a reference work. Therefore, headings and subheadings are essential in any extended brief. Judges must be able to leaf through it and see where points of interest are located. In longer briefs the headings and sub-headings are collected and set forth as the table of contents, so that the page locations can be seen at a glance. This is typically required by court rules.

When headings are interspersed within the argument itself they should be phrased in argumentative form, and not as mere topical references. If they are so worded, the judges will see immediately not only what the section concerns, but what the advocate argues. In the table of contents they will see the skeleton of the whole argument and, by comparison with the opposing brief, see where the main issues are.[18]

18. "Headings should always be argumentative rather than topical or even assertive." Weiner, Briefing and Arguing Federal Federal Appeals 67 (1961).

"Remember that the court usually gets its basic impression of the nature of your legal argument from these headings, because the usual practice is to turn to the index, where such headings should be inserted verbatim, and read it before reading the brief." Peters, The Preparation and Writing of Briefs on Appeal, 22 Cal. St. B.J. 175, 179-180 (1947).

A summary of argument is more than a mere restatment of the the headings, but includes key facts, principal authorities, and the essence of the advocate's reasoning. It is the argument itself, boiled down to the essentials, and stated in two or three or five pages instead of twenty or fifty. It permits a busy judge to grasp the core of an advocate's position before oral argument if he does not have time to read the brief itself. For this reason a few courts require it, although most do not. Whether or not it is necessary it is often advisable to include a summary of argument in a lengthy appellate brief. It may reach a judge who does not read the whole brief, and it may clarify the argument for the judges who do.[19]

The distinctions between headings and summaries of argument may be illustrated by the brief filed by the Secretary of Health, Education and Welfare in *Califano v. Aznavorian.* Grace Aznavorian had lost a portion of her Supplemental Security Income benefits because she had become ill during a trip to Mexico and had not returned to the United States within 30 days as required by the Social Seciruty Act. She filed a class action in the District Court and won on a holding that the relevant section of the Act was unconstitutional. The Secretary appealed. His argument clearly appears from the headings and subheadings in the index to his brief set forth as follows:

Argument
    I. The thirty-day rule of Section 1611(f) does not violate the Due Process Clause of the Fifth Amendment
        A. Section 1611(f) is constitutional if it bears a rational relation to a legitimate legislative purpose
        B. The 30-day rule is rationally related to legitimate governmental purposes
            1. Restricting eligibility for SSI benefits to United States residents
            2. Limiting benefits to those who need them for subsistence in the United States

19. Stern and Gressman, *supra* note 5, at 709.

II.   Retroactive monetary relief is barred by sovereign immunity

III. The district court acted within its discretion in limiting monetary relief to class members who are currently needy

In the same brief the Secretary's summary of argument is set forth in three pages. Four paragraphs are devoted to the points described under heading I. The following paragraph is illustrative.

> The right to travel abroad is not a "fundamental" right. It is "no more than an aspect of the 'liberty' protected by the Due Process Clause of the Fifth Amendment" and "[a]s such . . . can be regulated within the bounds of due process." *Califano v. Gautier Torres,* No. 77-88, decided February 27, 1978, slip op. 3 n.6. Section 1611(f) has no more than an incidental effect on the exercise of that constitutional liberty; the statute has no effect whatever on trips abroad that last less than 30 days, and it does not prohibit foreign travel of any duration.[20]

Thus the summary of argument is more than an outline. Although brief, it includes the essential reasoning contained in the argument.

INTRODUCTIONS AND CONCLUSIONS

Introductions can be useful for stating the essence of a case in simple language. Nothing else quite fulfills the same function: The statement of the issues is technical, the statement of facts is detailed, the summary of argument must summarize. If the brief writer therefore senses that he needs a spotlight right at the beginning—here is what this case is about, in a nutshell—he will draft such an introduction, trying to reach the nub of

20. U.S. Supreme Court Nos. 77-791 and 77-599, October Term 1977.

the case and at the same time to attract the interest of his audience.

Conclusions in briefs are usually extremely short, frequently no more than a statement of what the court is asked to do. Often there is no need for anything more. When, however, there have been numerous and complex arguments, with the most important stated first and the least important later on, the writer may very well use a brief summary to bring the judges back to the main points.

A conclusion of some length is often warranted when the judges have discretion as to whether or not to hear a case, or whether to grant broad or limited relief. Thus in *Smith v. Carberry*, a case in which it was alleged that medical care in the county jail was so substandard as to amount to cruel and unusual punishment, plaintiffs filed a posttrial brief that concluded with a two-page appeal to the court for action. The following excerpts are from the beginning and the end of the concluding section.

> The evidence on this first stage of the trial shows a pattern of continuing and pervasive neglect.
>
> The seriousness of the failure is no less, for those incarcerated, because no one official is solely at fault. To an inmate who is denied medical care it is no answer to say that responsibility is fragmented: that the doctors lack dilegence and devotion to professional standards; that the Sheriff fails to supervise his appointees; that the Mayor and the Supervisors fail to provide funds which they know to be necessary; that the public does not realize and possibly does not care what happens behind the walls. To the man with the chronic illness, the gastric disorder, the epileptic seizure, the draining abscess, the asthmatic attack, the cardiac arrest, the result is painfully the same, whatever the cause. . . .
>
> Official neglect is not likely to change, nor will the pattern of illegality be rectified, without the spur of the full catalytic and remedial powers possessed by the Court. With the aid of such powers the jails can be reformed. Plaintiffs urge the Court to accept the opportunity presented by this record.[21]

21. *Smith v. Carberry*, U.S. Dist. Ct. N.D. Cal., No. C-70-1244.

In this instance the brief writer reviews the essentials of the evidence, with concrete and telling examples. He stresses the point that other public officials have failed to adopt the necessary remedies and probably never will. He reminds the judge of his own unique and far-ranging powers and, in a final appeal, asks him to make full use of them.

9

VARIETIES OF BRIEFS

Each brief we file in a case has a different mission. We start in the trial court, let's assume, with a first brief dealing narrowly with the complaint: Closely parsed, the pleading is or is not sufficient to avoid dismissal. Or we plunge into the turmoil of an injunction hearing: One side will be irreparably damaged if injunctive relief is not promptly granted, the other side will be ruined if it is. Later we argue for or against a summary judgment, and still later we argue the admissibility or the weight or the legal significance of the evidence at trial. Then on to the court of appeals and perhaps beyond, to different briefs for different purposes, and for different audiences.

The wise practitioner will pay close attention to the varying functions of the briefs he writes and to the varying characteristics and powers of his readers. He will not repeat facts or source materials from earlier briefs simply because it is easy to do so but will make a reassessment in each case, asking himself anew the key questions:

In the present posture of the case what are my strongest positions, my most effective facts, my most persuasive authorities?
Before the present judge or judges what should I emphasize, and how should I write?

The present chapter deals with the varieties of assignments that the brief writer typically encounters and the ways in which he selects the content and style of each brief so as to carry out the mission at hand.

BRIEFS IN THE TRIAL COURT

When he writes for a single judge at the trial court level the advocate should learn what he can about the individual he writes for, and should keep sharply in mind the limitations under which he works, as previously discussed in Chapter 5.

The trial judge in the state court may have no clerk at all. In the federal court judges are allowed two clerks, but their cases are often complex and their dockets may be extensive. For these reasons the advocate should be careful not to burden the trial judge with invitations to engage in research. As far as he can, he should excerpt and describe in the brief itself whatever he wants the judge to consider.[1] Ordinarily the brief writer in the trial court should be guided by the following rules of thumb:

1. If testimony, an exhibit, a statute, or a case is important, quote the essentials in the brief itself.
2. Seldom be satisfied with a mere citation; give the trial judge descriptive detail.
3. If a piece of evidence or a legal authority is of only tangential or historical interest, omit it entirely.

Any trial judge is sharply limited in his ability to shape the law, for he must follow whatever is binding authority. Accordingly in a trial court brief the advocate will concentrate on the authorities he asserts are binding, or which his adversary asserts are binding, and delve into the secondary authorities or the persuasive cases from other jurisdictions only sparingly.

---

1. As stated bluntly in a recent article, "From what the judges say and from what I observe, the level of tolerance for the typical motion is about five pages of memorandum. More than that and the memorandum will either be scanned, referred to a clerk, or not read at all. If you want the judge to read your memorandum, be concise." Christenson, How to Write for the Judge, 9 Litigation 25 (Spring 1983).

Before making novel arguments or citing nonessential authorities he will ask himself the key questions:

> Assuming the judge agrees with this argument can he consider adopting it in view of the reasoning of the *Smith* case?
>
> This out-of-state case is directly in point but does it add anything to the *Baxter* holding from this jurisdiction, which I claim settles the matter?

These are considerations generally applicable to all trial court briefs. But the nature of the briefs themselves can vary widely, and the way they are written varies just as widely, depending on the purpose to be served.

The brief on demurrer or motion to dismiss is largely technical, like the pleading itself. The moving party emphasizes and quotes from the language he claims is decisive — because the actual and exact language of the pleading is determinative — and cites the most precise authorities he can find dealing with comparable wording. The opposing party emphasizes reasonable inferences from the document as a whole and also cites precise authorities tending to the contrary. On both sides there may be broad suggestions that the claim is or is not meritorious, but the judge is not likely to be swayed by such irrelevancies at the pleading stage. Is the claim adequately stated or is it not? That is the narrow question before him, and he will decide accordingly.

On motion for summary judgment or judgment notwithstanding the verdict the briefs are very different in emphasis and style, for now the parties no longer deal with a technical issue. The question is whether the issue should be tried at all, or whether, after trial by jury, the verdict should be nullified. Plainly the moving party has a heavy burden; if there is doubt, he loses. Accordingly his brief argues certainty throughout. The material facts are undisputed or beyond dispute; he quotes and cites extensively from affidavits and admissions to build an unbreachable wall of fact. His adversary, to the contrary, looks for chinks. Here, he points out, is an inconsistent fact, there a contrary inference, while over there is a gap in the evidence. The key conclusions cannot be drawn, or drawn as a matter of law, but are properly for resolution by the trier of fact after trial. He counters certainty by sowing the seeds of doubt.

On motion for a preliminary injunction or temporary restraining order the briefs are again very different, for here the parties no longer deal with certainties, but with probabilities. The judge must decide before any trial and often without live testimony whether to use his awesome powers of command. If he stops the defendant from doing something, or requires that he do something, will he maintain an orderly *status quo*, or will he create more mischief than he stops? If he fails to grant an order will the moving party be damaged in the interim, to the point that no judgment at trial can make him whole? The judge must make his best educated guess, from the untested assertions before him and from all he can judicially know or reasonably infer, as to what will result from his decision—and then hope he is right. Accordingly the effective brief will stress the common-sense realities in the case presented. The known facts, together with what they reasonably imply, are rounded out to produce a picture that is at least probable, if not fully proven. Likely scenarios are created on each side. If the advocate cannot cite chapter and verse, well then he cannot, but he appeals to the judge's broad experience in human affairs and calls on him to assess what is reasonably predictable.

Briefs dealing with depositions and discovery are so various that it is hardly useful to discuss them as a category. But they do have one characteristic in common with briefs on injunction questions, which is that they typically call for an assessment of probabilities. If the order is not granted as prayed, will the inquiring party be foreclosed from developing his best case, and thus be permanently prejudiced? If such-and-such a question is allowed, will it force the answering party to delve into confidential and essentially immaterial matters? If a far-reaching document search is ordered, will it result in mere harassment, or perhaps a burden so crushing as to force an unjust settlement? Here again the judge (or magistrate or commissioner) must make educated guesses, and the briefs will accordingly deal with probable scenarios. Because of the nature of these issues the brief writer should not neglect the potential value of affidavits to buttress his position. A sworn statement that certain facts, listed and identified, prefigure the relevance and importance of the inquiry, or that the inquiry will necessarily disrupt or harass the responding party in specific ways, or to a specific extent quantified in hours or dollars, can serve to dispel the judge's uncertainty.

Each of these types of briefs in the trial court should be concise, although the supporting factual material may be lengthy. Usually the governing law itself can be briefly stated.

BRIEFS BEFORE AGENCIES, COMMISSIONS, AND BOARDS

Briefs submitted to governmental agencies or to other organizations having quasi-governmental powers can be every bit as important as briefs submitted to a trial court.

Typically a governmental or quasi-governmental agency will have a special expertise and broad discretionary powers, so that its findings will be accorded deference in the courts. Once made, its decision will be difficult to reverse. Thus the practitioner should make every effort to win before the agency, and before he reaches the reviewing court.

Furthermore, an agency has a special need for a good brief. Because its powers may be relatively undefined in enabling statutes and appellate decisions, and its procedures and even its governing purposes may be relatively formless, its members need all the help they can get. A clear-cut and orderly written presentation can become the bright beacon, the one reliable guide, in a welter of emotional speechmaking and special-interest pleading.

Usually the members of an agency or its hearing officer will have little use for legalistic technicalities, but they will appreciate the lawyerly qualities of the trained advocate. Often the contents of the brief are left to the lawyer's discretion, for the agency may have no published rules regarding them. Before any agency, the advocate will be well advised to include the fundamentals of a brief such as he would submit to a court—

1. a definition of the issues or questions presented to the agency for decision
2. a carefully selected statement of the facts pertinent to the issues, with judicious mention of those facts generally relevant to the equities of the case
3. a discussion of any statutes, legislative history, regulations, or precedents that can serve as a standard or guide for the agency's decision

In particular cases it may be helpful to include as well a brief introduction or a conclusion requesting a specified result or disposition.

A definition of the issues is often left out or brushed over, but this is a crucial mistake. The agency cannot be expected to decide the issues without knowing what they are. If the parties do not define them, the agency must somehow identify them, or simply assume what they must be without the benefit of the parties' views. If one side defines them and the other does not, the first may have successfully chosen the battleground, and the other may be forced to meet him there.

The choice of relevant facts is always important, but especially so if the hearings have been loosely conducted, with the resultant admission of great quantities of immaterial evidence. The agency then badly needs the help of counsel in sorting out the undifferentiated mass of material received. What is relevant and what is not? What is reliable fact and what is raw speculation? The lawyer earns his keep when he puts it all in order and culls out the key facts on which a decision may be based.

Often there is little legal guidance for the agency, but if so there is all the more reason for the advocate to find and present whatever does exist. After all, the decision must be based on some standard, whether expressed or unexpressed, and the lawyer who can furnish it has provided what may be the winning basis for the agency's determination. Perhaps the agency's enabling statute or history will provide a general guide; perhaps there are pertinent regulations or procedures; perhaps policy statements or speeches; perhaps analogies can be drawn from cases in courts or before other agencies or under comparable statutes or from general experience. Somewhere there should be the raw materials for a suggested guide to a decision, and if the suggestion makes sense, and there is nothing to the contrary, it may win the day.

It is true of course that a brief before an agency may be more freewheeling than a brief filed in court, as the hearing itself may be. But in bringing a sense of order and logic to the agency's proceeding the brief will provide a telling and perhaps decisive contribution.

BRIEFS IN INTERMEDIATE
APPELLATE COURTS

When a case is on appeal, the first step for both sides is to recognize that a fundamental change has occurred. On its facts the case has already been won or lost. The winner has only to defend the proceedings below; the loser must show that those proceedings are indefensible.

Counsel sometimes have difficulty making the necessary adjustment. The losing trial advocate continues to argue questions of disputed fact as if they were still open for consideration; counsel for the winner falls into the same trap, forgetting the advantage he has won. Neither advocate adequately recognizes that he is now playing an entirely new game, with different rules and different objectives.

As Judge Prettyman of the District of Columbia Circuit put it, with his usual bluntness,

Let us begin with a correct conception of what an appellate proceeding is. It is a proceeding for the correction of errors. An appellate court is not a tribunal for a general review of proceedings in a trial court or before an administrative agency. Many lawyers seem to think the appellate court is just that. They tell the appellate bench how they should have won their case and how iniquitous the trial judge or the agency was. Every losing lawyer thinks that. But the place to win lawsuits is in the trial forum. The purpose of an appeal is to correct errors of law.

As he added, later in the same article,

[D]espite popular conceptions to the contrary, appellate judges are not persuaded to hold a trial court in error by a pointless general discussion of some topic, or by the characteristics, good or bad, of the parties, or by the passion of a plea for reversal. The appellate judge wants to know from the appellant what the alleged error was and why it was an error, and from the apellee the contrary.[2]

The point is not, of course, that the advocate for the appellant can rest with pointing out errors that do not affect the fundamentals of the trial below. The advocate must show that the errors are so serious as to be prejudicial, whereas the appellee's lawyer will defend the judgment in part by showing that, errors or not, the judgment is fundamentally right. Thus Judge Friedman of the Federal Circuit, while agreeing that the appellate lawyer's function is "to convince the tribunal that the lower court did or did not commit reversible error," has stressed the point that the appellant must also show that his case is fundamentally sound.

Perhaps the most important requirement—and one that many lawyers ignore—is to present your own affirmative case. A well-constructed and well-written brief should leave no doubt in the mind of the reader that the position is correct. It is not

2. Prettyman, Some Observations Concerning Appellate Advocacy, 39 Va. L. Rev. 285, 286, 292 (1953).

enough for the appellant to show that the lower court erred. That court's grounds for decision may be vulnerable, but even to invalidate that reasoning does not necessarily mean that the court's judgment will be reversed. The appellate court may discern other grounds on which the judgment should be upheld.[3]

If the appellant is to present his "affirmative case" successfully he must show what amounts to a miscarriage of justice. Not only was there error: Because of the nature of the case, as he describes it, the error or group of errors was fundamental to a fair trial of the issues, and the result is so tainted that it cannot be allowed to stand. In his style the brief writer will try to transmit the sense that his client has been grievously wronged, that basic principles have been ignored, that justice has gone awry. His language will be controlled and respectful, but it will have an undertone of urgency commensurate with the far-reaching consequences of the grave errors that occasion the appeal.

On the other side, the brief writer will, of course, try to refute each claim of error, or at least to minimize it. He will emphasize the reasons, as expressed or unexpressed by the court below, why it could properly have made each questioned decision. But he will also try to show that, overall, justice was done. He will balance the appellant's affirmative case with his own as necessary. Calmly and temperately, he will seek to leave the impression that this is still another trivial complaint from a loser, a routine appeal from a routine judgment that should routinely be affirmed.

Both sides in their briefs will feel freer than in the trial court to cite out-of-state cases and other secondary authorities, for the appellate court is typically more ready to consider them than the trial judge. The advocates may and they should emphasize principle, and not just authority. They will, however, recognize that the intermediate appellate court cannot ignore precedent from its court of last resort and will seldom be persuaded to reverse its own.

3. Friedman, Winning on Appeal, 9 Litigation 15 (Spring 1983).

BRIEFS IN COURTS OF LAST RESORT

When and if he reaches a court of last resort, such as the Supreme Court of California or the Court of Appeals of New York or, perhaps, the Supreme Court of the United States, the advocate will find that he is required to make another radical change in his approach to his case. In most instances the court will have decided to review the case for a limited purpose, but within those limits its powers will be extraordinarily broad. The brief writer must stick to the limited subject matter of the review; within that relevant area, however, he can make any argument he thinks will be appealing.

Where the law of its own jurisdiction is involved, the court of last resort is free to restate the relevant legal principles along traditional lines or, if it chooses, to reshape them in a new direction. The justices will neither ignore nor easily depart from precedent, but they do have the option of reinterpeting or modifying it in light of changed conditions or perceived errors. These choices they take seriously. They have only so many opportunities to deal with any one subject matter, and they know their decision may settle a point for years to come. Not surprisingly they seek to do more than parrot precedent, but instead will reexamine the reasons for it. If the machinery of the law is still in working order they will leave it alone, but if it needs an overhaul or a replacement part or a tune-up they will take the occasion to furnish it.

Accordingly counsel before a court of last resort will do their best to convince the justices that their position is fundamentally sound as legal doctrine, whether or not it is fully supported by precedent. As stated in Stern and Gressman's *Supreme Court Practice,*

> The first and most important factor for counsel to remember is that he is writing for a *supreme* court whose decisions are not reviewable by any higher tribunal. The necessary consequence is that the Court is not bound by authorities to any greater extent than it wishes to be, and that the Court is much freer to

165

reach what it regards as the correct or wise decision than any subordinate tribunal. This means that, although prior authority is not to be ignored, counsel should place great stress on convincing the Court on grounds of reason and principle, apart from authority.[4]

The authors in this passage are referring to the Supreme Court of the United States, but their observations are also applicable to the court of last resort in any state when it deals with its own state law.

In support of his arguments the Supreme Court advocate may properly use not only precedent and logic but any reliable factual material that bears on broad questions of policy. What will be the impact of a given decision? How will it affect the present parties, others similarly situated, and indirectly, the public as a whole? Judges sitting on courts of last resort are keenly interested in such questions. The "Brandeis brief" may help them to reach a result in harmony with contemporary conditions.

The advocate may also use, and should use liberally, secondary authorities from highly respected sources. Judges who have the power to approve or disapprove precedent at will may or may not be swayed by a subordinate judge's opinion. If, however, the leading authority in the field has written a passage on point they may find it highly persuasive. Any well-reasoned opinion or article, if directly applicable, is likely to be more convincing than lower-court authority alone.

The advocate will, of course, treat the court's own prior opinions fully and with the greatest respect, but these do not necessarily foreclose further argument. An opinion expressed by the court on one occasion may not be followed when on a later occasion the facts significantly differ, even where the reasoning and language seem indistinguishable. The makeup of the court may have changed. Even the justices who joined in the prior opinion may see the need for an exception or a modification. The advocate who can point the way to constructive change, for reasons powerfully supported and per-

4. Stern and Gressman, Supreme Court Practice 711-712 (5th ed. 1978).

suasively expressed, may have the satisfaction of bringing about a true change in the law.

AMICUS CURIAE BRIEFS

All too often briefs of amici curiae are a tedious waste of time for the clerks and judges who read them. They add nothing to the briefs of the parties except the fact, usually predictable, that a given person or organization supports one side of one of the issues.

Not infrequently amicus briefs are so hastily prepared that they do more harm than good. Counsel are retained at the last minute for a strictly limited fee and asked to produce a brief. With no more than a superficial understanding of the facts, the law, and the underlying issues, they dictate a rambling statement full of errors and logical lapses. The replies of their opponents, of course, are devastating.

Such harmful briefs can be avoided, and helpful briefs written, if the amicus and its counsel will keep in mind the unique purpose of such a presentation. It is not merely another brief on the issues. It states the interest of the amicus, in adequate detail, so that the judges can appreciate the organization's concern. It states why, in factual and practical terms, a decision one way will be beneficial to the group involved, whereas a decision to the opposite effect will be injurious. If the arguments in its favor are already adequately made it adopts them and does not repeat. If there is some argument closely tied to its own interests that the parties themselves have omitted, and if that argument is sound and persuasive, the amicus brief sets forth that argument alone. Usually the amicus brief should attempt no more. It should not be repetitive. The very last thing it should be is a warmed-up version of arguments already made. If it is, almost inevitably, the rehash will be weaker and more vulnerable than the original.

The strength of the amicus brief lies in the fact that its

author represents not merely an interested party, but usually some segment of the public as a whole. The brief writer should emphasize the breadth of his constituency, without exaggerating it, and adopt a statesmanlike attitude appropriate to his role. He can and should discuss the alternatives before the court in judicious language, as befits a friend of the court, and to the extent he does, he may be highly persuasive.

OPENING, RESPONDING, AND REPLY BRIEFS

When issues are briefed in a series, as they usually are, each successive paper is different in function and format from the one before.

Opening Briefs

Because it is the first to be filed the opening brief must perform an educational function. Judges typically read it through first, or read each section before reading the corresponding section of the next brief, and therefore look to it in the first instance to explain the issues, the relevant facts, and the applicable law. The opening brief should supply such information comprehensively and should explain as clearly as possible all technical terms, concepts, and little-known points of law.

To explain the case well is an added burden for the author, but it is also an important opportunity. If the drafter does a clear job of exposition, the stage is set for all later discussion. Indeed, to avoid quibbling, the author of the responding brief may have little choice but to agree with the substance of the opening statement of issues, and much of the facts and law as well.

The opening brief should be comprehensive and convincing by itself, so that if the response is weak or if by chance there is no response at all, the court will be satisfied to grant the relief requested. No affirmative points should be left for the reply or for an oral argument; the court should have the entire argument before it in one document, and the opposing party should have a fair chance to respond. If the advocate deliberately saves a material point to argue later, the·judges will resent what they will view as an effort to trap or sandbag the adversary. Typically they will permit the opposing attorney to answer the new argument in a supplementary brief, and thus the drafter will have annoyed the judges and at the same time will have forfeited the opportunity to have the last word.

It is one thing, however, to make one's own argument comprehensively; it is another to anticipate contrary arguments and then answer them. This the brief writer should carefully avoid. He may have a very good educated guess as to what his opponent's arguments may be. If so, it is tempting to satisfy his own ego and show off his mastery of the potential arguments on the one side. But he must control the urge, and keep his predictive abilities under wraps. Seldom can a lawyer be sure that an argument will actually be advanced until he sees or hears it. Never can he know just how it will be rationalized or how persuasively it will be phrased. If he answers an opposing contention in advance he will necessarily state what he expects the argument to be, and in so doing he may articulate it better than his adversary could have. He will also supply his intended answer, and in so doing he will necessarily help his adversary to avoid the impact of that answer. If he has a reply brief to do it in, it is certainly more prudent to wait and see what his opponent argues and how persuasively he actually argues it. Then, in the reply brief, it is time to let loose the counterpunch.

Responding Briefs

The responding brief is, in a sense, two briefs in one. It sets forth the affirmative position of the responding party and at the same time responds to the arguments made in the opening brief. Because there will be a reply the advocate has no chance for a last word on any issue.

He does, however, have a different tactical advantage of great importance, which is that he can study his opponent's opening contentions and ponder their implications before he need commit himself at all. Before he sees the opening brief he may have roughed out his own factual statement and his own arguments, but now he can test each of these, and see if it can be improved. In view of the opening statement of facts, can he safely omit one segment of his own, and summarize another, while strengthening still another with more detail? In view of the opening argument, should any of his points or authorities be abandoned as untenable, or as too weak to be persuasive? Should others be expanded or stressed in view of the gaps or concessions in the opening brief? Has his opponent, perhaps unwittingly, suggested an entirely new argument? The advocate can and should reassess his position, not only to reply to the opening brief but to stress affirmative points that strike where his adversary seems to be vulnerable.

In choosing the order for his argument the author of the responding brief will often elect to start with his own affirmative points and then reply to his opponent, in accordance with the general principle that the strongest points should go first. Thus, if he agrees with his opponents that the issues are *A, B,* and *C,* he will set forth his own arguments on issue *A* and then answer his opponent's arguments on issue *A,* and then proceed in a similar fashion with issue *B,* and then with issue *C.* If he does not agree on the issues (his opponent defines them as *A, B,* and *C,* but he believes the real issues are *X, Y,* and *Z*) he will set forth his arguments on *X, Y,* and *Z* and then reply to his opponent respecting *A, B,* and *C.*

Often, however, to destroy one's adversary's argument is to make one's own. If so, the brief writer will find that his best technique is first to reply to his opponent on issue *A,* then conclude with his own contrary version, and then do the same with issues *B* and *C.* An example is afforded by the brief for the plaintiffs-appellees in *Graves v. Barnes,* in which the authors were seeking to uphold the trial court's reward of attorneys' fees in a voting rights case. In the following segment the reply to appellants' arguments is merely the reverse of appellees' arguments on the same issues and is so treated.

Appellants next argue that if attorneys' fees are allowable against the State, in this case the allowance was excessive (A.O.B. 21-24). Appellants concede that plaintiffs below, appellees here, are the "prevailing parties" (A.O.B. 23). They do not claim that in this case "special circumstances would render such an award unjust." *See Newman v. Piggie Park Enterprises*, 390 U.S. 400, 402 (1967); *Panior v. Iberville Parish School Bd.*, 543 F.2d 1117 (5th Cir. 1976). They do not dispute the established law that plaintiffs-appellees' entitlement to fees date from the inception of the action. *See Kingsville Ind. School Dist. v. Cooper*, 611 F.2d 1109, 1114 (5th Cir. 1980). Thus their argument in this section of their brief assumes that fees are payable, and that the amount thereof should represent compensation for a decade of hard-fought, complex and important litigation, in which the voting rights of Texas citizens were considered on three different occasions by the Supreme Court of the United States.

To sustain their position that the amount of attorneys' fees is inflated or otherwise unreasonable, appellants must show no less than an abuse of discretion. . . . [Discussion showing that the trial court properly exercised its discretion in accordance with established guidelines]

Appellants suggest, rather than argue, that the enhancements of the attorneys' hourly rates by a factor of two makes the fee award excessive, but they fail to cite a single case so holding. In fact, the cases have repeatedly held that such an enhancement is permissible, in the trial court's discretion, as a recognition of the contingent nature of the compensation and the results achieved. . . . [Discussion of cases permitting comparable enhancements][5]

The Reply Brief

Last in the typical briefing series comes the reply brief. Here is where the authors of the opening brief have their best

5. *Graves v. Barnes*, U.S. Ct. App. 5th Cir. No. 81-1557.

opportunity. No longer do they have the task of educating the court. They need not set forth their principal arguments. All they need to do, and will if they can, is to find the major weaknesses in their opponent's positions, highlight them, and destroy those positions altogether.

The reply brief should be like a knockout punch—short, powerful, and right to the point. This is not the time to scatter one's energies or waste time on details that should have been set forth in earlier briefs. As Judge Friedman in the Federal Circuit expressed it,

> A reply brief should be short, punchy, and incisive. Do not file a reply brief, as some lawyers do, that is primarily concerned with correcting minor errors the other side has made. Such a brief is a sign of weakness: it suggests that you have no good answers on the merits, and therefore are nit-picking at the periphery.[6]

The reply brief is the perfect opportunity for pointing out omissions, for at this juncture there is no chance for one's adversary to supply what is missing. If, for example, the responding party wholly fails to meet an argument set forth in the opening brief or fails to address any significant set of facts or any pertinent line of cases, the omission should certainly be stressed in the reply. Sometimes it can be viewed as a virtual admission that no response can be made. The technique, however, can be overdone. As suggested by Judge Friedman's admonition, the reply should not be an occasion for seizing on minor errors and omissions. It should hammer the main weaknesses of the opponent's arguments and then show, by reference to the opening brief, how these reach to the very crux of the case.

6. Friedman, *supra* note 3, at 18.

10

METHODS OF
DRAFTING
AND EDITING

Brief writing is an art, but it is also a process of production. It requires planning and scheduling and problem solving and quality control. The success of the final product depends not only on the creative skills of the product designers but also, and importantly, on the methods and procedures used in the manufacture.

Production methods are the subject of this chapter; here we are concerned with procedures making for efficiency, not style or persuasive effect. However, such methods are not unrelated to the creative side of brief writing. In practical effect they make possible the full use of the persuasive skills that the brief writer possesses.

PREPARATION AND SCHEDULING

A brief should be written by a single lawyer, even if it will be long and complex. With rare exceptions, the facts and the law are so interrelated that to parcel out the job is to invite a hodge-podge of different styles and approaches in the draft that no later editing can quite correct. Of course, the lawyer who drafts it may be given all kinds of assistance by means of memoranda of law and fact and by suggested arguments and approaches; but the writing itself should be left in the drafter's hands alone.

The drafter must personally master the case. It is of no help at all if someone else knows the facts or the law and he does not, or if someone else has thought through the arguments and he has not. If, for example, another lawyer has tried the case that is now on appeal, the brief writer must himself study the exhibits and the transcript and the trial memoranda. He must master the facts as they relate to the issue on appeal. If some colleague has done the legal research the brief writer must himself read the authorities and relate them to the facts, and then search out such other authorities as the present issues require. He must master the relevant law. At that point the advocate will be in a position to construct arguments, using the ideas of his colleagues but integrating them all in a single plan. When he has the arguments firmly laid out and has begun to articulate them in his mind, he will be ready to write.

If the facts and legal issues are complex such preparation takes time, and so will the later drafting and revising and editing of a unified and persuasive argument. Thus, if the brief is to be extended, the first requisite for writing it well becomes apparent: The designated brief writer should do all he can to prepare as early as he can, and before the briefing schedule itself begins.

On appeal, for example, both sides can start their spadework when the notice of appeal is filed, or before, and certainly without waiting for the transcript on appeal. Any remaining legal research can also be completed beforehand. The trial exhibits are available, with notes and perhaps daily transcripts of the testimony, and all that is relevant can be categorized and summarized. Tentative arguments or position papers can be prepared, even by the lawyers for responding parties, for they can usually anticipate the opening brief well enough to justify the preparation. To delay is to squeeze the time available for writing and to do that is to jeopardize the effectiveness of the brief.

When the spadework has been done the writer should prepare an outline of his brief, in more or less final form, depending on whether he is opening or responding. In either case he will do best if he will draft tentative versions of the principal headings he expects to use and then group the relevant facts and the authorities under each. After this, with the aid of the materials he has so arranged, he will begin to see what his subheadings should be. A typical page of such a tentative outline may look something like this:

II. *The Complaint Was Barred by the Relevant Statute of Limitations*
    A. *Discovery of Claim*
        Admissions of John Anderson, Tr. 75-81, 243-47, esp. 295.
        Def. Exs. M, N, BB, GG, esp. Ex. N.
        Testimony of Shirley Morris, Tr. 406-16—no contradiction of Anderson—general agreement p. 415.
    B. *Fraud Claim Barred 3 Years After Discovery*
        § 338(4)—quote.
        Novak, v. *Brill* (leading case) (quote p. 434)
        Carney v. *Jackson* (similar facts)
        O'Shea v. *Dubinsky* (similar facts)
    C. Plaintiff's Cases Inapposite
        Simpson v. *Darling* (insufficient knowledge—criteria p. 390)
        Garfield v. *Parker Motors* (Fraudulent concealment)
        Conger v. *Greenaway* (pleading case)
        Shatner v. *Dugan Brothers* (pleading case).

Thus the brief writer organizes his materials to the point where he has manageable segments to work with and a general design for each segment. Each important fact or authority has a place to go, and the whole outline appears to hang together. It may not be perfect, and it certainly is subject to revision, but it is as developed as he can practically make it before he actually sits down to write.

As soon as he knows when the brief must be filed, and has checked to see how far his time may be extended, the writer should set himself a time schedule. He starts with the required filing date, including allowable extensions, and then counts backwards, estimating so many days before filing for final cite checking, reproduction and delivery, and so many days before that for examination and editing by those who will read and approve the draft. Now he has his personal deadline. At that point he can also decide when he will need further help, and from whom, and arrange it for their time.

Having fixed his own deadline, the brief writer will do well to impose on himself an interim goal, which is to produce a complete first draft by approximately the midpoint in his schedule. In this way he will allow for major revisions, if they prove to be necessary, and for intervening demands on his time. If he does not allow for the unexpected he is very likely to fall behind, and if he does, the quality of the finished product is bound to suffer.

In the same way those who may edit the draftsman's work — a senior colleague or in-house counsel for the client — should mark off their calendars with a date for the expected draft, not only to jog the draftsman, but to set aside their own time to examine and edit the work. They too must complete their revisions on a schedule if these are to be considered and incorporated successfully. A crash program at the very end of the process is certain to create confusion, uncertainty, and error. Thus the cardinal rule for all concerned is: Get in front of the briefing schedule and stay in front of it. At every stage, timeliness is a prerequisite.

ORDER OF WRITING

Once he starts writing the brief, the draftsman should, as a rule of thumb, write it straight through from beginning to end.[1] Ordinarily the only exception is the summary of argument. The brief writer does not need the summary to write the argument because he has a detailed outline to write from, but he does need the completed argument to write a good summary, because it must capture the essence of the completed argument. The other sections of a brief, however, are

1. *See* Weiner, Briefing and Arguing Federal Appeals, 129, 201-202 (1961).

each built on the one before, and it is seldom wise to take them out of order.

The foundation stone is the definition of issues. Counsel should set this out at the start, in an introduction or a separate statement of issues or questions presented, so that from then on his own mind will be focused. He needs the framework, just as the judges will when they read the brief, and there is nothing like writing it out to fix the issues in his mind. Many briefs are diffuse and rambling because the author has failed to do so. They are full of wandering thoughts and extraneous facts and irrelevant law because the writer has never settled on the issues at the beginning and stuck to them throughout the brief.

The statement of facts should be written next, and before the argument. If there is more than one statement of facts (for example, a general and preliminary statement followed by more specific statements placed before separate points in the argument), they should be written in the order they will appear. The reason is that unless the facts are extremely simple the writer needs to see them written out, precisely and in detail, before he can interrelate them with the law and express his reasoning precisely and in detail. Just as the judges need to assess the distinctive facts of the case before they can weigh the argument, so does the brief writer need to set them forth on paper, and then judge the strengths and weaknesses of the finished statement, before he can prepare an argument tailored to the facts he has.

Within the main sections of a brief there is more latitude. It may be possible, for example, to draft one separable subsection of a statement of fact first, although it will not appear first, or perhaps to draft some discrete point in the argument out of order. But there is always a problem in doing so if the sections are at all related: To what extent will some fact or authority have been previously described? The author does not know this if he drafts out of order; he must guess at it, and then revise as necessary after he writes the earlier sections, and the result may be unnecessary awkwardness. If he writes in order he can sense as he goes what facts and law the judges will need at each step, he can make his transitions more surely, and he can keep his own sense of continuity. Usually the result will be a better brief.

ROUGH DRAFTING AND REVISING

Drafting a brief of any degree of difficulty is like drafting a complex contract or will in that the shape and position of each part depends on some other part. Each segment must fit with the others to make a logically coherent whole. But the brief writer must do more than solve a complicated Chinese puzzle; he must make his work look simple, as if he were putting together a child's toy, for his aim is to produce clear, readable, and convincing prose.

Perhaps there are brief writers blessed with such fluency and such powers of concentration that they can dictate from notes and produce an adequate draft of a complex brief on their first try. Most of us cannot even begin to do so. We must write segments in longhand or dictate them in short bursts and then entirely rework the resulting rough drafts before anything coherent emerges, and that is just the beginning of the process.

For most of us, the only hope is to try, try, and try again. We follow our carefully devised outline, but the first rough draft of any section is seldom right or even acceptable. Almost certainly we will want to revise it on the spot, often with major changes. Later, as the brief progresses, we may need to revise it again, or perhaps expand it into two or three sections, or change the fundamental approach, or perhaps eliminate it altogether. This is what brief writing is like even for the highly experienced draftsman.

Once we fully accept this fact, brief writing becomes easier, not harder, for then we are on the way to recognizing a basic principle of drafting: Get something down on paper first, and then work from the draft.[2] If we try for perfection at the beginning we make the process so difficult that we cannot write at all; there are too many variables, too many complexities for us to hope to solve them all at once. Instead it is far better to rough out a good prototype, as if we were designing a new airplane, and then test it and refine the design and all the details until we have the production model.

The rough draft is an experiment throughout. We really cannot tell, until we see it in type, whether our description of an event or an exhibit or an important case is adequate. Have we included enough of the material facts, or too many? Is that quotation sufficient to give the context, or is it, perhaps, longer than necessary? Would a few key phrases be more emphatic than a whole paragraph? After we see the description in draft, placed in its setting as part of a thought sequence, the answer will usually leap out at us.

Especially is it necessary to experiment with comments, conclusions, and argumentative statements of all kinds, for here we must listen acutely for the judges' reactions. Is this passage too hesitant or too qualified? Is that one an overstatement at the present stage, or does it need, perhaps, a citation or quotation for convincing effect? Until the writer sees it on paper and listens as he reads, he cannot intelligently decide.

How the writer gets his first draft down on paper is almost wholly a matter of individual preference. Some lawyers find it natural to talk, and therefore to dictate. Some prefer to write in longhand, and then interlineate and scratch out and add inserts within inserts. All will be helped if their source materials are ready in front of them—their outline, their relevant notes and memos, and their photocopies of each principal transcript page and exhibit page, each statute or regulation or rule, each pertinent page of court opinions or law review articles, all appropriately marked off and underlined. These

2. "There is, as Brandeis commented, 'no such thing as good writing, only good rewriting.' Edit fiercely; reduce your language to muscle and bone." Kaufman, Appellate Advocacy in the Federal Courts, 79 F.R.D. 165, 170 (1978).

sources should be devoured before the writing begins until they are part of the writer's mind, until his ideas start to form naturally into words and phrases and sentences. Before he actually starts to compose he should be ready as a fighter is ready in his corner when the bell rings, straining to get at his adversary.

When he does draft, the writer should write right through a section if he can, so that he can hold to his thoughts and keep his momentum. This means that he should have an uninterrupted block of time sufficient for the purpose, but it also requires a determination not to be sidetracked. Many writers find it helpful to set themselves a deadline for drafting purposes (*e.g.*, "I'm going to get this section out in draft before I go home") because then they will take full advantage of the only purpose of a first draft, which is to get something down on paper. The next time they see the section it will be in type, ready for a fresh and searching look.

When the first rough draft of a section is typed, the writing really begins. Now that the writer has a text to work with, he does a great many things at once, as well as he can on a first rewriting:

1. reconsiders the basic organization of the section and changes it if it does not proceed step by step
2. tests each statement of fact and law for accuracy, and revises accordingly
3. adds to and subtracts from citations and quotations as necessary
4. reviews each paragraph to see that it states and adequately develops an idea
5. sharpens his sentences so that each is simple, clear, and emphatic
6. sharpens his words and phrases for impact and persuasive effect
7. deletes all excess verbiage—words, phrases, sentences, and paragraphs
8. listens, as he reads and rewrites, with the ears of the judges

If all this is too much to do at once the brief writer can revise in stages. His first job is any major organizational revision that may be necessary; if the section does not hang together logically and must be rewritten entirely, then he must do what amounts to another first draft. In a second phase he can work with his authorities, revising as appropriate, and in a third phase with his modes of expression.

However he goes about it, the section should normally be completed to the author's satisfaction before he goes on to the next. Minor details can wait, but in essence the advocate should know the value of what he has written—how strong it is, how persuasive it is—before proceeding. He should work through the harder parts, and not skip to the easier parts, for it is always better to write his ideas progressively, in the same order that the judges will read them.

RESOURCEFULNESS IN WRITING

There are times when any brief writer hovers between frustration and despair. The section he has just finished does not seem convincing, and the writer is not sure why. He tries to write the next section, but he cannot find a way to express his thought. Something is wrong. Is it the choice of language or is it perhaps the thought itself? Is the whole argument misconceived? The writer must find the answer, and soon, for a deadline inexorably approaches.

Such a paralysis of thought, sometimes called writer's block, calls for a fresh approach.[3] Now the writer needs to be resourceful. If he cannot get past his obstacle one way, he must try another. Below are described some of the techniques that help writers to surmount the common obstacles.

Say what you mean. Brief writers can get lost in their prose because they are self-consciously writing, rather than talking

3. A variety of solutions to the problem of writer's block are suggested in Mack and Skjei, Overcoming Writing Blocks (1979).

to a friend. If, however, they are interrupted by a colleague and asked to explain what they have written, they will say it simply: "What I really mean is that. . . ." Suddenly they have the words; they are not inhibited by writing for judges, clients, and posterity. Accordingly one of the writer's most effective techniques is to keep asking himself questions such as these: What is the essence of this point? What do I really intend to say? Have I said what I really mean? If he does this he will get rid of his inhibitions and write, candidly and directly, what he meant to say from the beginning.

Get to the point. Closely related to the inhibited frame of mind is the tendency to postpone. Some lawyers spend too many sentences and paragraphs leading up to the point they want to make, prefacing it with unnecessary generalities, peripheral considerations, and premature qualifications, holding the point itself in reserve as if they were afraid to reach it. The writer gets bogged down (to say nothing of the reader) because nothing he is writing has much significance until he states the point itself. As soon as he comes to it he will be able to see whether his related observations have a legitimate place or are mere sputtering. Often they are better omitted.

Say it step by step. If a thought sequence refuses to come clear when written out it may be because it is badly written or because the sequence itself is illogical. If the thought itself is faulty, then no wonder the writer cannot express it to his satisfaction; the writing process typically forces the writer to recognize such errors. One way to find out the cause of the block is to break up the thought into its smallest components and then express it that way, in one short sentence after another. Does each sentence then follow in a logical sequence? If it does the writer can revise it, using the shorter sentences or some improved combination of them. If it does not, he has discovered the point where his logic breaks down, and can now revise the thought sequence itself.

Return to the sources. If analysis and rewriting do not solve a problem by themselves, perhaps the original sources will. Often if the writer goes back and browses in the transcript or in the pertinent cases, focusing on his present problem, something will show up: perhaps some express or implied admission he had not noticed before, perhaps some language in an opinion suggesting a new point of distinction, perhaps some reasoning that suggests a different argument. The original sources keep yielding up their insights as the brief progresses. In the same way source books help in finding words to express the writer's half-formed thoughts. There is no point in his staring at his draft and searching his mind for adequate words when he has a dictionary and a thesaurus and a Fowler's in his bookshelf or his library. Now is the time to get them out and use them.

Try a new viewpoint. Writers can often unblock their minds by trying radical new approaches. Perhaps they have blinders on, and do not see some simple solution to a problem. They need a new viewpoint. A brainstorming session with a willing colleague can be helpful, for another lawyer will not be encumbered with the writer's thought patterns nor any of the details of the case. To his fresh eye a new approach may be obvious. But the writer himself can also keep his mind flexible and resourceful by forcing himself into new ways of looking at his problem. He can think about it from the point of view of his adversary (what facts or cases or arguments would he fear the most?) or the man in the street (what would appeal to him the most?). He can think of how his current section would read if he reversed the present order, or omitted this portion or that, or broke it up into two sections, or wrote it to emphasize a key fact or a principal case, or perhaps conceded his present argument altogether and tried to turn the concession to his advantage. The important thing is to dare to try anything on for size, to let one's imagination run free. The exercise may seem like daydreaming, and it is, but from such unconventional thinking some idea may emerge, and the idea may break the logjam.

Put the brief aside. Any writer's mind will go numb after a period of concentrated effort, and when it does there is no point in continuing. One can turn to the record or the cases, or do some minor editing, or take a break or quit for the day, but to write one needs a fresh and agile mind. It is time to put the brief aside and allow one's brain to recuperate—for an hour or two or overnight—and then try again. Often the block will have disappeared by morning.

REVISING

Once the writer has worked through the brief section by section, it is time for him to sit back and look at it as a whole. Is each part so strong that it cannot be attacked successfully by his adversary? If a judge reads through the whole brief will it hold his attention? Will it convince him at each stage and leave him persuaded at the end?

The writer should be his own severest critic, because he is in the best position to make changes. By the time he has progressed this far no one else knows the facts and the law and the possible arguments as well as he does, even if someone else has tried the case, and even if someone else will orally argue the present issues. The writer has created the brief and therefore has faced and solved each of the problems presented by it. He knows what are the available options and now, with a searching new look, should make his decisions. If the brief needs changes, it is time to be ruthless about it, and reconstruct the whole draft if necessary.

In short, the writer should revise his own work just as far as he can, to the point where he is satisfied with its organization and its substance and its wording, before he turns it over to a colleague or the client for editing or approval. It is safest to assume that if he has not gotten it right, no one else will.

EDITING

It behooves the editor of a brief to be cautious, for the same reason a thoracic surgeon is cautious. He wields his scalpel in the body of a complex structure of interrelated parts, most of which perform a useful function. If he excises some portion in haste, it may be missed. If he implants some device of his own design, it may not fit within the structure. Thus, when a brief is generally well reasoned and well written the editor will do well to leave it largely alone. If he tries to put his own imprint on it he is likely to disturb the flow of thought or muddle the argument without realizing he is doing so. It is important for the editor to recognize, with some humility, that whereas he may be more experienced than the drafter he has not mastered the law and the facts, he has not analyzed the issues and the arguments, he has not sweated through the problems of drafting, and accordingly he is less qualified in these respects than the lawyer who wrote the brief.

What the editor can do, however, even when the brief is well prepared, is to read it through with the eyes of a judge. Because he has not written it, he can react to it as judges would, and flag those parts that would not appeal to them. Perhaps this section needs more emphasis or that section is obvious and should be reduced. Here is an unduly emotional phrase; there the point is too blandly stated and would not be noticed. The editor marks such places and then calls in the drafter for a conference. He does not so much direct the changes as point out the trouble spots he sees. Together they decide on solutions.

If the brief is not well done, and major surgery is necessary, the editor must himself become intimately involved with the analysis and the drafting. His first question is diagnostic: Has the drafter failed to analyze the issues and the arguments, or has he failed to write effectively, or both? The editor cannot afford to jump to conclusions, but must get to the bottom of the problem. This means getting out at least the key factual material and the principal authorities and reading or rereading them, and then walking through the arguments with the drafter. Perhaps the solution is simpler than it seems—change the order here, provide a transition there, put that point directly and not obliquely—but it may not be. Perhaps a whole new approach is necessary and the brief needs to be rewritten from beginning to end.

It is this worst-case possibility that underscores the need for getting ahead of the briefing schedule. If at all possible the draft of a brief should be completed and ready for editing early enough so that if necessary it can be rewritten completely and still be filed on time.

FINAL CHECKING AND FILING

Judges would like to be able to take for granted that every citation and every quotation in a brief is accurate, but they cannot. Too often briefs are sloppily produced at the very end of the process.

The entire brief must be proofread and cite-checked and Shepardized and reviewed for conformance to local rules after the draft is otherwise edited and ready to file, not because all the essential steps have not already been carried out, but because new errors will appear. Parts of the text have been changed in the editing process. The whole text has been retyped for the word processing machine or has been set in type by the printer. At any of these times mistakes will be made — not may be made, but will be made. It is rare indeed that a final check will not uncover errors.

Usually such final checks are made by legal assistants or secretaries or docket clerks or proofreaders, and in general they should be. Lay personnel, assigned to look for errors alone, are more likely to spot them than the lawyers. But the drafter should make his own last minute check as well, for his own expertise is unique. Here is an important citation to the record: Is the drafter sure that it includes the pages he wants, which he and his editor have discussed? Here are citations to a crucial line of cases: Has that latest case in the series, the one that was argued four months ago, been decided in the last week or two?

Here is a conclusion written in an early draft: Is it consistent with that revised paragraph appearing five pages later, and should either statement be modified? These are the kinds of final checks that only the drafter can make effectively.

In the end the brief must be filed, and filed on time, or it may be rejected entirely. This very last step in the process may be mechanical, but it is crucial, just like getting signatures on a contract or a will. Without it the lawyer has accomplished nothing. Accordingly the responsible lawyer will check on the filing of his brief like a mother hen to make sure there is no hitch—the messenger is actually on his way to the local court-house, the courier has actually reported from the distant city. He knows that there is always the possibility of human error and he does all he can to prevent any such disaster. If worse comes to worst he will file it himself; he will hike to the court-house through a blizzard; but no brief that he has written will fail to reach the attention of the court.

APPENDIX A

SUPREME COURT BRIEFS AND OPINIONS ON THE APPEAL IN KAHN v. SHEVIN

Comment: This appendix presents an example of briefing in a closely contested case on appeal where the facts are substantially undisputed. A further example showing the treatment of disputed facts on an appeal is offered in Appendix B.

The reader may completely examine each brief in this appendix in turn or read them as a judge might, examining first a section from the opening brief and then the corresponding section from later briefs, and so on. At the end are the Supreme Court opinions, where the reader should note which points from the briefs proved to be decisive.

Mel Kahn, a widower residing in Florida, filed a class action asserting that he and other widowers were deprived of equal protection and due process rights by a Florida statute limiting a tax exemption to widows. The American Civil Liberties Union Foundation became associated with his cause. The Circuit Court for Dade County, Florida, ruled in his favor, finding an unconstitutional sex discrimination, but the Florida Supreme Court reversed. On Kahn's appeal the case was then briefed and argued before the Supreme Court of the United States.

The first brief set forth below is the Brief for Appellants, with inserted comments by this author.

Supreme Court of the United States

MEL KAHN, etc.,

Appellants,

— v. —

ROBERT L. SHEVIN, et al.,

Appellees.

ON APPEAL FROM THE SUPREME COURT OF

THE STATE OF FLORIDA

BRIEF FOR APPELLANTS

Opinions Below

The opinion of the Supreme Court of the State of Florida is reported at 273 So. 2d 72. The opinion of the Circuit Court, 11th Judicial District, Dade County, Florida, is unreported. Copies of both opinions are set forth in the Appendix to the Jurisdictional Statement (J.S. at A1-A7).

Jurisdiction

On February 7, 1973, the Supreme Court of the State of Florida entered the judgment which is the subject of this appeal. Notice of Appeal to the Supreme Court of the United States was filed in the Supreme Court of Florida on May 4, 1973 (A.17a). The Jurisdictional Statement was filed on July 6, 1973, and probable jurisdiction was noted on October 23, 1973.

The jurisdiction of the Supreme Court to review this decision of the Supreme Court of Florida on appeal is conferred by Title 28 U.S.C., Section 1257(2). The following decisions sustain the jurisdiction of the Supreme Court to review the judgment on appeal in this case *In re Gault,* 387 U.S. 1 (1967); *Loving v. Virginia,* 388 U.S. 1 (1967); *Levy v. Louisiana,* 391 U.S. 68 (1968).

Statutes Involved

Florida Statue §196.191(7) provides:[1]

A widow is entitled to exempt $500 yearly from her property tax. Other persons entitled to exempt $500 include: those who have lost a limb or become disabled in war, by military hostilities or by misfortune and are residents of the state.

Comment: The foregoing sections were inserted to comply with Supreme Court rules and practice. The reader will notice that they are set forth as concisely as possible and with no adversary flavor added.

Questions Presented

Whether Fla. Stat. §196.191(7), which provides that widows are entitled to a property tax exemption of up to $500, but makes no provi-

1. Fla. Stat. §196.191 was repealed by Laws 1971. c. 71-133. §15, effective December 31, 1971. Section 196.202, replacing §196.191(7), was added by Laws 1971, c. 71-133, §12, effective December 31, 1971. Section 196.202 reads:

196.202 Property of widows, blind persons, and persons totally and permanently disabled
Property to the value of five hundred dollars ($500) of every widow, blind person, or totally and permanently disabled person who is a bona fide resident of this state shall be exempt from taxation.

The Florida Constitution sets forth the basis for this property tax exemption. Article IX, Section 9 of the 1885 Florida Constitution provided

... [T]here shall be exempt from taxation property to the value of five hundred dollars to every widow *and* to every person who is a bona fide resident of this state, and has lost a limb or been disabled in war or misfortune.

The provisions of former Article IX, Section 9 of the 1885 Florida Constitution, were incorporated in its successor, Article VII, Section 3(b) of the 1968 Florida Constitution, which provides:

There shall be exempt from taxation, cumulatively, to every head of a family residing in this state, household goods and personal effects to the value fixed by general law, not less than one thousand dollars, and to every widow or person who is blind or totally and permanently disabled, property to the value fixed by general law not less than five hundred dollars.

sion for men similarly situated, denies appellant, a widower, the equal protection of the laws.

Comment: This formulation of the question presented is concise and clear enough because the question is simple. An alternative method, discussed in Chapter 6, is to set forth the background facts first and then state the question itself. For example,

> Fla. Stat. §196.191(7) provides that widows are entitled to a property tax exemption of up to $500, but makes no provision for men similarly situated. The question is whether such a statute denies appellant, a widower, the equal protection of the laws.

Essentially the statement is nonargumentative, except perhaps in referring to "men similarly situated": the opposition would presumably argue that men are not similarly situated because of their superior earning power. In any case, as the reader will see, this phrase has been omitted from the oppposing version of the question presented.

Statement of the Case

Appellant Mel Kahn is a widower who resides in Florida. He applied, in January, 1971, to the Dade County Tax Assessor's office for a $500 property tax exemption under Fla. Stat. §196.191(7). That statute provides a property tax exemption for widows, but does not specifiy a similar exemption for widowers. Widower Kahn was denied the tax exemption.

Appellant then sought declaratory relief in the Circuit Court for Dade County, Florida; he argued that §196.191(7) in unconstitutional as a violation of the equal protection clause of the fourteenth amendment to the United States Constitution and Art. 1, §2, Declaration of Rights, Florida Constitution, 1968, insofar as widowers are denied the exemption accorded widows. The Circuit Court held that §196.191(7), as it applies to the female gender only, is "discriminatory and arbitrary and unconstitutional" under the equal protection clause of the fourteenth amendment to the United States Constitution (J.S. at A3). On defendant's appeal, the Supreme Court of Florida reversed, holding §196.191(7) a valid legislative enactment. 273 So. 2d at 74 (J.S. at A7).

Comment: Under Supreme Court rules the Statement of the Case includes a statement of the facts. Because there were no disputed facts in this test case, the statement can be very short.

The reader will notice that appellants' statement discusses and briefly quotes the reason for the decision in the Circuit Court, which was favorable, but states only the result reached by the Supreme Court of Florida. The emphasis is the opposite in appellees' Statement of the Case; *see* page 217 *infra.*

Summary of Argument

I

Fla. Stat. §196.191(7), providing a property tax exemption of up to $500 to all Florida widows, but not widowers, denies appellant the equal protection of the law guaranteed by the fourteenth amendment.

Historically, women have been treated as subordinate and inferior to men. Although discrimination against women persists and equal opportunity has by no means been achieved, women simultaneously have been placed on a pedestal and given special benefits. Both discrimination against, and special benefits for, women stem from stereotypical notions about their proper role in society.

Special benefits for women such as the tax exemption here at issue result in discriminatory treatment of similarly situated men, themselves victims of male sex-role stereotypes. Absent firm constitutional foundation for equal treatment of men and women by the law, individuals seeking to be judged on their own merits will continue to encounter law-sanctioned obstacles.

II

The distinction between widows and widowers established by Fla. Stat. §196.191(7) creates an "invidious classification" requiring close judical scrutiny. Although the legislature may distinguish between individuals on the basis of their need or ability, it is presumptively impermissible to distinguish on the basis of an unalterable identifying trait over which the individual has no control and for which he or she should not be disadvantaged by the law.

III

Upon finding that the sex-based classification in Fla. Stat. §196.191(7) violates the fourteenth amendment, this Court should remand to the court below for consideration whether, consistent with the dominant legislative purpose, the constitutional infirmity should be remedied by holding the exemption avaiable to all widowed property owners.

Comment: Here the authors have chosen not to summarize their argument in any detail nor to cite principal authorities, but instead they have kept the summary simple and conclusionary. The choice is understandable because the argument itself rests on a wide variety of legal and factual authorities and on an equally wide variety of approaches.

The broad-brush statement appearing as Point I of the summary, with its plea for a "firm constitutional foundation for equal treatment of men and women by the law," reflects the fact that the relevant law was in a state of flux and that the conclusion asserted as Point II might or might not be sustained.

ARGUMENT

I. The gender-based classification in Fla. Stat. §196.191(7), established for a purpose unrelated to any biological difference between the sexes, constitutes an invidious discrimination in violation of the equal protection clause of the fourteen amendment.

A. The Challenged Classification Is Based on a Stereo-type That Lacks Correspondence With Reality for Millions of Families in the United States.

The classification embodied in Fla. Stat. §196.191(7), granting property tax exemptions to widows but not to widowers, reflects a familiar stereotyping of sex roles: a woman left alone by the death of her husband is thought economically disabled; a man is believed to suffer scant financial loss upon the death of his wife, and even to be relieved of the burden of supporting her.

The division of the widowed population into two distinct classes, self sufficient men and disabled women, is hardly tenable in this latter half of the twentieth century. Widowhood may have a devastating impact on a man whose age disqualifies him from pursuing economic opportunities, and who must cope with loss of myriad services once performed for him by his spouse. On the other hand, many women, during marriage, are self supporting and may contribute importantly to the support of their families. Hardly atypical is the older couple with a wife in good health who assumes financial responsibility for an ailing husband. Moreover, widowed women do not constitute a clear economic class. On the contrary, the Florida population undoubtedly includes a substantial number of affluent widows who need a tax exemption far less than widowers of limited means.

In short, Fla. Stat. §196.191(7) reflects a stereotypical view of the economic roles of men and women which does not correspond with reality for millions of persons in the United States. In April, 1971, approximately 32 million women, 42.7% of all women 16 years of age or older, were in the labor force, compared with 28.9% in March, 1940. U.S. Bureau of Labor Statistics, Dept. of Labor, Employment and Earnings 34-35 (May 1971). By 1973, more than 33 million women were in the labor force; of these women, 19.25 million, or 58.5% of working women, were married and living with their husbands. U.S. Women's Bureau, Dept. of Labor, Why Women Work 1 (rev. ed. June 1973). This is almost twice the rate of 1940. U.S. Women's Bureau, Dept. of Labor, Bull. No. 294, Handbook of Women Workers 39 (1969). From 1960 to 1970, nearly half the increase in the labor force was accounted for by married women. Waldman, Changes in the Labor Force Activity of Women, 93 Monthly Labor Rev. 10, 11 (June 1970). And in recent years, married women have made up the largest portion of the annual increase in the civilian labor force. Waldman & Young, Marital and Family Characteristics of Workers, 94 Monthly Labor Rev. 46 (March 1971). Married women of all ages are increasing their rate of labor force participation while other groups are not. A. Ferriss, Indicators of Trends in the Status of American Women 103 (1971). In well over 40% of families where both spouses were present, both were employed. *Id.* at 95.

Moreover, despite the discrimination against women workers still characteristric of the labor market, many married women earn more than their husbands. The Census Bureau reports that in 1970, wives earned more than husbands in 3.2 million or 7.4% of American families. *See* N.Y. Times, Mar. 19, 1973, at 40, col. 1. The 1970 Census also reveals that women accounted for two-thirds of the increase in total employment in the 1960s and for half or more of the gain in certain jobs, ranging from bookkeeping to bartending. *See* Occupation by Industry, PC-7C, 1970.

It may be that decades ago Florida's widow's exemption did correlate "fairly and substantially" with the ability of women property owners to pay taxes. In 1892, the exemption was applicable only to the "widow dependent on her own exertions, that has a family dependent upon her for support."[2]

By the turn of the century, the dependent family requirement was dropped, but the exemption remained conditioned in the widow's "dependen[ce] upon her own exertions."[3]

Since 1941, the exemption has been available, without qualification, to "every widow."[4]

In light of the significant changes in women's opportunities for and pursuit of gainful employment in the course of this century, the progression from needy widow to any widow, and continued exclusion of widowers, defies rational explanation.

Comment: The pertinent facts in this case derive not from a trial record but from governmental and other trustworthy

2. Fla. Const. art. IX, §9 (1885); Fla. Laws 1891, c. 4010, §4(7), p. 2.
3. Fla. Laws 1895, c. 4322 §4(7), p. 4.
4. Constitutional development: Fla. Const. art. IX, §9 (1885), *as amended,* general election 1940 (Amendment of 1940 proposed by Fla. Laws 1939, H.J.R. No. 375, p. 1666); Fla. Const. art. VII, §3 (1968). Satutory development: Fla. Stat. §192.06(7) (1941), *as noted in* Fla. Laws 1943, c. 21742, §1(7), p. 154; *amended by* Fla. Laws 1969, c. 69-55, §§1, 2, p. 240 and *renumbered* Fla. Stat. §196.191(7); Fla. Stat. §196.191(7) (1969) *repealed by* Fla. Laws 1971, c. 71-133, §15, p. 409 and *replaced by* Fla. Stat. §196.202, Fla. Laws 1971, c. 71-133, §12, p. 408.

sources, and are therefore directly cited to the Court in Brandeis-brief fashion. The authors have chosen to lead off with statistics designed to show that the statute under review is so out of step with reality that it "defies rational explanation," and thus to lay a foundation for their later argument that gender-based discrimination cannot be sustained. This order of argument offers the advantage of laying out the relevant factual material first, just as in the usual case a statement of the disputed facts is placed before a discussion of the law.

B. The Equal Protection Clause of the Fourteenth Amendment Does Not Tolerate Legislative Line-Drawing on the Basis of Sex Stereotypes.

In 1971, this Court, departing from a century old decisional course,[5] declared constitutionally impermissible a classification similar to the one challenged here. In *Reed v. Reed*, 404 U.S. 71 (1971), the Court invalidated an Idaho statue that preferred men over women for appointment as estate administrators. The statutory preference was based on the stereotypical assumption that men have more business experience than women. *Reed v. Reed*, 93 Idaho 511, 514, 465 P.2d 635, 638 (1970). Explicitly repudiating one-eyed sex role thinking as a predicate for legislative distinctions, this Court held in *Reed:*

> [The statute] provides that different treatment be accorded to the applications on the basis of their sex; it thus establishes a classification subject to scrutiny under the Equal Protection Clause. 404 U.S. at 75.

Recognizing that the governmental interest urged to support the Idaho statute was "not without some legitimacy," 404 U.S. at 76, the Court nonetheless termed "arbitrary" the major premise of the Idaho court, and found the legislation constitutionally infirm because it provided "dissimilar treatment for men and women who are . . . similarly situated." 404 U.S. at 77.

5. *Bradwell v. Illinois*, 83 U.S. (16 Wall.) 130 (1873); *Minor v. Happersett*, 88 U.S. (21 Wall.) 162 (1874); *Muller v. Oregon*, 208 U.S. 412 (1908); *Goesaert v. Cleary*, 335 U.S. 464 (1948); *Hoyt v. Florida*, 368 U.S. 57 (1961); *see generally* Johnson & Knapp, Sex Discrimination by Law: A Study in Judical Perspective, 46 N.Y.U.L. Rev. 675 (1971).

Reed was assessed by both courts[6] and commentators[7] as a sign of fundamental change in this Court's perspective with regard to gender-based classifications. It was apparent that the Court had departed significantly from the traditional equal protection analysis familiar in review of social and economic legislation. Sex-based distinctions were subject to "scrutiny," a word until *Reed* typically reserved for race discrimination cases where the term was accompanied by the requirement that the legislation meet a "compelling state interest" standard. "Traditional" equal protection rulings, by contrast, mandate judicial tolerance of a legislative classification unless "patently arbitrary": "A statutory discrimination will not be set aside if any state of facts reasonably may be conceived to justify it." *McGowan v. Maryland*, 366 U.S. 420, 426 (1961). *See also Jefferson v. Hackney*, 406 U.S. 535, 546 (1972); *Dandridge v. Williams*, 397 U.S. 471, 485 (1970).

On May 14, 1973, in *Frontiero v. Richardson*, 411 U.S. 677 (1973), this Court made explicit the incurable flaw in governmental schemes that treat males and females differently solely on the basis of gender, schemes that rest upon stereotypical judgments concerning distinct roles for men and women. In *Frontiero*, a statutory presumption that husband is breadwinner, wife dependent, was declared a constitutionally impermissible means of determining entitlement to government benefits. 411 U.S. at 681. Four members of the Court, in a plurality opinion written by Mr. Justice Brennan, declared gender classifications subject to strict judicial scrutiny:

> [S]ince sex, like race and national origin, is an immutable characteristic determined solely by accident of birth, the imposition of special disabilities upon the members of a particular sex because of their sex

6. *See Brenden v. Independent School District*, 477 F.2d 1292 (8th Cir. 1973); *Eslinger v. Thomas*, 476 F.2d 225 (4th Cir. 1973); *Green v. Waterford Board of Education*, 473 F.2d 466 (10th Cir. 1972), *cert. denied*, 412 U.S. 906 (1973); *La Fleur v. Cleveland Board of Education*, 465 F.2d 1185 (6th Cir. 1972), *cert. granted* 411 U.S. 947 (1973); *Lamb v. Brown*, 456 F.2d 18 (10th Cir. 1972); *Heath v. Westerville Board of Education*, 345 F. Supp. 501 (S.D. Ohio 1972); *Reed v. Nebraska School Activities Ass'n*, 341 F. Supp. 258 (D. Neb. 1972); *Williams v. San Francisco Unified School District*, 340 F. Supp. 438 (N.D. Calif. 1972); *Robinson v. Rand*, 340 F. Supp. 37 (D. Colo. 1972); *Shull v. Columbus Municipal Separate School District*, 388 F. Supp. 1376 (N.D. Miss. 1972); *Bray v. Lee*, 337 F. Supp. 934 (D. Mass. 1972); *Matter of Patricia A.*, 31 N.Y.3d 83, 335 N.Y.S.2d (1972).

7. Gunther, The Supreme Court, 1971 Term, Forward: In Search of Evolving Doctrine on a Changing Court: A Model for a Newer Equal Protection, 86 Harv. L. Rev. 1, 34 (1972); Note, Pregnancy Discharges in the Military: The Air Force Experience, 86 Harv. L. Rev. 568, 583-588 (1973).

would seem to violate "the basic concept of our system that legal burdens should bear some relationship to individual responsibility...." *Weber v. Aetna Casualty & Surety Co.*, 406 U.S. 164, 175 (1972). And what differentiates sex from such nonsuspect statuses as intelligence or physical disability, and aligns it with the recognized suspect criteria, is that the sex characteristic frequently bears no relation to ability to perform or to contribute to society. 411 U.S. at 686.

The 8-1 judgment in *Frontiero* invalidated a fringe benefit scheme that awarded male members of the military housing allowances and medical care for their wives, regardless of dependency, but authorized benefits for female members only if they in fact supported their husbands. The differential at issue in the case at bar is sharper than the one held unconstitutional in *Frontiero*. There, husband qualified if wife supplied more than half his support. Here, under no circumstances may a man qualify for the exemption.

The message of *Frontiero* is clear: persons similarly situated, whether male or female, must be accorded evenhanded treatment by the law; lump treatment of men, on the one hand, and women on the other is constitutionally impermissible. Legislative classifications may legitimately take account of need or ability; they may not be premised on sex-role stereotypes or unalterable sex characteristics that bear no necessary relationship to an individual's need, ability or life situation.[8] Recently, the Solicitor General, speaking for the United States and all its agencies, expressed with precision the significance of the *Reed-Frontiero* development (Memorandum for the United States as *Amicus Curiae* at 8, *Cohen v. Chesterfield County School Board* and *Cleveland Board of Education v. La Fleur,* in U.S.S.C. Nos. 72-777 and 72-1129, filed October, 1973):

It is now settled that the Equal Protection Clause of the Fourteenth Amendment ... does not tolerate discrimination on the basis of sex. *Frontiero v. Richardson,* 411 U.S. 677 (1973); *Reed v. Reed,* 404 U.S. 71 (1971).[9]

8. Enlightened judges in state courts take a similar view of gender-based classifications. *See, e.g., Sail'er Inn v. Kirby,* 5 Cal. 3d 1, 485 P.2d 529 (1971), a unanimous decision of the California Supreme court explicitly denominating sex a suspect classification.
9. *Accord, Smith v. City of East Cleveland,* 363 F. Supp. 1131 (N.D. Ohio 1973) (minimum height and weight requirements for municipal police officers discriminate invidiously on the basis of sex); *Healy v. Edwards,* 363 F. Supp. 1110 (E.D. La. 1973) (three-judge court), *juris. statement filed,* 42 U.S.L.W. 3307 (Nov. 12, 1973) (exemption of women from jury service held unconstitutional); *Bowen v. Hackett,* 361 F. Supp. 854

While instances of discrimination against women dominate the growing body of case law, the constitutional mandate is equally applicable to men. For, as *Frontiero* graphically illustrates, gender-based discrimination frequently impacts adversely on both sexes. Laws defining women as a dependent class reinforce societal attitudes that "separate but equal" is a concept appropriately applied to men and women. Women as workers may be denied equal opportunities and fringe benefits because in the world outside the home they are regarded as secondary. As "compensation," women are recognized as principal caretakers of home and children and therefore as financially disabled.

In *Stanley v. Illinois*, 405 U.S. 645 (1972), this Court emphasized the fundamental unfairness to men as well as women of legislative lines based on sex stereotypes. Unwed fathers, the Court ruled, may not be deprived of custody absent a hearing of the same quality accorded unwed mothers and wed parents. Acknowledging that "[i]t may be, as the State insists, that most unmarried fathers are unsuitable and neglectful parents," this generalization is not true of *all* unwed fathers. 405 U.S. at 654. Consequently, the legislative presumption was impermissible, despite its convenience and its correspondence to reality in perhaps the majority of cases.

Similarly, lower courts have rejected disadvantageous treatment of men unsupported by strong affirmative justification. *E.g., Moritz v. Commissioner of Internal Revenue*, 469 F.2d 466 (10th cir. 1972), *cert. denied*, 412 U.S. 906 (1973) (never-married man declared entitled to parent-care tax deduction provided by Congress for never-married women); *Healy v. Edwards*, 363 F. Supp. 1110, 1113-14 (E.D. La. 1973) (three-judge court), *juris. statement filed*, 42 U.S.L.W. 3307 (Nov. 12, 1973) (rejecting jury service exemption for women as inconsistent with "[t]he minimum requirement of Equal Protection" that "dissimilar treatment may no longer constitutionally be provided for men and women who are similarly situated *with respect to the objectives of the legislation*") (emphasis by the court); *Ballard v.*

(D.R.I. 1973) (dependent child allowance must be furnished disabled and unemployed men and women on the same basis); *Ballard v. Laird*, 360 F. Supp. 643 (S.D. Calif. 1973) (three-judge court) (Navy must grant commissioned servicemen same tenure legislatively guaranteed to servicewomen); *Aiello v. Hanson*, 359 F. Supp. 792 (N.D. Calif. 1973) (three-judge court), *juris. statement filed sub nom. Geduldig v. Aiello*, 42 U.S.L.W. 3247 (Oct. 12, 1973) (employees disabled by pregnancy-related condition entitled to compensation from state insurance fund under same terms and conditions as those applicable to all other disabled employees).

Laird, 360 F. Supp. 643 (S.D. Calif. 1973) (three-judge court) (whether the discrimination favors the female or the male is irrelevant in utilizing the teaching of *Frontiero*—cost of granting male officers same 13 year guaranteed tenure as female officers does not justify infringement of the constitutional guarantee); *Lamb v. Brown,* 456 F.2d 18 (10th Cir. 1972) (16 (male)/18 (female) sex/age differential for juvenile offender treatment discriminates unconstitutionally against men).

Nor does the provision here at issue enjoy special immunity from constitutional scrutiny because tax exemption is a matter of "legislative grace." For it is now beyond debate that "[a] minimum demand of uniformly reasonable rules in the management of public largess is surely an unexceptional requirement of constitutional government." Van Alstyne, The Demise of the Right-Privilege Distinction in Constitutional Law, 81 Harv. L. Rev. 1439, 1461 (1968); *see Shapiro v. Thompson,* 394 U.S. 618, 627 n.6 (1969).

Two cases, closely analogous to the one at bar, underscore the point: *In re Estate of Legatos,* 1 Cal. App. 3d 657, 91 Cal. Rptr. 910 (1969); *Moritz v. Commissioner of Internal Revenue, supra.* In *Estate of Legatos,* the court declared inconsistent with equal protection an inheritance tax imposed on certain property when devised by husband to wife but not when devised by wife to husband:

> Equality of burden is a fundamental pricinple of taxation. Equal protection demands that similar property be taxed by the same yardstick to those similarly situated. . . . Both in their incidence and innate characteristics tax moneys are sexless and soulless. 1 Cal. App. 3d at 661, 662, 81 Cal. Rptr. at 913.

The court also noted that "[a]dministrative convenience such as preventing loss of revenue to the state is not a valid basis for classification." 1 Cal. App. 3d at 662, 81 Cal. Rptr. at 913.

In *Moritz,*[10] the Court of Appeals for the Tenth Circuit concluded that a tax classification "premised primarily on sex" constituted an "invidious discrimination." 469 F.2d at 470. In sharp contrast to the Florida Supreme Court's assertion that because "women workers as a class do not earn as much as men" a widows-only tax exemption has a "fair and substantial relation" to a permissible legislative objective, 273 So. 2d at 73, the Tenth Circuit reasoned:

10. Cited with apparent approval in *Frontiero v. Richardson,* 411 U.S. 677, 691 n.25 (1973).

If Congress had desired to give relief to persons in low income brackets ... means were available through classifications geared to such objectives without using the invidious discrimination based solely on sex. *Cf., Stanley v. Illinois,* 405 U.S. 645, 656, 657. 469 F.2d at 470.

In sum, denial to widowers of the property tax exemption granted widows cannot survive constitutional review. Exclusion of widowers, based solely on their sex, reflects arbitary and stereotypical notions of the differences between women and men, is wholly unrelated to any biological difference between the sexes, and is not fairly and substantially related to individual need.

Comment: In this section the authors set forth their principal affirmative legal argument, choosing to leave to the next section their treatment of the authorities cited by the Supreme Court of Florida. The United States Supreme Court authorities are discussed first, followed by lesser authorities that seem particularly apt and persuasive. The reader will notice that the authors select and discard until they reach the relevant essence of each case. A few key facts, the crux of the decision, a pinpoint quotation or two, a few words showing the impact of the case—these are all that remain after final editing.

C. Gender Classification as a Proxy for Some Other Individual or Social Characteristic, Such as Physical or Economic Capability or Need, Once Regarded as Favorable to or Protective of Women Is Now Recognized as Ultimately Harmful to Them.

The court below, citing *Hoyt v. Florida,* 368 U.S. 57 (1961), concluded that gender classifications are permissible "for the purpose of according a privileged status to women." 273 So. 2d at 73 n.3. In fact, *Hoyt,* is a classic example of the invidious effect of classifications once thought by well-intentioned jurists to operate "benignly" in women's favor. *See* Johnston & Knapp, Sex Discrimination by Law: A Study in Judicial Perspective, 46 N.Y.U.L. Rev. 675, 708-21 (1971).

Hoyt upheld the constitutionality of a Florida statute limiting service of women on juries to volunteers. The limitation was considered reasonable because "woman is still regarded as the center of home and family life." 368 U.S. at 62. Hence, she was entitled to "favored" treatment, indeed, the best of both worlds: the right to serve for the asking, immunity from responsibilty if she preferred not to serve.

Decisions in the wake of *Hoyt* demonstrate that favors of this kind come at an exorbitant price.[11] *See* Motion to Affirm, *Edwards v. Healy,* U.S.S.C. Docket No. 73-759 (December, 1973). For example, in a 1970 decision, a New York trial court rejected the challenge of a female plaintiff to a jury system with automatic exemption for women. As a result of this exemption, women constituted less than twenty percent of the available pool. In his published opinion, the judge relied on *Hoyt* to explain to the complainant that she was "in the wrong forum." Accurately reflecting the impact of laws "for women only," the judge stated that plaintiff's "lament" should be addressed to her sisters who prefer "cleaning and cooking, bridge and canasta, the beauty parlor and shopping, to becoming embroiled in plaintiff's problems. . . ." *De Kosenko v. Brandt,* 63 Misc. 2d 895, 898, 313 N.Y.S.2d 827, 830 (Sup. Ct. 1970). *See also Goldblatt v. Board of Education,* 52 Misc. 2d 238, 275 N.Y.S.2d 550 (1966), *aff'd,* 57 Misc. 2d 1089, 294 N.Y.S.2d 272 (Sup. Ct. 1968) (regulation authorizing full salary less jury fees for male, but not female, teachers was "reasonable" because a woman could avoid jury duty by claiming exemption).

The implications of *Hoyt* were better understood by the three-judge federal district court in *Healy v. Edwards, supra.* Recognizing that *Reed* had eroded, and *Frontiero* crevassed the foundation of *Hoyt,* the court reasoned:

> When today's vibrant principle is obviously in conflict with yesterday's sterile precedent, trial courts need not follow the outgrown dogma. Hence we consider that *Hoyt* is no longer binding. 363 F. Supp. at 1117.

Other "favors" once accorded women by chivalrous or paternalistic legislatures have undergone similar reassessment. Thus, the indeterminate sentence for women, subjecting them to potentially longer

11. *Cf.* S. Grimke, Letters on the Equality of the Sexes and the Condition of Women; addressed to Mary Parker, President of the Boston Female Anti-Slavery Society 10 (1838):

We ask no favors for our sex. All we ask of our brethren is that they take their feet off our necks. . . .

prison terms than men, has been recognized as an invidious classification, despite the favor it bestowed: early release for females who promptly reformed under the special supervision accorded them. *See U.S. ex rel. Robinson v. York,* 281 F. Supp. 8 (D. Conn. 1968); *New Jersey v. Chambers,* 36 N.J. 287, 307 A.2d 78 (1973); *Commonwealth v. Daniel,* 430 Pa. 642, 243 A.2d 400 (1968); *Commonwealth v. Stauffer,* 211 Pa. Super. 113, 251 A.2d 718 (1969); *Liberti v. York,* 28 Conn. Supp. 9, 246, A.2d 106 (1968).

In contrast to the assumption of the court below that distinct classification of widows and widowers asists women to achieve equality, administrators and courts charged with implementation of national fair employment policy recognize that special treatment of women perpetuates sex stereotypes and thereby retards women's access to equal opportunity in economic life. Thus, Sex Discrimination Guidelines, 29 C.F.R. §§1604.1-1604.10, issued by the Equal Employment Opportunity Commission pursuant to Title VII of the Civil Rights Act of 1964, 42 U.S.C. §§2000e *et seq.,* provide:

> It shall be an unlawful employment practice for an employer to make available benefits for the wives and families of male employees where the same benefits are not made avaiable for the husbands and families of female employees.... 29 C.F.R. §1604.9(d)....
>
> It shall be an unlawful employment practice for an employer to have a pension or retirement plan which establishes different optional or compulsory retirement ages based on sex, or which differentiates in benefits on the basis of sex. 29 C.F.R. §1604.9(f).

These Guidelines, issued in 1972 and applicable to state and municipal employment as well as to the private sector, reflect consistent administrative and judicial interpretation of Title VII. For example, in 1969, the Equal Employment Opportunity Commission found reasonable cause to believe that Title VII was violated by a death benefit plan providing an automatic pension for widows of male employees, but no pension for widowers of female employees unless physically or mentally incapable of self-support. "Title VII of the Civil Rights Act of 1964," the Commission stated, "is intended to protect *individuals* from the penalizing effect of . . . presumptions based on the collective characteristics of a sexual group." EEOC Decisions, Case No. YNY9-034, CCH Emp. Practices Guide ¶6050 (June 16, 1969). (Emphasis in the original.) For court confirmation of the principle underlying this EEOC decision, *see Rosen v. Public Service Elec. & Gas Co.,* 477 F.2d 90 (3rd Cir. 1973) (Title VII violated by pension arrangement allowing women to retire earlier on full pension); *Diaz v. Pan American World Airways*, 442 F.2d 385 (5th Cir. 1971) (invalidating a ban on hiring male flight attendants); *Hays v. Potlatch Forests, Inc.*, 465 F.2d 1081 (8th Cir. 1972) (reconciling state law with Title VII by extending premium overtime law to men).

The insistence on equal benefits for men and women, husbands and wives, widowers and widows evident in Title VII administration is also a feature of other legislation designed to eradicate sex-based discrimination.[12] For example, in December, 1971, Congress amended §2108 of Title 5 of the United States Code "to provide equality of treatment for married women federal employees with respect to (veteran's) preference, eligible employment benefits, cost of living allowances in foreign areas, and regulations concerning marital status generally . . . ." P.L. 92-187, 85 Stat. 644. This legislation, covering all employees of the federal government except members of the uniformed services, added the following subparagraph to 5 U.S.C. §7152:

> (c) Notwithstanding any other provision of law, any provision of law providing a benefit to a male Federal employee or to his spouse or family shall be deemed to provide the same benefit to a female Federal employee or to her spouse or family.

This provision had the following effects: (a) It equalized the tests under 5 U.S.C. §8133 for payment of death benefits to widows and widowers of federal employees dying from injury sustained in the performance of duty. Previously, widows were entitled to benefits if they were "living with or dependent for support on the decedent at the time of his death or living apart for reasonable cause or because of desertion." 5 U.S.C. §8101(6). A widower, however, was entitled to benefits only if, "because of physical or mental disability, [he] was wholly dependent for support on the employee at the time of her death." 5 U.S.C. §8101(11). (b) It equalized the tests under 5 U.S.C. §8110 for payment of augmented compensation to spouses of dis-

---

12. Similarly, administrators of Executive Orders designed to promote equal employment opportunity target elimination of sex-role stereotypes as the essential task. *See, e.g.,* H.E.W. Higher Education Guidelines, issued pursuant to Executive Order 11246, 3 C.F.R. 418 (1965), as amended by Executive Order 11375, 32 Fed. Reg. 14303 (1968), at 13 (Oct. 1, 1972) (child care leave should be available to men and women on an equal basis).

abled federal employees. Previously, a wife was eligible for augmented compensation if she lived in the same household as the employee or received regular contributions from him, or if he was under court order to contribute to her support. A husband was eligible for augmented compensation only if he was wholly dependent on the employee for support because of physical or mental disability.

In January, 1971, Congress amended 5 U.S.C. §8341[13] which defines persons qualified for Federal Civil Service survivor's annuities. A surviving widow qualified automatically, but a surviving widower qualified only if he was incapable of self-support because of mental or physical disability and received more than half his support from his wife. The amendment gave widowers the same automatic qualification as widows. The House Committee Report states the reasons for the amendment:

> In the Committee's judgment, the present provision is discriminatory in that it runs counter to the facts of current-day living, whereby the woman's earnings are significant in supporting the family and maintaining its standards of living. Accordingly, the bill removes the dependency requirements applicable to surviving widowers of female employees, thus according them the same treatment accorded widows of deceased male employees. H.R. Rep. No. 91-1469, 91st Cong., 2d Sess., 1970 U.S. Code Cong. & Ad. News, Vol. III, 5931, 5934.

In December, 1971, Congress amended 5 U.S.C. §2108,[14] which defines persons eligible for veterans preference in the federal civil service. Previously, the "unmarried widow," but not the unmarried widower, of a veteran, and "the wife," but not the husband, of "a service-connected disabled veteran" meeting certain other requirements were eligible. The amendment made widowers and husbands eligible under the same conditions as widows and wives.

In the same act, Congress amended 5 U.S.C. §5924, which provides cost of living allowances to dependents of federal employees living in a foreign area. The allowance, previously payable to "the employee's wife or his dependents, or both," was made payable to "the employee's spouse or dependents, or both."

In October, 1972, Congress amended 38 U.S.C. §102(b) which defines the term "dependent" for the purpose of determining the

13. P.L. 91-658, 84 Stat. 1961.
14. P.L. 92-187, 85 Stat. 644.

amount of the education assistance allowance armed forces veterans are eligible to receive.[15] A veteran with dependents, as defined, is eligible for a substantially higher allowance.[16] Section 102(b) previously provided that the wife of a male veteran was automatically classified as a dependent while the husband of a female veteran was classified as dependent only if he "is incapable of self-maintenance and is permanently incapable of self-support due to mental or physical disability. . . ." The amendent redefines "dependent" to include all husbands of eligible female veterans without regard to incapacity or dependency. And on July 9, 1973, 37 U.S.C. §401 was amended to eliminate the differential at issue in *Frontiero*.[17]

Before amendment, the provisions cited above imposed a test of actual dependency for husbands or widowers, but authorized benefits for wives or widows regardless of dependency. The change in each case was to extend to husbands or widowers the automatic benefits already enjoyed by wives or widows. The "administrative convenience" of prior arrangements was rejected as a justification for differentials in benefits. Rather, the prior arrangements were recognized as "discriminatory" and inconsistent with "the facts of current-day living."

Although aware that "steps have been . . . taken toward the elimination of legal barriers to equality of the sexes," 273 So. 2d at 73, the court below found support for its decision in *Gruenwald v. Gardner*, 390 F.2d 591 (2d Cir.), *cert. denied*, 393 U.S. 982 (1968). *Gruenwald* found no constitutional infirmity in a statutory scheme that accorded women more favorable treatment than men in computing social security benefits upon retirement at age 62.

But if *Hoyt* represents sterile precedent, *Gruenwald* must be regarded as similarly stripped of vitality. *Gruenwald* antedated *Reed*, *Stanley*, and *Frontiero*. When *Gruenwald* was presented to the Second Circuit, that court had as its guide an unbroken line of this Court's decisions sanctioning legislation that drew "a sharp line between the sexes."[18] Post-*Reed*, the Second Circuit promptly signalled its willingness to examine gender classifications from the new perspective. *See Green v. Waterford Board of Education*, 473 F.2d 629 (2d Cir. 1973). And indicative of heightened public consciousness of the invidious

15. P.L. 92-540, 86 Stat. 1074.
16. 38 U.S.C. §1682.
17. P.L. 93-64, 87 Stat. 147. Although the effective date of the statute is July 1, 1973, the Comptroller General has declared the *Frontiero decision fully retroactive*. 53 Comp. Gen. — (B 178979, Aug. 31, 1973).
18. *Goesaert v. Cleary*, 335 U.S. 464, 466 (1948). *See* cases cited note 2 *supra*.

character of sex-based distinctions, Congress has eliminated the *Gruenwald* differential. The more favorable computation once reserved for women has been extended to men. 42 U.S.C. §414 (Supp. 1972), *amending* 42 U.S.C. §414.

Moreover, the distinction approved in *Gruenwald* had at least a tenuous relationship to discrimination encountered by women in the labor market. The benefit calculation applied to amounts earned by women; it was thus linked in an arguably direct way to disparities in salary and promotion opportunities for male and female wage earners. In the case at bar, on the other hand, the tax exemption is not tied in any way to discrimination encountered by women in economic activity. Totally unrelated to the needs or economic capabilities of widows, it is available on the same terms to the heiress who has never engaged in gainful employment and to the woman who has functioned as her family's sole breadwinner.

In sum, the *noblesse oblige* to "the weaker sex" exhibited by the court below does not aid women to achieve equality[19] and discriminates unfairly against men. In particular, Fla. Stat. §196.191(7) perpetuates the myth that widows cannot, without assistance, make financial ends meet, but widowers can. Far from having any substantial relationship to a legitimate state interest, the classification at issue reflects stereotypical attitudes toward the roles of married men and women, hence, the financial status of widowers and widows. One-eyed sex-role thinking of this kind no longer accords with reality for a substantial and growing portion of the population.

Comment: In this section of their argument, the brief writers boldly attack as outmoded the prior Supreme Court decision in *Hoyt v. Florida,* which was relied on by the court below. They might have been content with distinguishing the case on its facts, but the authors apparently concluded that their overall argument would be better served by asking the Court to disapprove or ignore it. Such an approach permits them to show a variety of recent developments in Congress, federal

19. Generalized provisions based on gender stereotypes of the variety here at issue must be distinguished from affirmative action measures tailored narrowly and specifically to rectify the effects of past discrimination against women in a particular setting. Such measures deal directly with economic and social conditions that underlie and support a subordinate status for women. *See, e.g,* H.E.W. Higher Education Guidelines, *supra* note 12; Galbraith, Kuh and Thurow, The Galbraith Plan to Promote the Minorities. N. Y. Times, Aug. 22, 1971 (Magazine) at 9.

agencies, and the lower courts, all suggesting that the *Hoyt* case is no longer in tune with contemporary notions of equality and that legislative favors to females are more of a hindrance than a help.

Although the Court is asked to repudiate the "sterile precedent" of the *Hoyt* decision, it is not urged to make new law. Instead, the authors offer the Court a far easier ground for decision, arguing that the reasoning of *Reed v. Reed* and *Frontiero v. Richardson* has already undercut the basis of *Hoyt*, making that decision unsound.

II. Upon determining that the gender-based classification in Fla. Stat. §196.191(7) violates the fourteenth amendment, this Court should remand to the court below for consideration whether, consistent with the dominant legislative purpose, the constitutional infirmity should be remedied by holding the exemption available to all widowed property owners.

Both the trial court and the Supreme Court of Florida acknowledged the obvious point that when the legislature provided an exemption for widows, it intended to benefit females only. In part because women are vastly under-represented in this Nation's decision-making councils,[20] laws are drafted from a masculine perspective. Ordinarily, absent an express provision to the contrary or something in the subject or context inconsistent with such construction, statutory terms importing the masculine gender apply to females as well.[21] But, with rare exception,[22] words in a statute importing the female gender are subject to grammatical construction — they mean "for women only." Although legislative intent to exclude widowers is thus beyond debate, that intent should supply the starting point, not the terminus, for judicial analysis of the appropriate remedy in this case.

The remedial choice was never addressed by the Florida Supreme

20. *See Frontiero v. Richardson.* 411 U.S. 677, 686 n.17 (1973).
21. *Cf.* 1 U.S.C. §1.
22. *See* P.L. 92-540, 86 Stat. 1092, *amending* 38 U.S.C. §102(b) (wife includes husband, widow includes widower); Fla. Stat. §1.01 (2) ("The masculine includes the feminine and neuter and *vice versa.*") (emphasis added).

Court since it concluded that the "widows only" exemption was constitutional. The trial court, while identifying the constitutional infirmity, failed to perceive the further obligation imposed on a responsible judiciary "to decide whether it more nearly accords with [the legislature's] wishes to eliminate its policy altogether or extend it in order to render what [the legislature] plainly did intend, constitutional." *Welsh v. United States*, 398 U.S. 333, 355-56 (1970) (Harlan, J. concurring); *see Skinner v. Oklahoma ex rel. Williamson*, 316 U.S. 535, 542-543 (1942). The nature of the necessary inquiry was succinctly described by the Supreme Court of New Jersey:

> ... The judiciary cannot enlarge the reach of the statute, for this is solely a legislative function. The proposition is obvious enough, and it is equally true that a court may not restrict the scope of a statute. But neither proposition is involved when the question is whether a statute must fall because of a constitutional defect. Rather the question is whether the Legislature would want the statute to survive, and that inquiry cannot turn simply upon whether the statute, if adjusted to the constitutional demand, will cover more or less than its terms purport to cover. Although cases may be found which seem to speak in such mechanical terms, we think the sounder course is to consider what is involved and to decide from the sense of the situation whether the Legislature would want the statute to succumb. *Schmoll v. Creecy*, 541 N.J. 194, 202, 254 A.2d 525, 529-30 (1969).

Similar reasoning is implicit in this Court's judgment in *Frontiero v. Richardson, supra*. The *Frontiero* judgment reflects a determination that extension of benefits to spouses of female members of the uniformed services would better serve the legislative purpose than would judicial destruction of the spousal benefit scheme. The same approach, preferring salvage to demolition, is indicated in diverse decisions of this Court involving state as well as federal laws. *E.g., U.S. Dept. of Agriculture v. Moreno*, 41 U.S.L.W. 5105 (U.S. June 25, 1973) (federal food stamps); *Gomez v. Perez*, 409 U.S. 535 (1973) (child support under state law); *New Jersey Welfare Rights Organization v. Cahill*, 411 U.S. 619 (1973) (state aid to families of working poor); *Richardson v. Davis*, 409 U.S. 1069 (1972), *aff'g* 342 F. Supp. 588 (D. Conn. 1972) and *Richardson v. Griffin*, 409 U.S. 1069 (1972), *aff'g* 346 F. Supp. 1226 (D. Md. 1972) (social security child benefits); *Weber v. Aetna Cas. & Sur. Co.*, 406 U.S. 164 (1972) (state workmen's compensation child benefits); *Graham v. Richardson*, 403 U.S. 365 (1971) (state public assistance); *Shapiro v. Thompson, supra* (state and District of Columbia public assistance); *Levy v. Louisiana*, 391 U.S. 68, *rehearsing denied*, 393 U.S. 898 (1968) and *Glona v. American Guaranty & Liability Ins. Co.*, 391 U.S. 73, *rehearing denied*, 393 U.S. 898 (1968) (state wrongful death recoveries).

The remedial issue was noted and treated explicitly in *Moritz v. Commissioner of Internal Revenue, supra,* a decision of particular relevance to the instant case, for it involved a tax benefit available to never married women, but not to never married men. After determining that discriminatory tax treatment could not be justified by generalizations based on sex stereotypes, the Tenth Circuit further declared:

> [Next], we must determine the effect of the invalidity of provisions denying the deduction to men who have never married. Where a court is compelled to hold such a statutory discrimination invalid, it may consider whether to treat the provision containing the discriminatory underinclusion as generally invalid or whether to extend the coverage of the statue. 469 F.2d at 470.

The Tenth Circuit concluded that extension of the coverage of the deduction provision was "logical and proper," and accordingly ruled that "the benefit of the deduction . . . should be texted to [Moritz]."[23] *Accord, Ballard v. Laird, supra* (13 year tenure for women in Navy's commissioned service must be extended to men); *cf. In re Estate of Legatos, supra* (property exempt from tax when devised by wife to husband must also be exempt when devised by husband to wife); *Hays v. Potlatch Forests, Inc., supra* (consistent with Title VII's employment discrimination prohibition, premium overtime law by its term applicable to women only must be applied by employer to men as well as women).

Nor is the propriety of extension of benefits a recent judical discovery. As explained by Mr. Justice Brandeis writing for the Court over four decades ago in *Iowa-Des Moines National Bank v. Bennett,* 284 U.S. 239, 247 (1931), the legislature eventually may decide to remove the benefit from all, but in the meantime, the Court may prescribe an extension cure. Similar extensions were authorized in *Yale & Towne Mfg. Co. v. Travis,* 262 F. 576 (S.D.N.Y. 1919), *aff'd,* 252 U.S. 60 (1920) (tax exemption granted by statute only to state citizens extended to citizens of other states); *Burrow v. Kapfhammer,* 284 Ky. 753, 145 S.W. 2d 1067 (1940), *noted in* 54 Harv. L. Rev.

23. The remedial route in *Moritz* was noted by this Court in *Frontiero v. Richardson,* 411 U.S. 677, 691 n.25 (1973).

1078 (1941) (exempt class extended to cure unconstitutional exclusion); *Quong Ham Wah Co. v. Industrial Accident Comm'n,* 184 Cal. 26, 192 P. 1021 (1920), *appeal dismissed,* 255 U.S. 445 (1921) (workmen's compensation benefits extended to nonresidents to cure constitutional infirmity).

It should be stressed that invalidation of a statutory benefit is an anomalous response to a plaintiff who seeks extension of the benefit to him. Appellant Kahn, like the complainants in *Frontiero* and *Moritz,* does not subscribe to the mutual suffering theory and has no interest in pursuing a claim to withdraw benefits from others. *Cf. Iowa-Des Moines National Bank v. Bennett, supra* at 247 (person subjected to discriminatory taxation cannot be expected to seek payment of increased taxes by others). In this light, the trial court's disposition appears illogical and improper. If that court was unable "to decide from the sense of the situation whether the Legislature would want the [widow's exemption] to succumb,"[24] it might at least have adopted an intermediate position, declaring the statute unconstitutional as written, but leaving the choice of cures to the legislature. Precisely this middle ground was adopted in *White v. Crook,* 251 F. Supp. 401 (M.D. Ala. 1966), where the three-judge federal district court declared unconstitutional Alabama's exclusion of women from jury service, but deferred further relief to permit the legislature to recast the statute.

Indeed, the course taken from the trial court, *i.e.,* nullification of the widow's exemption, collides head-on with Florida's constitutional and statutory stipulations; the extension remedy sought by Appellant Kahn, on the other hand, is consistent with the dominant purpose expressed in the Florida Constitution and statute.[25] Population statistics alone indicate that the judiciary would disserve legislative intent were it to invalidate the exemption: the Florida population

24. Some indication of legislative preference is provided by Fla. Stat. §61.08 (1972), requiring alimony and child support to be determined in accordance with a sex-neutral standard. Moreover, the Floria judiciary has clearly indicated that extension is the appropriate remedial route to eliminate legal barriers to equality of the sexes. *Compare Gates v. Foley,* 247 So. 2d 40 (Fla. 1971) (extending to wife right to sue for loss of consortium) *with Ellis v. Hathaway,* 27 Utah 2d 143, 493 P.2d 985 (1972) (establishing equality between the spouses by forbidding either to sue for loss of consortium).

25. In *Burrows v. Kapfhammer,* 284 Ky. 753, 761-62, 145 S.W.2d 1067, 1072 (1940), the court pointed out that judicial elimination of the statutory exemption there at issue would run directly contrary to "express legislative provision"; extension of the exemption to the excluded class was therefore viewed as the only judicial course consistent with "logic, common sense [and] reason."

aided by the exemption (widows) is four times larger than the population excluded (widowers).[26] Moreover, most of the widowed men in Florida are over 65,[27] at or beyond the age when labor force participation terminates with attendant and often drastic reduction in income. Surely the Florida legislature was not so intent on denying the exemption to widowers, a relatively small class of predominantly elderly persons, that it would prefer invalidation of the exemption for the relatively large class of widows to adjustment of the statute to meet the constitutional demand.

Comment: In this second and separate portion of the appellant's brief the authors deal with the remedial issue in the case. The following points are neatly set forth in order: a remedial issue exists; extension of benefits has been at least impliedly approved by the Supreme Court; lower courts have explicitly ordered such extension; and denial of this extension would be anomolous under the circumstances. Effective phraseology is used at a number of places in the presentation—"the starting point, not the terminus," "preferring salvage to demolition," "does not subscribe to the mutual suffering theory," and so on.

As will be seen in the majority and dissenting opinions, the Court never reached the remedial issue argued in this Section.

CONCLUSION

For the reasons stated above, the decision of Florida Supreme Court should be reversed, and Florida Statute §196.191(7) should be declared unconstitutional insofar as it differentiates between widowed persons solely on the basis of gender.

On remand, the court below may preserve the express constitu-

26. In 1970, of males aged 14 years and over, 3.4% were widowers, while 14.0% of the females in the same age group were widows. U.S. Bureau of Census, Census of Population: 1970, Detailed Characteristics, Final Report PC(1)-D11 Florida, October, 1972, at 679-80, noted in Appellees' Motion to Dismiss or Affirm at 4.

27. Approximately 70% of all widowers and 64% of all widows in Florida are over 65. Bureau of Census, *supra* note 26 at 679.

tional and statutory stipulations for a widow's exemption by declaring §196.191(7) applicable to all widowed residents.

Respectfully submitted,

RUTH BADER GINSBURG
MELVIN L. WULF
BRENDA FEIGEN FASTEAU
CHRISTINE CASSADY CURTIS
American Civil Liberties Union
Foundation
22 East 40th Street
New York, New York 10016
WILLIAM HOPPE
Second Floor, Concord Building
Miami, Florida 33130

Attorneys for Appellants

Comment: Thus the Appellants' Brief ends with a simple conclusion limited to a statement of the action the court is asked to take. Overall the brief has accomplished its mission. It has shown the Justices persuasive reasons for concluding, *prima facie,* that a reversal may be required.

The Brief for Appellees follows, again with inserted comments. As the reader will see, it does not so much contradict appellants' version of the facts and the law as offer a different viewpoint with different points of emphasis.

MEL KAHN, etc.,

Appellants,

— v. —

ROBERT L. SHEVIN, *et al.,*

Appellees.

ON APPEAL FROM THE SUPREME COURT OF

THE STATE OF FLORIDA

[273 So. 2d 72]

BRIEF FOR APPELLEES

*Report of Opinions Below, Jurisdiction, and Statutes
Involved*

Pursuant to Rule 40, Supreme Court Rules, and Paragraph 3 thereof, Appellees adopt Appellant's Report of Opinions Below, Jurisdiction, and Statutes Involved.

Comment: Because the appellees do not differ with appellants on these required statements they adopt appellants' statements of them, as the rules require.

Question Presented

Whether the exemption from ad valorem taxation of property to the value of $500 yearly, provided by Art. VII §3(b), Fla. Const. and Fla. Stat. §196.191(7) for widows, but not widowers, denies appellant, a widower, the equal protection of the laws.

Comment: This statement explicitly refers to the pertinent section of the Florida constitution as well as to the pertinent Florida statute, thus emphasizing its importance to the people of Florida, whereas the Appellants' Brief relegates the constitutional section to a footnote. The statement omits appellants' phrase "makes no provision for men similarly situated," presumably because the authors will later stress that there is a continuing economic disparity between the sexes, which the statute is designed to alleviate.

Statement of the Case

The Appellant, a widower, applied to the Dade County Tax Assessor for, and was denied, an exemption from ad valorem taxation for property to the value of $500 under Fla. Stat. §196.191(7), which statute extends such an exemption to persons who are blind, persons who are totally and permanently disabled, and to widows, but not to widowers.

Appellant then filed his complaint for declaratory relief as a class action pursuant to Rule 1.220 Fla. R.C.P., and Fla. Stat. §86.011, alleging denial of his application for exemption under Fla. Stat. §196.191(7) and asserting that as a widower he and others similarly situated were deprived of equal protection and due process of law by the language and application of the statute. The Circuit Court ruled in Appellant's favor and a timely appeal was taken to the Florida Supreme Court which reversed the judgment of the Circuit Court. The Supreme Court held that there was a "fair and substantial relation" between the objective of reducing the factually existent disparity between the economic capabilities of the sexes and the statute affording to women who have lost a spouse by death a slight economic advantage. (J.S. at A7) Thus, the Florida Supreme Court concluded that Fla. Stat. §196.191(7) is constitutionally valid. (J.S. at A7)

Comment: This statement is similar to appellants' Statement of the Case except that it merely mentions the unfavorable ruling of the Circuit Court below but sets forth the essence of the favorable decision in the Supreme Court of Florida.

Appendix A

Summary of Argument

I

The granting of a $500 property tax exemption to widows, among others, but not to widowers by Fla. Stat. §196.191(7) and Art. VII §3(b), Fla. Const. is based on valid social and economic policy determinations and does not deny Appellant the equal protection of the law under the fourteeth amendment.

Although women make up an ever-increasing portion of the work force, they are still far behind in obtaining equality of economic opportunity. The gap between salaries for comparably qualified women and men in like positions is is fact increasing rather than decreasing. Thus, widows, like other women, are not in as favorable a position to support themselves as are other members of society, including widowers, and Florida has taken this into consideration in granting a slight tax advantage to widows.

Such a determination is properly within the broad discretion granted states in allowing tax exemptions, having a fair and substantial relation to the object of the legislation and is in no way palpably arbitrary.

II

Classifications based on sex are properly found to be valid where they bear a rational relationship to a proper state object, and such classifications are not inconsistent with the equal protection clause of the fourteenth amendment. The attempt by Florida, through a small tax exemption, to reduce the economic disparity between the sexes in the case of widows is a proper use of the state's power to classify, as it is a proper state policy, based upon social as well as economic considerations, to alleviate the hardship to women resulting from the inequality of economic opportunity.

III

Even should classifications based upon sex be considered to be inherently suspect, the compelling interest of the state in reducing the economic disparity between the sexes, and the resulting encouragement of the elderly to locate in Florida justifies the classification

218

set out in Fla. Stat. §196.191(7) and Art. VII, §3(b), Fla. Const., and is consistent with the equal protection requirements of the fourteenth amendment.

IV

Should the classifications based on sex be held unconstitutional as violative of the equal protection clause of the fourteenth amendment, this cause should not be remanded to the court below for consideration of whether to judicially expand the definition of widow to include widowers. This issue has already been fully briefed, argued and considered by the court below. The extension of benefits granted by a provision of the state constitution by judicial redefinition of the term "widow" to include widowers would be improper.

Comment: Here the authors have chosen to make their summary brief and conclusionary, as the appellants did, and generally to follow appellants' format. In Point I they differ with appellants on the question of which of the pertinent facts are most significant, stressing the point that women today remain economically disadvantaged. In Points II and III they first take issue with the constitutional test proposed in appellants' Point II and then meet it in its own terms. In Point IV they briefly deal with the secondary issue discussed in Point III of appellants' summary.

ARGUMENT

I. The property tax exemption for widows provided by
Fla. Stat. §196.191(7) and Art. VII, §3(b), Fla. Const.
is based on valid economic considerations and consti-
tutes a reasonable classification determined by actual
difference and valid state policy and is properly within
the taxing classification power of the state.

A. Any classification for purposes of taxation is per-
missible which has a reasonable relation to a legiti-

mate end of governmental action and only if it
appears that there is no rational basis for the classification so as to make it patently arbitrary may it
be set aside as invidious discrimination in violation
of the equal protection clause of the fourteenth
amendment.

It has long been the position of this Court that, in the selection of
the subjects of taxation, broad discretion is allowed to the states.[1]
Thus, in *Royster Guano Co. v. Virginia*, 253 U.S. 412, 415 (1920), this
Court stated that "the latitude of discretion is notably wide in the
classification of property for purposes of taxation and the granting
of partial or total exemptions upon grounds of policy." And the
Court observed in *Madden v. Kentucky*, 309 U.S. 83, 87-88 (1940):

> The broad discretion as to classification possessed by a legislature in
> the field of taxation has long been recognized. This Court fifty years
> ago concluded that "the Fourteeth Amendment was not intended to
> compel the State to adopt an iron rule of equal taxation," and the
> passage of time has only served to underscore the wisdom of that
> recognition of the large area of discretion which is needed by a legisla-
> ture in formulating sound tax policies. Traditionally classification has
> been a device for fitting tax programs to local needs and usages in
> order to achieve an equitable distribution of the tax burden. It has,
> because of this, been pointed out that in taxation, even more than in
> other fields, legislators possess the greatest freedom in classification.
> Since the members of a legislature necessarily enjoy a familiarity with
> local conditions which this Court cannot have, the presumption of
> constitutionality can be overcome only by the most explicit demonstra-
> tion that a classfication is a hostile and oppressive discrimination
> against particular persons and classes. The burden is on the one at-
> tacking the legislative arrangement to negative every conceivable basis
> which might support it.

So long as the state proceeds on a rational basis having some
ground of difference bearing a fair and substantial relation to the
object of the legislation, and does not resort to a classification which
is palpably arbitrary, the classification has been upheld.[2] "If the se-

1. *Lehnhausen v. Lake Short Auto Parts Co.*, 410 U.S. 356 (1973); *Allied Stores of Ohio,
Inc. v. Bowers*, 358 U.S. 522 (1959); *Madden v. Kentucky*, 309 U.S. 83 (1940); *Lawrence v.
State Tax Commission of Mississippi*, 286 U.S. 276 (1932).
2. *Lindsley v. National Carbonic Gas Co., Inc.*, 220 U.S. 61 (1910); *Louisville Gas &
Electric Co. v. Coleman*, 277 U.S. 32 (1928); Ohio Oil Co. v. Conway, 281 U.S. 146
(1930).

lection on classification is neither capricious nor arbitrary, and rests upon some reasonable consideration or difference or policy, there is no denial of equal protection of the law." *Brown-Forman Co. v. Kentucky*, 217 U.S. 563, 573 (1910). "That a statute may discriminate in favor of a certain class does not render it arbitrary if the discrimination is founded upon a reasonable distinction, or difference in state policy."[3] *Allied Stores of Ohio, Inc. v. Bowers*, 358 U.S. 522, 528 (1959). In such a case, the proper test in defining the limits placed by the equal protection clause on state power is whether the classification is "palpably arbitrary" or "invidious." *Lehnhausen v. Lake Shore Auto Parts Co.*, 410 U.S. 356 (1973).

The classification in this case effects an exemption from taxation for property owned by widows, blind persons and persons who are totally and permanently disabled, to the value of $500. Such a classification is far from being palpably arbitrary, and in fact rests on a recognition that these groups are likely to face certain economic hardships with which the general population does not have to cope.[4] As to widows, the Supreme Court of Florida reasonably and properly noted that:

> It has been ably pointed out that the object of the legislation here in question is "to reduce to a limited extent the tax burden on widows who own property to the value of $500 and . . . thereby to 'reduce the disparity between the economic . . . capabilities of a man and a woman,' . . ." As recognized in *Gruenwald v. Gardner*, supra, women workers as a class do not earn as much as men. Certainly this has a "fair and substantial relation" to the ability of women owners to pay taxes on property of even minimal value.
>
> We recognize that steps have been and are continuing to be taken toward the elimination of legal barriers to equality of the sexes. Among the significant steps toward this end is the legislative provision for alimony and child support payments by women as well as men.

3. Citing *American Sugar Refining Co. v. Louisiana*, 179 U.S. 89 (1900); *Stebbins v. Riley*, 268 U.S. 137, 142 (1925).

4. Appellant cites *Moritz v. Commissioner of Internal Revenue*, 469 F.2d 466 (10th Cir. 1972), *cert. denied* 412 U.S. 906 (1973) as support for the proposition that a classification based on sex constitutes invidious discrimination. A careful reading of that option, however, indicates that the Court recognized the economic considerations. The Court asserted that "relief" to persons in low income brackets and bearing special burdens of dependence could be achieved. The Court then indicated that "the lack of a basis related to the income of women is illustrated further by the fact that the statute allows the deduction to widowers and divorcees." Thus, that court appeared to indicate that had the statute in question in fact been based upon the inferior income of women, it would have been upheld. 469 F.2d at 470, n.4.

Appendix A

This provision, however, provides a means of taking into consideration the factual economic capability of each woman involved through judicial supervision and control.

Significantly, the provisions of the statute under review do not provide any means for similar consideration. Therefore, until the steps taken toward legal equality result in equality in fact, a finding of identity between the sexes at this time would rest on fiction and not fact. (J.S. at A6-A7)

Appellant, in arguing that women are not in such an economically inferior position, emphasizes heavily that women have been increasing as a percentage of the work force. (Brief of Appellant, P. 6). He chooses to ignore the fact that this has not benefited women in regard to earning capacity. In reality, inequality of income is a severe and current problem. Women who work at full-time jobs the year round earn, on the average, only *$3 for every $5 earned by men* similarly employed.[5] The gap, in fact, was greater in 1970 than it was in 1955. Women's median wage or salary income as a proportion of men's fell from almost 64 percent in 1955 to 59.4 percent in 1970.[6]

5. S. Rep. No. 689, 92d Cong., 2d Sess. 9 (1972).
6. The U.S. Dept. of Labor, Women's Bureau Fact Sheet on the Earnings Gap, Dec., 1971 (Rev.), contained the following chart:

Median Earning of Full-time Year Round Workers,[a] by Sex, 1955-70[b]

| Year | Median Earnings | | Women's median earnings as percent of men's |
	Women	Men	
1970	$5,323	$8,966	59.4
1969	4,977	8,227	60.5
1968	4,457	7,664	58.2
1967	4,150	7,182	57.8
1966	3,973	6,848	58.0
1965	3,823	6,375	60.0
1964	3,690	6,195	59.6
1963	3,561	5,978	59.6
1962	3,446	5,794	59.5
1961	3,351	5,644	59.4
1960	3,293	5,417	60.8
1959	3,193	5,208	61.3
1958	3,102	4,927	63.0
1957	3,008	4,713	63.8
1956	2,827	4,466	63.3
1955	2,719	4,252	63.9

a) Worked 35 hours or more a week for 50 to 52 weeks.

b) Data for 1967-70 are not strictly comparable with those for prior years, which are for wage and salary income only and do not include earning of self-employed persons.

These same discrepancies in incomes due to sex and the resulting hardship are as equally applicable to Florida as to the nation generally. For example, in Florida in 1969, of all families which had a male head of household, 9.8% were below the poverty level, while of those which had a female head, 35.8% were below the poverty level.[7] The average income in 1969 for all Florida families was $10,120, while that for Florida families with a female head of household was only $5,718.[8] Florida also has a much higher percentage of widows than widowers. In 1970, of males, age 14 years and over, 3.4% were widowers, while 14.0% of the females in the same age group were widows.[9]

Thus women, although joining the working population in increasing numbers, are nevertheless subject to a clear economic disadvantage in the area of comparability of incomes. On this basis, it can hardly be said that there was no rational basis on which the citizens of the State of Florida could have determined the subject classification nor, therefore, could it be said that the classification is patently arbitrary.

Comment: In this section the appellees set forth the undeniable fact that undergirds their argument on the law. Women still earn much less than men in comparable positions, which means, in turn, that there is a rational basis for the modest preference granted to widows. They might have stressed their key fact even more by setting it up as a separate point with its own appropriate subheading, but the table they included was striking enough. As the reader will see, the majority opinion seized on it.

B. Distinctions based on sex may properly be found to exist, and the proper test of the validity of such distinctions should be whether the classification bears a rational relationship to a state object that is sought to be advanced in a manner which is consis-

7. U.S. Bureau of the Census, Census of Population: 1970 General Social and Economic Characteristics, Final Report PC(1)-C11 Florida, April 1972, at 203.
 8. *Id.* at 233.
 9. U.S. Bureau of the Census, Census of Population: 1970 Detailed Characteristics, Final Report PC(1)-D11 Florida, October 1972, at 679-80.

**tent with the equal protection clause of the four-
teenth amendment.**

The Court has long held that the equal protection clause of the
fourteenth amendment does not require identity of treatment for all
citizens, or preclude a state, by legislation, from making classifications and creating differences in the rights of different groups.[10] It is
only when the discriminating treatment and varying standards, as
created by the legislative classifications, are arbitrary and wanting in
any rational justification that they offend the equal protection
clause.[11] Specifically, a legislative classification based on sex has often
been held to be constitutionally permissible.[12]

In *Reed v. Reed*, 404 U.S. 71 (1971), the Court struck down a
sex-based classification in an Idaho statute. The language of the
Court was substantially in accordance with prior cases however:

> In applying that clause, this Court has consistently recognized that
> the Fourteenth Amendment does not deny to States the power to treat
> different classes of persons in different ways. *Barbier v. Connolly*, 113
> U.S. 27 (1885); *Lindsley v. Natural Carbonic Gas Co.*, 220 U.S. 61 (1911);
> *Railway Express Agency v. New York*, 336 U.S. 106 (1949); *McDonald v.
> Board of Election Commissioners*, 394 U.S. 802 (1969). The Equal Protec-
> tion Clause of that amendment does, however, deny to States the power
> to legislate that different treatment be accorded to persons placed by a
> statute into different classes on the basis of criteria wholly unrelated to
> the objective of that statute. A classification "must be reasonable, not
> arbitrary, and must rest upon some ground of difference having a fair
> and substantial relation to the object of the legislation, so that all per-
> sons similarly circumstanced shall be treated alike." *Royster Guano Co. v.
> Virginia*, 253 U.S. 412 (1920). The question presented by this case, then,
> is whether a difference in the sex of competing applicants for letters of
> administration bears a rational relationship to a state objective that is
> sought to be advanced by the operation of §§15-312 and 15-314. . . .

10. *Brown-Forman Co. v. Kentucky*, 217 U.S. 563, 573 (1910); *State Board of Tax
Commissioners v. Jackson*, 283 U.S. 527, 533 (1931); *American Sugar Refining Co. v.
Louisiana*, 179 U.S. 89 (1900). See *Williams v. McNair*, 316 F. Supp. 134, 136 (D.S.C.
1970), *aff'd without opinion*, 401 U.S. 951 (1971).

11. *Bell's Gap R. Co. v. Pennsylvania*, 134 U.S. 232, 237 (1890); *Magoun v. Illinois
Trust & Savings Bank*, 170 U.S. 283, 293 (1898); *Allied Stores of Ohio, Inc. v. Bowers*, 358
U.S. 522, 527 (1959).

12. See *West Coast Hotel Co. v. Parrish*, 300 U.S. 379, 394-395 (1937); *Radice v. New
York*, 264 U.S. 292, 296-298 (1924); *Goesaert v. Cleary*, 335 U.S. 464 (1948); *Hoyt v.
Florida*, 368 U.S. 57 (1961); *Williams v. McNair*, 316 F. Supp. 134 (D.S.C. 1970), *aff'd
without opinion*, 401 U.S. 951 (1971); *Forbush v. Wallace*, 341 F. Supp. 217 (M.D. Ala.
1971), *aff'd without opinion*, 405 U.S. 970 (1972).

... To give a mandatory preference to members of either sex over members of the other, *merely to accomplish the elimination of hearings on the merits,* is to make the very kind of arbitrary legislative choice forbidden by the Equal Protection Clause of the Fourteenth Amendment; and whatever may be said as to the positive values of avoiding intrafamily controversy, the choice in *this context* may not lawfully be mandated solely on the basis of sex.

... By providing dissimilar treatment for men and women who are thus similarly situated, the challenged section violates the Equal Protection Clause. *Royster Guano Co. v. Virginia, supra.* 404 U.S. at 75-77. (Emphasis supplied.)

Thus, while striking down a classification established merely for the administrative convenience of eliminating hearings, the Court reaffirmed that, even where sex is the basis of classification, a classification which is reasonable, and not arbitrary, and which rests upon some ground of difference having a fair and substantial relation to the object of the legislation, so that all persons similarly circumstanced are treated alike, does not violate the equal protection clause of the fourteenth amendment. In setting out this test, the Court cited only *Royster Guano Co. v. Virginia,* 253 U.S. 412 (1920), in support of its determination. The test of equal protection as stated in *Royster Guano Co. v. Virginia* was that:

It is unnecessary to say that the "equal protection of the laws" required by the 14th Amendment does not prevent the states from resorting to classification for the purposese of legislation. Numerous and familiar decisions of the court establish that they have a wide range of discretion in that regard. But the classification must be reasonable, not arbitrary, and must rest upon some ground of difference having a fair and substantial relation to the object of the legislation, so that all persons similarly circumstanced shall be treated alike. The latitude of discretion is notably wide in the classification of property for purposes or total exemptions upon grounds of policy.... Nevertheless, a discriminatory tax law cannot be sustained against the complaint of a party aggrieved if the classification appears to be altogether illusory. 253 U.S. at 415.

It does not appear, therefore, that *Reed v. Reed, supra,* determined that the state had the same burden, where sex is the basis of a classification, as it would have where certain classifications such as race,[13]

---

13. *Bolling v. Sharpe,* 347 U.S. 497 (1954); *McLaughlin v. Florida,* 379 U.S. 184 (1964); *Loving v. Virginia,* 388 U.S. 1 (1967).

Appendix A

nationality[14] and alienage[15] were challenged. Those cases subject the classification to the "most rigid scrutiny," *Korematsu v. United States,* 323 U.S. 214, 216 (1944), and the showing of a "compelling state interest." *Shapiro v. Thompson,* 394 U.S. 618 (1969)..

Further indication that the test for sex-based distinctions remained as it had historically been treated exists. Four months after the *Reed* decision, this Court affirmed without opinion[16] the holding of a three judge District Court in *Forbush v. Wallace,* 341 F. Supp. 217 (M.D. Ala. 1971). In that case, the District Court upheld both the requirement that a wife upon marriage take her husband's surname and the requirement that she use that name in order to obtain a driver's licencse. The District Court reasoned that:

> This judicial pronouncement, as with any state statute or regulation, must have a rational basis. It is well settled that "the Equal Protection Clause does not make every difference in the application of laws to different groups a violation of our constitution." *Williams v. Rhodes,* 1968, 393 U.S. 23, 30. Thus, as a general rule, a law is not violative of the Fourteenth Amendment, despite the existence of discrimination in the technical or broad sense, where the law at issue maintains some rational connection with a legitimate state interest. *E.g., McDonald v. Board of Election Commissioners,* 1969, 394 U.S. 802, 808-09; *Kotch v. Board of River Port Pilots Commissioners,* 1947, 330 U.S. 552. Furthermore, when a court is presented with a challenge to a seemingly valid state law on equal protection grounds, it must sustain that law if it can discern any rational basis. *E.g., Dandridge v. Williams,* 1970, 397 U.S. 471; *Metropolitan Casualty Insurance Co. v. Brownell Industries,* 1935, 294 U.S. 580; *Borden's Farm Products Co. v. Baldwin,* 1934, 293 U.S. 194. 341 F. Supp. at 222.

In *Frontiero v. Richardson,* 411 U.S. 677 (1973), the Court once again examined the question of the degree of justification necessary for classification based on sex. While four members of the Court indicated a willingness to extend the "inherently suspect" test to sex classifications, the majority of the Court refused to do so.[17] Mr.

14. *Hirabayashi v. United States,* 320 U.S. 81 (1943); *Korematsu v. United States,* 323 U.S. 214 (1944); *Oyama v. California,* 332 U.S. 633 (1948).

15. *Graham v. Richardson,* 403 U.S. 365 (1971).

16. 405 U.S. 970, *aff'g* 341 F. Supp. 217 (M.D. Ala. 1971).

17. Mr. Justice Stewart, in concurring with the result, limited his finding to a determination that the statutes involved worked an "invidious" discrimination. Mr. Justice Rehnquist dissented on the grounds stated by the district Court. Mr. Justice Powell, joined by the Chief Justice and Mr. Justice Blackmun, concurred, but for the reasons set out in the text, *infra.*

Justice Powell, joined by the Chief Justice and Mr. Justice Blackmun stated:

> I agree that the challenged statutes constitute an unconstitutional discrimination against service women in violation of the Due Process Clause of the Fifth Amendment, but I cannot join the opinion of Mr. Justice Brennan, which would hold that all classifications based upon sex, "like classifications based upon race, alienage, and national origin," are "inherently suspect and must therefore be subjected to close judicial scrutiny." Supra at 682. It is unnecessary for the Court in this case to characterize sex as a suspect classification, with all of the far-reaching implications of such a holding. *Reed v. Reed,* 404 U.S. 71 (1971), which abundantly supports our decision today, did not add sex to the narrowly limited group of classifications which are inherently suspect. In my view, we can and should decide this case on the authority of *Reed* and reserve for the future any expansion of its rationale. 411 U.S. at 691-92.

This reasoning is sound and is a recognition that distinctions based on sex may be rational and beneficial to both sexes. Such is the case before us. Women are in an inferior economic position as previously noted, which does not appear to be correcting itself in spite of the legislative efforts which have been made. In fact, as previously noted, the situation has become even more aggravated over the years. To try to limit the extent of this burden is a proper policy determination of the state and the statutory exemption constitutes a rational means for doing so. As noted by the Second Circuit Court of Appeals in *Gruenwald v. Gardner,* 390 F.2d 591 (2d Cir. 1968), where the court held that a statute granting women more favorable treatment than men in computing social security benefits does not violate the Civil Rights Act:

> The appellant concedes that women, as a class, earn less than men, that their economic opportunities in higher age groups are less, and that higher benefits will operate as an inducement for their earlier retirement, but disputes "the unequal treatment of two individuals solely because of sex" and argue that a "classification must rest upon a difference which is real. . . ."
> There is here a reasonable relationship between the objective sought by the classification, which is to reduce the disparity between the economic and physical capabilities of a man and a woman — and the means used to achieve that objective in affording to women more favorable benefit computations. There is, moreover, nothing arbi-

trary or unreasonable about the application of the principle underlying the statutory differences in the computations for men and women. Notwithstanding the favorable treatment granted to women in computing their benefits, the average monthly payments to men retiring at age 62 still exceeds those awarded women retiring at that age. Social Security Bulletin, Annual Statistical Supplement 1965, U.S. Dept. of Health, Educa. and Welfare, at 47, 56, 64, 69. Social Security Bulletin, Annual Statistical Supplement 1963, *supra* at 47. 390 F.2d at 592.

A recent decision by a three judge District Court in New Jersey in *Wiesenfeld v. Secretary of Health, Education, and Welfare*, 42 L.W. 2326 (1973), concurred in this analysis of *Reed* and *Frontiero*. In reviewing a section of the social security act providing widows, but not widowers, with survivors' benefits while caring for children entitled to insurance benefits, the Court stated:

> ... The Supreme Court has declined to add sex to the list of inherently suspect classifications. *Frontiero v. Richardson*, 411 U.S. 677, 41 L.W. 4609 (1973); *Reed v. Reed*, 404 U.S. 71, 40 L.W. 4013 (1971). . . .
> In *Reed* and *Frontiero* we do not discern a "general shift" of standards nor the establishment of a "new intermediate" equal protection test, and we reject those cases which adopt such standards. We do, however, perceive an expression of deep concern by the Supreme Court to analyze statutory classifications based upon sex in more pragmatic terms of this everyday modern world rather than in the stereotyped generalizations of the Victorian age. . . ." 42 L.W. at 2326-72.

The District Court then reviewed the matter first under the "traditional" test and determined that it satisfied that standard:

> ... [W]e must first proceed to an analysis of whether Section 402(g) is rationally related to some valid public purpose.
> When this standard is applied to Section 402(g), we find that this measure is a rational attempt by Congress to protect women and families who have lost the male head of the household. This choice by Congress is not arbitrary because it is very evident that women have been and continue to be unable to earn income equal to that of men even though Congress has clearly indicated that job discrimination on the basis of sex shall be unlawful. 42 L.W. at 2327.[18]

18. While that court then applied the "close judicial scrutiny" test, and found the provision to violate that test, it did so only after determining that the legislation, in fact, discriminates against some of those it intends to protect:

Clearly the granting to widows, as an economically disadvantaged group, a small exemption from ad valorem property taxation does bear a rational relationship to the goal of reducing the existent economic gap and is valid under the fourteenth amendment. To determine otherwise would be to ignore the realities of economic hardship faced by widows in our society.

Comment: In the section above, the authors deal with the crucial and hotly debated question whether classifications based on gender alone are subject to an especially close scrutiny. As did the appellants, they gingerly pick their way among the differing opinions in *Reed* and *Frontiero* and reach their own conclusions, being especially careful to avoid overstatement and to quote for accuracy. The reader will notice that throughout this argument, there is no backbiting and no bickering. The authors recognize that the views of their opponents will be treated with respect and that the winning brief will be the one that offers the more balanced and reasonable position on a highly controversial question.

C. Even if sex classifications are considered to be inherently suspect, the classification found in Fla.

... [E]ven though Congress may have intended that this section rectify the effects of past and present discrimination against women, it operates to "heap on" additional economic disadvantages to women wage earners such as [the deceased wife]. During her employment as a teacher, maximum social security payments were deducted from her salary. Yet, upon her tragic death, her surviving spouse and child receive less social security benefits than those of a male teacher who earned the same salary and made the same social security payments.

While affirmative legislative or executive action may satisfy a compelling governmental interst to undo the past discrimination against such suspect groups as racial minorites, such action cannot meet the higher equal protection standard if it discriminates against some of the group which it is designed to protect. Because Section 402(g) discriminates against women ... who have successfully gained employment as well as against men and children who have lost their wives and mothers, we find this section violates the Fifth Amendment. 42 L.W. at 2327.

Such is not the situation in the case at hand. The statute is intended to benefit widows, who, as a group, are subject to economic disadvantages, but none of whom, unlike the *Wiesenfeld* situation, are potentially discriminated against by the legislation.

Appendix A

Stat. §196.191(7), is justified when subjected to strict judicial scrutiny, as the state has a compelling interest in protecting widows.

In *Frontiero v. Richardson, supra,* 411 U.S. at 689, it is indicated by four members of the Court that classifications based upon sex, like classifications based on race, alienage, and national origin, are inherently suspect and should therefore be subjected to close judicial scrutiny. This was the first indication by any members of the Court that such scrutiny should be given to this area. While this approach, we submit, does not recognize the realities of the differences between men and women which justify classifications where they are rational, nevertheless, should the Court determine to apply the strictor test, the State of Florida does in fact have a compelling interest which is being furthered.

Unlike the situation in *Frontiero,* the purpose of the provision in Florida's Constitution and statutes is not merely "administrative efficiency" and is not subject to the conclusion of the Court in that case that:

> . . . by according differential treatment to male and female members of the uniformed services for the *sole purpose* of achieving *administrative convenience,* the challenged statutes violate the Due Process Clause of the Fifth Amendment insofar as they require a female member to prove the dependency of her husband." (emphasis supplied) 411 U.S. at 690-91.

It is to be noted that, while the Court refused to recognize sex differentiation for the *sole* purpose of achieving administrative convenience as a compelling state interest, the Court did indicate that if the Government could affirmatively show that money was saved it would suffice:

> The Government offers no concrete evidence however, tending to support its views that such differential treatment in fact saves the Government any money. In order to satisfy the demands of strict judicial scrutiny, the Government must demonstrate, for example, that it is actually cheaper to grant increased benefits with respect to *all* male members, than it is to determine which male members are in fact entitled to such benefits and to grant increased benefits only to those members whose wives actually meet the dependence requirement. Here, however, there is substantial evidence that, if put to the test,

many of the wives of male members would fail to qualify for benefits. And in light of the fact that the dependency determination with respect to the husbands of female members if presently made solely on the basis of affidavits, rather than through the more costly hearing process, the Government's explanation of the statutory scheme is, to say the least, questionable. 411 U.S. at 689-90.

Florida is not solely concerned with saving money or administrative convenience. To grant an exemption to widows in fact is a considerable expense to the state in lost revenues. Nevertheless, the state recognizes the plight of women in the economic area and the decreased ability, through no fault of their own, to sustain themselves in today's job market.[19] Florida, with its large elderly population, has a special concern for widows who may be faced with this problem and has a compelling interst in giving them special tax consideration. This fact is bolstered by the anticipation that such action will encourage this group to continue to seek retirement homes in Florida. Such economic and social considerations are certainly not in a class with mere administrative convenience, nor even with the money-saving basis which the Court indicated in *Frontiero* could satisfy their strict judicial scrutiny. Considering these compelling intersts of the citizens of Florida, it should be determined that sufficient reason exists to uphold the statute even under such strict scrutiny.

Comment: In this final prong of their principal argument the authors try to sustain the point that even under a strict-scrutiny test the Florida statute should be upheld because its interest in the legislation is compelling. Factually they have little evidence in support of the argument, but they can and do at least suggest why Florida should be concerned with widows' problems and conclude that such concern should be enough within the meaning of the cases. Because the argument is not strong, standing alone, the authors have quite appropriately put it last in the series under Point I.

19. This is akin to the situation suggested in *Wiesenfeld v. Secretary of Health, Education, and Welfare,* 42 L.W. 2326 (1973), where the New Jersey District Court suggested that "affirmative legislative or executive action may satisfy a compelling governmental interest to undo the past discrimination against such suspect groups as racial minorities. . . ." 42 L.W. at 2327.

Appendix A

II. Should the ad valorem tax exemption granted to widows by Art. VII, §3(b), Fla. Const., and Fla. Stat. §196.191(7) be held to be unconstitutional, this cause should not be remanded to the court below for consideration of judicially expanding the word "widow" to include widowers.

Appellant urges that should this Court determine that the gender-based classification in §196.191(7), Fla. Stat. and Art. VII, §3(b), Fla. Const., violate the fourteenth amendment to the United States Constitution, this cause should be remanded to the Florida Supreme Court for consideration of whether the constitutional infirmity could be remedied by holding the exemption available to all persons, otherwise qualified, who have lost a spouse by death. Appellant has asserted that "[t]he remedial choice was never addressed by the Florida Supreme Court since it concluded that the 'widows only' exemption was constitutional." Appellants' Brief at 210. Contrary to this assertion, both the trial court, in holding the statute to be unconstitutional, and the Florida Supreme Court, in reversing that holding, did consider the propriety of "expanding" the definition of "widow" to include males as well as females and held that they were unable to do so.[20] This point was fully briefed

---

20. The Trial Judge held "this Court is powerless to expand the meaning of 'widow' to include both women and men. . . ." (J.S. at A3) The Florida Supreme Court was in accord:

> We agree that the term "widow" may not be judicially redefined to include a man who has lost his wife since the legislative intent obviously limits the application of the term only to a woman who has lost her husband by death. This definition is in conformance with the unvarying legislative and judicial use of the term in other areas. [Citing *City of Jacksonville Beach v. State*, 151 So. 2d 430 (Fla. 1963); *Wilson v. Fridenburg*, 19 Fla. 461 (1882); *In re Estate of Yohn*, 229 So. 2d 612 (Fla. App. 1st, 1969), *In re Beacher's Estate*, 177 So. 2d 838 (Fla. App. 3rd, 1965).] (J.S. at A5-A6)

In *Brinson v. State*, Case No. 43932 (Fla. Sup. Ct., filed Jan. 9, 1974), *rev'g*, 278 So. 2d 317 (1 D.C.A. Fla. 1973), the Florida Supreme Court held that Florida's rape statute, Fla. Stat. §794.01, could not be judicially construed to apply to a defendant accused of forcible carnal knowledge of a male:

> It is not the province of the judiciary to legislate; therefore, for the Court to change the definition of "female" found in Florida Statutes, §794.01, to be the same as the more inclusive word "person" is to invade the province of the Legislature. Slip Opinion at 3.

and argued before the Florida Supreme Court by both Appellant and Appellees.

It should also be pointed out that the gender-based classification under consideration here is not simply one instituted by the legislature, but is an expression of the will of the people of Florida who ratified the provisions of Art. VII, §3(b), Fla. Const., in November of 1968. Thus, if this cause were to be remanded, the Florida Supreme Court would have to consider not what the legislature intended by enacting Fla. Stat. §196.191(7), but what the people of Florida intended when they ratified the mandatory, self-executing exemption provision of Art. VII, §3(b), of the 1968 Florida Constitution. The universally accepted definition of the word "widow" to refer only to females was undoubtedly in the minds of the people when they ratified this provision of our constitution, and there can be little question but that their understanding of the provision and their intention in ratifying it was to grant the exemption only to a woman who has lost her spouse by death.

Appellant has cited numerous cases in support of his proposition that a judicial extension of benefits under an otherwise unconstitutional statute is proper.[21] In those cases the courts have generally looked to the overall legislative purpose of the statutes involved in order "to decide whether it more nearly accords with [the legislature's] wishes to eliminate its policy altogether or extend it in order to render what [the legislature] plainly did intend, constitutional." *Welsh v. United States*, 398 U.S. 333, 355-56 (1970) (Harlan, J., Concurring). Appellant has cited no case in which the courts have extended the benefits provided by a provision of a state *constitution*. The reason for such judicial restraint is sound. When a court extends the benefits of a legislative enactment, it does so because it feels that is what the legislature itself would do in the face of having the provision otherwise fall for some constitutional infirmity. However, should the court misread the will of the legislature, it is usually a relatively simply matter for the legislature to reappeal the provision altogether. The situation is entirely different when the benefits sought to be extended are provided not by statute, but by an expression of the will of the people in a state constitution. Should the court misread the will of the people in this situation, it can be rectified only by a constitutional amendment. The process of amending Florida's Constitution is far more costly and lengthy than the legislature's

21. *See* Appellant's Brief at page 211.

Appendix A

enacting a statute,[22] and until it is amended, public funds will be lost by virtue of extending a tax exemption to a class of person which the people have not expressly provided for. On the other hand, should the Court hold the widow's exemption provision of Florida's Constitution to be invalid, then the people of Florida would have the opportunity to affirmatively express their will and desire to extend an exemption to both widows and widowers.

Comment: In this concluding section the authors rely primarily on the fact that the Court here deals with not only a statute but a section of the Florida constitution. They address the point which appellants have not; How can a court know what the people would have voted if they had been presented with a different proposal, modified to conform to the Constitution? The authors have no authority to cite on this point but this does not stop them. They argue on reason alone.

CONCLUSION

For the reasons stated above, the decision of the Florida Supreme Court should be affirmed and Art. VII, §3(b), Fla. Const., and Fla. Stat. §196.191(7) should be declared to provide a proper classification within the taxing power of the State of Florida, not in violation of the equal protection clause of the fourteenth amendment.

However, should the Court hold the gender-based classification to be unconstitutional, this cause should not be remanded for consideration of whether to judicially redefine the term "widow" to include widowers.

22. The procedure for amending Florida's Constitution is provided in Article XI, Fla. Const. (1968). The proposed amendment may orginate either by joint resolution agreed to by three-fifths of the membership of each of the two houses of Florida's Legislature (Art. XI, §1), or by an initiative petition "signed by a number of electors in each of one half of the congressional districts of the state, and of the state as a whole, equal to eight percent of the votes cast in each of such districts respectively and in the state as a whole in the last preceding election in which presidential electors were chosen." (Art. XI, §3) In either case, the proposed amendment must be approved by a vote of the electors before it may become effective. (Art. XI, §5)

Respectfully submitted,

ROBERT L. SHEVIN
Attorney General
SYDNEY H. MCKENZIE, III
Assistant Attorney General
The Capitol
Tallahassee, Florida 32304

Attorneys for Appellees
State of Florida

Comment: Thus the Appellees' Brief, like the appellants', ends with a brief conclusion in the usual form.

The brief as a whole is essentially a statement of Florida's own affirmative position on the significant facts and the significant law; it does not so much take issue with appellants' arguments as to by-pass them. It says, in substance, "Well, those points are all very well, but here is what really matters." The result, so far in the briefing, is a clear-cut choice between competing policies.

IN THE

Supreme Court of the United States
OCTOBER TERM, 1973

No. 73-78

MEL KAHN, etc.,

Appellants,

— v. —

ROBERT L. SHEVIN, *et al.*,

Appellees.

ON APPEAL FROM THE SUPREME COURT OF

THE STATE OF FLORIDA

REPLY BRIEF FOR APPELLANTS

I. A dispensation setting women apart from similarly situated men does not assist in undoing inequalities in economic opportunity women encounter.

Appellees justify the gender line set by the widows tax exemption (Fla. Stat. §196.191(7)) as a reasonable means of serving state policy "to alleviate the hardship to women resulting from the inequality in economic opportunity."[1] The theme is familiar. Last term, this Court was asked to approve the gender differential challenged in *Frontiero v. Richardson,* 411 U.S. 677 (1973), because the statute dealt with "economic benefits" and reflected "the realities of American life" — women's dependence on men.[2] Similarly, in *Moritz v. Commissioner of Internal Revenue,* 469 F.2d 466 (10th cir. 1972), *cert. denied,* 412 U.S. 906 (1973), the Court of Appeals was asked to approve exclusion of never married men from a tax benefit granted never married women because "employment opportunities and pay scales for women remain more restricted than for men."[3] The justification

---

1. Brief for Appellees at 218.
2. Brief for Appellees, *Frontiero v. Richardson,* No. 71-1694, at 7, 10, 11-12.
3. Brief for Appellee, 10th Cir. No. 71-1127, at 14; *see also* (Solicitor General's) Petition for a Writ of Certiorari, No. 72-1298, at 8-11.

should fare no better here than it did in *Frontiero* and *Moritz*, for "benign dispensations" that set females apart from similarly situated males shore up the very attitudes and traditions that have so long served to keep women "in their place."[4]

It should be stressed that wide latitude of discretion in classifying *property* for tax purposes is not at issue in this case. What is in controversy is the breadth of discretion to classify *persons* solely on the basis of an immutable birth trait that bears no necessary relationship to need or ability. *Cf. In re Estate of Legatos,* 1 Cal. App. 3d 657, 662, 81 Cal. Rptr. 910, 913 (1969) ("Both in their incidence and innate characteristics tax moneys are sexless and soulless.") If appellees' rationale is accepted, then Florida could, with at least equally "compelling" justification, dispense tax exemption solely on the basis of race or national origin.

Overlooked or misapprehended in appellees' presentation is the critical distinction between lump treatment of women as the inferior and therefore needier sex, and measures designed to undo the inequalities in economic opportunity women encounter. Continued exclusion of widowers from a tax exemption initiated in 1885 simply perpetuates the policy of a society in which women were separate and unequal.[5] The exemption surely does not address "the plight of women in the economic area" through means calculated to aid them

---

Appellees' reading of the *Moritz* opinion (Brief for Appellees at 221 n.4) is selective rather than "careful." Use of a gender classification in lieu of an income classification was the invidious means upon which the opinion focused. The further point made by the *Moritz* court concerning allowance of the deduction to widowers and divorcées but not to never married men, responded to a wholly distinct argument made by Moritz, *i.e.*, that the statute diffentiated irrationally between members of the same sex: "It merits emphasis that, in addition to its wholly irrational distinction between single sons and daughters, the statute capriciously prefers sons who are widowed or divorced to sons who are lifelong bachelors." Brief for Appellant, *Moritz v. Commissioner of Internal Revenue,* 10th Cir. No. 71-1127, at 24-25. Cf. text at notes 8-10 *infra*.

4. *See generally,* K. M. Davidson, R. B. Ginsburg & H. H. Kay, Text, Cases and Materials on Sex-Based Discrimination, Ch. 1 (Constitutional Aspects), especially at 8-10, and 53-57 (1974).

5. "So great a favourite [was] the female sex of the laws of [Florida]" that women were accorded a widows exemption long before they achieved the franchise. *Cf.* 1 Blackstone, Commentaries 442-45 (1765). Similar solicitude was exhibited by this Court in *Quong Wing v. Kirkendall,* 223 U.S. 59 (1912) (upholding license fee exemption for women operators of hand laundries where no men were employed), and *Breedlove v. Suttles,* 302 U.S. 277 (1937) (upholding poll tax legislation more onerous for men than for women — women not required to pay for years in which they did not vote).

"to sustain themselves in today's job market."[6] For such means address the problem at its source; principal examples are laws prohibiting gender discrimination in education, employment, financing, housing, and public accommodations.[7] Significantly, Florida's utilization of this means to undo inequalities has been minimal.[8]

Moreover, appellees' heartwarming statement of Florida's policy "to alleviate hardship to women" who must cope with the world without a male partner, and appellees' statistical references,[9] highlight a further irrationality in the statutory scheme. No gender-based exemption is accorded the female head of household who never married, or whose marriage was terminated by divorce. The unmarried or divorced woman has no greater economic opportunities than her widowed sister, indeed she may encounter sharper prejudice in the job market.[10] Further, she receives no statutory share in a man's estate, as does the widow,[11] to ease her plight.

Decades ago Burnita Shelton Matthews[12] commented: "It is of course disappointing to women that men of the legal profession are unable to see equality as equity when applied as between men and women." Women Should Have Equal Rights With Men, A Reply, 12 A.B.A.J. 117, 120 (1926). While benefits for widows, but not for widowers, originated in all-male chambers, the direction taken by women allowed to speak for themselves is clear: groups and legislators dedicated to the elimination of discrimination against women

6. Brief for Appellees at 231 (text at note 19). In this respect, Florida's exemption resembles the "favor" supplied by the differential in *Gruenwald v. Gardner*, 390 F.2d 591 (2d Cir.), *cert. denied*, 393 U.S. 982 (1968), discussed in Brief for Appellants at 208. More recently legislatures and courts have become increasingly skeptical of such "favors." *See, e.g., Chastang v. Flynn and Emrich Co.*, 365 F. Supp., 957, 965-67 (D. Md. 1973).

7. *See, e.g.*, Griffiths, The Law Must Reflect the New Image of Women, 23 Hastings L.J. 1 (1971).

8. While Florida prohibits sex discrimination in government employment, Fla. Stat. §§112.041, 112.042 (1967), 110.092 (1969), most of its anti-discrimination laws omit gender from the catalogue. *See* Fla. Stat. §§409.026 (1970) (prohibiting discrimination on the basis of race, color, or religion, but not sex, in the administration of social services), 509.092, 509.141 (1970) (discrimination in certain places of public accomodation — covers race, religion and national origin, but not sex).

9. Brief for Appellees at 223.

10. *See, e.g., Doe v. Osteopathic Hospital*, 333 F. Supp. 1357 (D. Kan. 1971) (termination of employment of unwed expectant mother); *Cirino v. Walsh*, 66 Misc. 2d 450, 321 N.Y.S.2d 493 (Sup. Ct. 1971) (unwed mother who met all objective criteria for school crossing guard position found "not qualified" by police department because birth status of her children showed she lacked "good character").

11. *See Simons v. Miami Beach First National Bank*, 381 U.S. 81 (1965).

12. Then counsel to the National Women's Party, later United States District Judge for the District of Columbia.

have emerged as principal proponents of protection on an equal basis to both men and women.[13]

Finally, appellees's analysis[14] of *Wiesenfeld v. Secretary of Health, Education and Welfare*, Civil Action No. 268-73, D.N.J. December 11, 1973, 42 U.S. Law Week 2326, misses the essential point. Indeed, the claims of Stephen Wiesenfeld and Mel Kahn are barely distinguishable. In *Wiesenfeld*, 42 U.S.C. §402(g) was declared unconstitutional "insofar as it discriminates against widowers on the basis of their sex"; defendant was enjoined "from denying benefits . . . to widowers solely on the basis of sex." Had Paula Wiesenfeld died in Florida, no "benign dispensation" would have been accorded her surviving spouse under Fla. Stat. §196.191(7), despite the tragic impact of her death upon her family. Whether the female partner contributes to the economic welfare of her family through gainful employment or homemaking services[15] or, as is increasingly the reality, through productive effort both on the job and at home, surely recognition of her worth would be enhanced by declaring Fla. Stat. §196.191(7) equally applicable to widows and widowers.

II. The remedial choice on remand.

Based upon Alice-in-Wonderland reasoning, appellees would foreclose consideration of any remedial route other than elimination of the widows exemption.[16] Demolition of the exemption policy, "relief"

13. *E.g.*, Griffiths, *supra* note 7, at 8-9. Prime sponsors of full extension of widows benefits to widowers under Social Security are Representatives Martha Griffiths and Bella Abzug. *See, e.g.*, H.R. 9,715, 90th Cong., May 8, 1967; H.R. 841, 91st Cong. January 3, 1969; H.R. 3,289, 92d Cong., 1st Sess., February 2, 1971 (all introduced by Representative Griffiths); H.R. 15,528, 16,036, 16,101, 92d Cong., 2d Sess., June 15, 1972, July 26, 1972, and July 31, 1972 (introduced by Representative Abzug); H.R. 1570, 93d Cong., 1st Sess., January 9, 1973 (introduced by Representative Griffiths). The fact that the commission that wrote the 1968 Florida Constitution included only one woman among thirty-six members may well explain why the 1885 widows exemption emerged unchanged and was not converted to a widowed persons exemption. See 25A Fla. Stat. Ann. at ix.

14. Brief for Appellees at 228, 231 and nn. 18, 19.

15. *See* Walker & Gauger, The Dollar Value of Houshold Work (College of Human Ecology, Cornell Univ. 1973).

16. The Florida Supreme Court considered only the threshold question, whether the word "widow" could be defined to mean "widowed person." It ruled against such expansive definition. That court's further ruling that the gender line was constitutional left it without occasion to consider the remedial choice posed by an underinclusive classification. Nor is *Brinson v. State* (Fla. Sup. Ct., January 9, 1974, cited in Brief for Appellees at 232) relevant to a tax exemption constitutionally infirm for under-

surely not sought by appellant, is urged by appellees because: (1) the people of Florida ratified a revised Constitution in 1968; (2) that Constitution, among its many provisions, carried forward from the 1885 Constitution provision for a widows tax exemption; (3) curing the underinclusive classification by extending the exemption to widowers risks misreading the will of the people. Left out of this assessment is the larger risk of misreading that a demolition course entails. The exemption is currently available to approximately three-quarters of the widowed population.[17] Inclusion of the remaining quarter is a small adjustment in comparison to the radical change effected by elimination of the exemption.

Moreover, the 1968 Constitution, including the widows tax exemption authorization, was presented to the people on a take-it-or-leave-it basis. The voters' acceptance of a three-quarter loaf, all that was offered them, surely does not indicate that they would have refused the whole, much less that they would have preferred abstinence to a full portion. On the contrary, the voters' approval of two new constitutional provisions suggests precisely the opposite. The 1968 Constitution substitutes for the former provision that "all men are equal before the law," the guarantee that "all natural persons are equal before the law,"[18] and further stipulates that "there shall be no distinction between men and women in the holding, control, disposition, or encumbering of their property."[19] In short, a declared purpose of the exemption, to encourage the elderly "to continue to seek retirement homes in Florida,"[20] signals the direction for a judiciary concerned with preservation rather than destruction of legislative policy and the will of the people.[21]

---

inclusion. *Brinson* involved a criminal charge; judicial extension of a criminal statute, the Florida Supreme Court point out, is barred by the due process clause. No such impediment exists when the issue is extension of a benefit.

17. *See* Brief for Appellant at 214 n.26.

18. Art. 1, §2.

19. Art. 10, §5.

20. Brief for Appellees at 25.

21. *Cf. Guinn v. United States*, 238 U.S. 347, 366-67 (1925); Note, 55 Harv. L. Rev. 1030, 1034-36 (1942). On remand, at the very least, the Florida Supreme Court should have the opportunity to consider whether it wishes to adopt a remedial approach in harmony with this Court's precedent. *See, e.g., Frontiero v. Richardson*, 411 U.S. 677, 691 n.25 (1973), where the annual cost factor for the benefit extended was an estimated $3.5 million in the Air Force and $1 million in the Navy. *See* Hearings Before the Special Subcomm. on the Utilization of Manpower in the Military of the House Comm. on Armed Services, 92d Cong., 1st & 2d Sess. 12502-12503 (1972) (estimates for the other armed services not reported). Considerably higher costs were

In any event, since widows were accorded the exemption during the period herein question, the denial of equal protection to appellants can be repaired only by according exemption to them for that period.

CONCLUSION

For the reasons presented by appellants, the decision of the Florida Supreme Court should be reversed, and Fla. Stat. §196.191(7) should be declared unconstitutional insofar as it differentiates between widowed persons solely on the basis of gender.

Respectfully submitted,

RUTH BADER GINSBURG
MELVIN L. WULF
BRENDA FEIGEN FASTEAU
CHRISTINE CASSADAY CURTIS
American Civil Liberties Union
Foundation
22 East 40th Street
New York, New York 10016
WILLIAM HOPPE
Second Floor, Concord Building
Miami, Florida 33130

Attorneys for Appellants

Comment: Appellants' Reply Brief is concise, as it should be. In the first four paragraphs the authors come right to the point, seeking to demolish their opponents' reasoning with a series of short, logical arguments. The brief writers choose not to reargue in their reply the meaning and application of *Reed* and *Frontiero,* the key cases discussed in the earlier briefs.

---

entailed in, *e.g., Shapiro v. Thompson,* 394 U.S. 618 (1969); *Graham v. Richardson,* 403 U.S. 365 (1971); and *New Jersey Welfare Rights Organization v. Cahill,* 411 U.S. 619 (1973). *See also In re Estate of Legatos,* 1 Cal. App. 3d 657, 81 Cal. Rptr. 910 (1969) (gender-based tax exemption judicially extended to cure underinclusion).

Appendix A

Whereas the brief is in general moderate in its tone (*e.g.*, appellees are said to have "overlooked or misapprehended" a "critical distinction," p. 237) the authors on one occasion resort to sarcasm ("appellees' heart-warming statement," p. 238) and on another to epithet ("Alice-in-Wonderland reasoning," p. 239) — phraseology that may or may not have aided their position.

Following submission of briefs and argument the Supreme Court affirmed, Justices Brennan, Marshall, and White dissenting. 416 U.S. 351 (1974). The opinions are quoted below with some final comments.

MR. JUSTICE DOUGLAS delivered the opinion of the Court.

Since at least 1885, Florida has provided for some form of property tax exemption for widows.[1] The current law granting all widows an annual $500 exemption, Fla. Stat. § 196.202 (Supp. 1974-1975), has been essentially unchanged since 1941.[2] Appellant Kahn is a widower who lives in Florida and applied for the exemption to the Dade County Tax Assessor's Office. It was denied because the statute offers no analogous benefit for widowers. Kahn then sought a declaratory judgment in the Circuit Court for Dade County, Florida, and that court held the statute violative of the Equal Protection Clause of the Fourteenth Amendment because the classficiation "widow" was based upon gender. The Florida Supreme Court reversed, finding the classification valid because it has a "fair and substantial relation to the object of the legislation,' "[3] that object being the reduction of "the disparity between the economic capabilities of a man and a woman." Kahn appealed here, 28, U.S.C. §1257(2), and we noted probable jurisdiction, 414 U.S. 973. We affirm.

1. Article IX, § 9, of the 1885 Florida Constitution provided that: "There shall be exempt from taxation property to the value of two hundred dollars to every widow that has a family dependent on her for support, and to every person that has lost a limb or been disabled in war or by misfortune."

2. In 1941 Fla. Stat. §192.06 (7) exempted "[p]roperty to the value of five hundred dollars to every widow. . . ." That provision has survived a variety of minor changes and renumbering in substantially the same form, including Fla. Stat. §196.191 (7) (1971) under which appellant was denied the exemption. Currently Fla. Stat. §196.202 provides: "Property to the value of five hundred dollars ($500) of every widow, blind person, or totally and permanently disabled person who is a bona fide resident of this state shall be exempt from taxation."

3. Quoting *Reed v. Reed*, 404 U.S. 71, 76.

242

There can be no dispute that the financial difficulties confronting the lone woman in Florida or in any other State exceed those facing the man. Whether from overt discrimination or from the socialization process of a male-dominated culture, the job market is inhospitable to the woman seeking any but the lowest paid jobs.[4] There are, of course, efforts under way to remedy this situation. On the federal level, Title VII of the Civil Rights Act of 1964 prohibits covered employers and labor unions from discrimination on the basis of sex, 78 Stat. 253, 42 U.S.C. §§2000e-2(a)(c), as does the Equal Pay Act of 1963, 77 Stat. 56, 29 U.S.C. §206(d). But firmly entrenched practices are resistant to such pressures, and, indeed, data compiled by the Women's Bureau of the United States Department of Labor show that in 1972 a woman working full time had a median income which was only 57.9% of the median for males—a figure actually six points lower than had been achieved in 1955.[5] Other data point in the same

4. In 1970 while 40% of males in the work force earned over $10,000 , and 70% over $7,000, 45% of women working full time earned less than $5,000, and 73.9% earned less than $7,000. U. S. Bureau of the Census: Current Population Reports, Series P-60, No. 80.

5. The Women's Bureau provides the following data:

| Year | Median earnings | | Women's median earnings as percent of men's |
	Women	Men	
1972	$5,903	$10,202	57.9
1971	5,593	9,399	59.5
1970	5,323	8,966	59.4
1969	4,977	8,227	60.5
1968	4,457	7,664	58.2
1967	4,150	7,182	57.8
1966	3,973	6,848	58.0
1965	3,823	6,375	60.0
1964	3,690	6,195	59.6
1963	3,561	5,978	59.6
1962	3,446	5,794	59.5
1961	3,351	5,644	59.4
1960	3,293	5,417	60.8
1959	3,193	5,209	61.3
1958	3,102	4,927	63.0
1957	3,008	4,713	63.8
1956	2,827	4,466	63.3
1955	2,719	4,252	63.9

Note:—Data for 1962-72 are not strictly comparable with those for prior years, which are for wage and salary income only and do not include earnings of self-employed persons.

Source: Table prepared by Women's Bureau, Employment Standards Administration, U.S. Department of Labor, from data published by Bureau of the Census, U. S. Department of Commerce.

direction.[6] The disparity is likely to be exacerbated for the widow. While the widower can usually continue in the occupation which preceded his spouse's death, in many cases the widow will find herself suddenly forced into a job market with which she is unfamiliar, and in which, because of her former economic dependency, she will have fewer skills to offer.[7]

There can be no doubt, therefore, that Florida's differing treatment of widows and widowers " 'rest[s] upon some ground of difference having a fair and substantial relation to the object of the legislation.' " *Reed v. Reed,* 404 U.S. 71, 76, quoting *Royster Guano Co. v. Virginia,* 253 U.S. 412, 415.

This is not a case like *Frontiero v. Richardson,* 411 U.S. 677, where the Government denied its female employees both substantive and procedural benefits granted males "*solely* . . . for administrative convenience." *Id.,* at 690 (emphasis in original).[8] We deal here with a state tax law reasonably designed to further the state policy of cushioning the financial impact of spousal loss upon the sex for which that loss imposes a disproportionately heavy burden. We have long held that "[w]here taxation is concerned and no specific federal right, apart from equal protection, is imperiled, the States have large leeway in making classifications and drawing lines which in their judgment produce reasonable systems of taxation." *Lehnhausen v. Lake Shore Auto Parts Co.,* 410 U.S. 356, 359. A state tax law is not arbitrary although it "discriminate[s] in favor of a certain class . . . if the discrimination is founded upon a reasonable distinction, or difference in state policy," not in conflict with the Federal Constitution. *Allied Stores v. Bowers,* 358 U.S. 522, 528. This principle has weathered nearly a century of Supreme Court adjudica-

6. For example, in 1972 the median income of women with four years of college was $8,736—exactly $100 more than the median income of men who had never even completed one year of high school. Of those employed as managers or administrators, the women's median income was only 53.2% of the men's, and in the professional and technical occupations the figure was 67.5%. Thus the disparity extends even to women occupying jobs usually thought of as well paid. Tables prepared by the Women's Bureau, Employment Standards Administration, U. S. Department of Labor.

7. It is still the case that in the majority of families where both spouses are present, the woman is not employed. A. Ferriss, Indicators of Trends in the Status of American Women 95 (1971).

8. And in *Frontiero,* the plurality opinion also noted that the statutes there were "not in any sense designed to rectify the effects of past discrimination against women. On the contrary, these statutes seize upon a group—women—who have historically sufffered discrimination in employment, and rely on the effects of this past discrimination as a justification for heaping on additional economic disadvantages." 411 U. S., at 689 n.22 (citations omitted).

tion,[9] and it applies here as well. The statute before us is well within those limits.[10]

Affirmed.

MR. JUSTICE BRENNAN, with whom MR. JUSTICE MARSHALL joins, dissenting.

The Court rejects widower Kahn's claim of denial of equal protection on the ground that the limitation in Fla. Stat. §196.191(7) (1971), which provides an annual $500 property tax exemption to widows, is a legislative classification that bears a fair and substantial relation to "the state policy of cushioning the financial impact of spousal loss upon the sex for which that loss imposes a disproportionately heavy burden." *Ante,* at 355. In my view, however, a legislative classifcation that distinguishes potential beneficaries solely by reference to their gender-based status as widows or widowers, like

9. See *Bell's Gap R. Co. v. Pennsylvania,* 134 U.S. 232, 237; *Madden v. Kentucky,* 309 U.S. 83, 87-88; *Lawrence v. State Tax Comm'n,* 286 U.S. 276; *Royster Guano Co. v. Virginia,* 253 U.S. 412.

10. The dissents argue that the Florida Legislature could have drafted the statute differently, so that its purpose would have been accomplished more precisely. But the issue, of course, is not whether the statute could have been drafted more wisely, but whether the lines chosen by the Florida Legislature are within constitutional limitations. The dissents would use the Equal Protection Clause as a vehicle for reinstating notions of substantive due process that have been repudiated. "We have returned to the original constitutional proposition that courts do not substitute their social and economic beliefs for the judgment of legislative bodies, [which] are elected to pass laws." *Ferguson v. Skrupa,* 372 U. S. 726, 730.

Gender has never been rejected as an impermissible classification in all instances. Congress has not so far drafted women into the Armed Services, 50 U.S.C. App. §454. The famous Bandeis Brief in *Muller v. Oregon,* 208 U.S. 412, on which the Court specifically relied, *id.,* at 419-420, emphasized that the special physical structure of women has a bearing on the "conditions under which she should be permitted to toil." *Id.,* at 420. These instances are pertinent to the problem in the tax field which is presented by this present case. Mr. Chief Justice Hughes in speaking for the Court said:

> The States, in the exercise of their taxing power, as with respect to the exertion of other powers, are subject to the requirements of the due process and the equal protection clauses of the Fourteenth Amendment, but that Amendment imposes no iron rule of equality, prohibiting the flexibility and variety that are appropriate to schemes of taxation. . . . In levying such taxes, the State is not required to resort to close distinctions or to maintain a precise, scientific uniformity with reference to composition, use or value. To hold otherwise would be to subject the essential taxing power of the State to an intolerable supervision, hostile to the basic principles of our Government and wholly beyond the protection which the general clause of the Fourteenth Amendment was intended to assure. *Ohio Oil Co. v. Conway,* 281 U. S. 146, 159.

classifications based upon race,[1] alienage,[2] and national origin,[3] must be subjected to close judicial scrutiny, because it focuses upon generally immutable characteristics over which individuals have little or no control, and also because gender-based classifications too often have been inexcusably utilized to stereotype and stigmatize politically powerless segments of society. *See Frontiero v. Richardson,* 411 U.S. 677 (1973). The Court is not, therefore, free to sustain the statute on the ground that it rationally promotes legitimate governmental interests; rather, such suspect classifications can be sustained only when the State bears the burden of demonstrating that the challenged legislation serves overriding or compelling interests that cannot be achieved either by a more carefully tailored legislative classification or by the use of feasible, less drastic means. While, in my view, the statute serves a compelling governmental interst by "cushioning the financial impact of spousal loss upon the sex for which that loss imposes a disproportionately heavy burden," I think that the statute is invalid because the State's interest can be served equally well by a more narrowly drafted statute.

Gender-based classifications cannot be sustained merely because they promote legitimate governmental interests, such as efficacious administration of government. *Frontiero v. Richardson, supra; Reed v. Reed,* 404, U.S. 71 (1971). For "when we enter the realm of 'strict judicial scrutiny,' there can be no doubt that 'administrative convenience' is not a shibboleth, the mere recitation of which dictates constitutionality. *See Shapiro v. Thompson,* 394 U.S. 618 (1969); *Carrington v. Rash,* 380 U.S. 89 (1965). On the contrary, any statutory scheme which draws a sharp line between the sexes, *solely* for the purpose of achieving administrative convenience, necessarily commands 'dissimilar treatment for men and women who are . . . similarly situated,' and therefore involves the 'very kind of arbitrary legislative choice forbidden by the [Constitution]. . . .' *Reed v. Reed,* 404 U.S., at 77, 76." *Frontiero v. Richardson, supra,* at 690. But Florida's justification of §196.191(7) is not that it serves administrative convenience or helps to preserve the public fisc. Rather, the asserted justification is that §196.191(7) is an affirma-

1. *See Loving v. Virginia,* 388 U.S. 1, 11 (1967); *McLaughlin v. Florida,* 379 U.S. 184, 191-192 (1964); *Bolling v. Sharpe,* 347 U.S. 497, 499 (1954).

2. *See Graham v. Richardson,* 403 U.S. 365, 372 (1971).

3. *See Oyama v. California,* 332 U.S. 633, 644-646 (1948); *Korematsu v. United States,* 323 U.S. 214, 216 (1944); *Hirabayashi v. United States,* 320 U.S. 81, 100 (1943).

tive step toward alleviating the effects of past economic discrimination against women.[4]

I agree that, in providing special benefits for a needy segment of society long the victim of purposeful discrimination and neglect, the statute serves the compelling state interest of achieving equality for such groups.[5] No one familiar with this country's history of pervasive sex discrimination against against women[6] can doubt the need for remedial measures to correct the resulting economic imbalances. Indeed, the extent of the economic disparity between men and women is dramatized by the data cited by the Court, *ante*, at 243-244. By providing a property tax exemption for widows, §196.191(7) assists in reducing that economic disparity for a class of women particularly disadvantaged by the legacy of economic discrimination.[7] In that circumstance, the purpose and effect of the suspect classification are ameliorative; the statute neither stigmatizes nor denigrates widowers not also benefited by the legislation. Moreover, inclusion of needy widowers within the class of beneficiaries would not further the State's overriding interest in remedying the economic effects of past sex discrimination for needy victims of that discrimination. While doubtless some widowers are in financial need, no one suggests that such need results from sex discrimination as in the case of widows.

4. Brief for Appellees 230-231. The State's argument is supported by the Florida Supreme Court which held that the object of §196.191 (7) was to help " 'reduce the disparity between the economic . . . capabilities of a man and a woman. . . .' " 273 So. 2d 72, 73 (1973).

5. Significantly, the Florida statute does not compel the beneficiaries to accept the State's aid. The taxpayer must file for the tax exemption. This case, therefore, does not require resolution of the more difficult questions raised by remedial legislation which makes special treatment mandatory, *See* Note, Developments in the Law— Equal Protection, 82 Harv. L. Rev. 1065, 1113-1117 (1969).

6. *See Frontiero v. Richardson*, 411 U. S. 677 (1973); *Sail'er Inn, Inc., v. Kirby*, 5 Cal. 3d 1, 485 P. 2d 529 (1971). *See generally* The President's Task Force on Women's Rights and Responsibilities, A Matter of Simple Justice (1970); L. Kanowitz, Women and the Law: The Unfinished Revolution (1969).

7. As noted by the Court, *ante*, 243-244:

[D]ata compiled by the Women's Bureau of the United States Department of Labor show that in 1972 a women working full time had a median income which was only 57.9% of the median for males—a figure actually six points lower than had been achieved in 1955. . . . The disparity is likely to be exacerbated for the widow. While the widower can usually continue in the occupation which preceded his spouse's death, in many cases the widow will find herself suddenly forced into a job market with which she is unfamiliar, and in which, because of her former economic dependency, she will have fewer skills to offer. (Footnotes omitted.)

Appendix A

The statute nevertheless fails to satisfy the requirements of equal protection, since the State has not borne its burden of proving that its compelling interest could not be achieved by a more precisely tailored statute or by use of feasible, less drastic means. Section 196.191(7) is plainly overinclusive, for the $500 property tax exemption may be obtained by a financially independent heiress as well as by an unemployed widow with dependent children. The State has offered nothing to explain why inclusion of widows of substantial economic means was necessary to advance the State's interst in ameliorating the effects of past economic discrimination against women.

Moreover, alternative means of classification, narrowing the class of widow beneficiaries, appear readily available. The exemption is granted only to widows who complete and file with the tax assessor a form application establishing their status as widows. By merely redrafting that form to exclude widows who earn annual incomes, or possess assets, in excess of specified amounts, the State could readily narrow the class of benficiaries to those widows for whom the effects of past economic disciimination against women have been a practical reality.

MR. JUSTICE WHITE, dissenting.

The Florida tax exemption at issue here is available to all widows but not to widowers. The presumption is that all widows are financially more needy and less trained or less ready for the job market than men. It may be that most widows have been occupied as housewife, mother, and homemaker and are not immediately prepared for employment. But there are many rich widows who need no largess from the State; many others are highly trained and have held lucrative positions long before the death of their husbands. At the same time, there are many widowers who are needy and who are in more desperate financial straits and have less access to the job market than many widows. Yet none of them qualifies for the exemption.

I find the discrimination invidious and violative of the Equal Protection Clause. There is merit in giving poor widows a tax break, but gender-based classifications are suspect and require more justification than the State has offered.

I perceive no purpose served by the exemption other than to alleviate current economic necesity, but the State extends the exemption to widows who do not need the help and denies it to widowers who do. It may be administratively inconvenient to make individual determinations of entitlement and to extend the exemption to needy men as well as needy women, but administrative efficiency is not an adequate justification for discriminations based purely on sex. *Frontiero v. Richardson*, 411 U.S. 677 (1973); *Reed v. Reed*, 404 U.S. 71 (1971).

It may be suggested that the State is entitled to prefer widows over widowers because their assumed need is rooted in past and present economic discrimination against women. But this is not a credible explanation of Florida's tax exemption; for if the State's purpose was to compensate for past discrimination against females, surely it would not have limited the exemption to women who are widows. Moreover, even if past discrimination is considered to be the criterion for current tax exemption, the State nevertheless ignores all those widowers who have felt the effects of economic discrimination, whether as a member of a racial group or as one of the many who cannot escape the cycle of poverty. It seems to me that the State in this case is merely conferring an economic benefit in the form of a tax exemption and has not adequately explained why women should be treated differently from men.

I dissent.

Comment: The majority accept the essential reasoning of the Florida brief. In particular, they incorporate in their opinion the tables furnished in that brief that show that women's incomes remain significantly less than men's and that demonstrate that the Florida statute has a reasonable basis within the rationale of *Reed*. They also accept that brief's analysis distinguishing *Frontiero*.

Justices Brennan and Marshall, dissenting, are also impressed by the data cited by appellees and persuaded that the Florida statute is "ameliorative." (Page 247 *supra*). In their opinion, however, Florida must achieve this end by a more precisely tailored statute. Justice White concludes that "gender-based classifications are suspect and require more justification than the State has offered." (Page 248 *supra*.)

As the reasoning and the citations in these opinions show, the briefs have performed their essential task. They have illuminated the issues and helped to guide and persuade the Justices.

APPENDIX B

FACTUAL PORTIONS OF APPELLATE BRIEFS AND COURT OPINION IN THE CASE OF DIAZ v. KELSEY-HAYES COMPANY

Comment: In this appendix appear factual statements and arguments based on fact from the briefs and the court opinion in *Diaz v. Kelsey-Hayes Company, Inc.*, 1 Civil No. 49258 in the Court of Appeal of the State of California, First Appellate District, Division Three.

Pedro Diaz, an agricultural worker, was killed when a lettuce-hauling truck backed up and ran over him. His heirs brought a wrongful death action against the manufacturers of the truck, claiming that it should have been equipped with an audible back-up alarm. Their legal theories were (1) negligent design and manufacture, (2) strict liability for product defect resulting in injury, and (3) breach of the implied warranties of merchantability and fitness for use. The jury's verdict was in favor of the defendant manufacturer, Kelsey-Hays Company, but on plaintiff's motion the judge granted a new trial, finding the jury's verdict to be "clearly against the weight of the evidence." Kelsey-Hays appealed.

In their opening brief on appeal the Kelsey-Hays attorneys conceded that the trial judge had a broad area of discretion in ruling on a motion for a new trial, but nevertheless insisted that the evidence in its favor was more than adequate to justify the jury verdict, and hence the judge's order was an abuse of discretion. They presented the evidence at trial in separate sections of their brief—first a general statement of largely undisputed fact, and later summaries of pertinent evidence inserted at appropriate points in their argument. The first, or general, statement is quoted below.

Statement of Facts

The accident which forms the basis of this wrongful death action occurred on June 11, 1974, in Salinas, California. The decedent, Pedro Diaz, was killed when run over by a lettuce hauling truck during lettuce harvesting operations. The truck was manufactured and sold in 1968 by the Fabco Division of defendant and appellant, Kelsey-Hayes Company. A full understanding of the issues presented in this appeal requires a description of the lettuce harvesting process as well as a description of the vehicle's design history.

The truck involved in the subject accident was a Wide Track Model 206 (WT206). The basic chassis, including the frame, suspensions, axles, power train, engine and transmissions, was designed by appellant (RT 221). Some of the chassis' components were selected and installed by appellant but manufactured by others (RT 221). The body and cab were designed by other manufacturers and assembled by appellant (RT 221).

Prior to 1954, trucks used to harvest lettuce were converted or modified two axle chassis designed and built by Ford Motor Company, General Motors, and other truck manufacturers. In 1954, appellant designed and manufactured a wide track chassis, with a designation WT201, to specifications provided by a customer (RT 234, 264). The specifications dictated the cab configuration, wheel base, cargo capacity, tire size, engine size and vehicle length (RT 264). Both the WT201 and WT206 chassis were tailored to meet the specific needs and requirements of lettuce harvesting. The WT201 designed in 1954 and the WT206 sold in 1968 were identical except for minor modifications to the undercarriage (RT 234).

The truck was designed with an 80 inch tread width to correspond with the distance between several furrows in the lettuce field. This permitted the truck to be driven through the fields without causing excessive damage to the growing crops. To provide sufficient traction for the muddy field conditions that were often encountered during harvesting, the WT206 chassis was equipped with three driving axles (RT 261, 742).

During the harvesting operation, cartons of packed lettuce are loaded by laborers onto the truck as the truck proceeds slowly through the field. This requires that the vehicle have the capacity to travel through muddy conditions at a slow, steady rate of speed. After the cartons of lettuce are loaded, they must be transported to the grower's cooler as quickly as possible to assure high quality produce for shipment. Thus, the truck must also have the capacity to travel at highway speeds since the grower's cooler facilities are often located some distance from the fields where the lettuce is grown. The WT206 is able to perform both functions by means of three separate transmissions. Depending upon the gear selection made with respect to each of the transmissions, the truck can travel at low speeds through adverse field conditions and at highway speeds (RT 741-746).

The main transmission of the WT206 has five forward speeds and a reverse gear. There is a three speed auxiliary transmission behind the main transmission which contains direct, underdrive, and overdrive gears. The third transmission, or transfer case, transfers power to the front axle and contains direct and underdrive gears (RT 267). Utilizing the underdrive selections in the auxiliary transmission and the transfer case increases the gear reduction and results in lower speeds and added power to the wheels. Selecting direct in the auxiliary transmission and direct in he transfer case allows the truck to attain higher speeds (RT 743-746).

The WT206 involved in the subject accident was sold to Bruce Church, Inc., in 1968. Agricultural equipment manufactured and sold in 1968 did not come equipped with back-up warning devices. No governmental regulations required the installation of back-up devices on agricultural vehicles.

The WT206 measures 22¼ feet from the front axle to the rear of the bed. The bed is 95½ inches wide (RT 527, 554). To aid rear view visibility, the truck is equipped with large mirrors mounted on both sides of the cab. When fully loaded, the loaded cartons create a blind spot which cannot be eliminated (RT 598-601).

The decedent was working with a crew that was harvesting lettuce by the "naked pack" method. This method differs from the other harvesting method normally used where lettuce is packaged after being wrapped in cellophane. The naked pack method utilizes a crew of approximately 32 laborers. The crew is divided into "trios" consisting of two lettuce cutters and one packer. Each trio cuts and then packs the lettuce into cardboard boxes. The cartons into which the lettuce is packed are folded and stapled by machines located on a "stitcher truck" that follows the crew through the field. The empty cartons are stacked, one inside the other. They are then placed in the rows by the cutters before the lettuce is cut (RT 152-156). The packed lettuce is sprinkled with water and the boxes are closed, stapled, and loaded onto the hauler truck which follows the crew as it proceeds through the field. When the truck is fully loaded, the load is tied down and the truck immediately leaves the field. Depending upon the location of the truck in the field and whether there is uncut lettuce in front of the truck, it may leave the field in either a forward or reverse direction.

The decedent was employed by Bruce Church, Inc., as a lettuce cutter. His crew had been working northward through a field and, just prior to the accident, they had reached a point near the end of the field. The hauler truck was to the southwest of the crew and it was facing north. The stitcher truck was facing south, in a position approximately 20 yards to the west of the hauler truck (RT 628, 631). Because the lettuce growing directly north of the hauler truck was too small to harvest, the crew began to work the field in a southerly direction, beginning at a point northeast of the hauler truck.

At the time of the accident, the decedent was carrying a stack of approximately 16 empty cartons that extended several feet above his head. Balancing the stack of boxes on his left hip and with his vision of the truck totally obstructed, he proceeded east from the stitcher truck, apparently intending to place the empty cartons to the south of where the crew was working. In doing so, he passed five to seven feet behind the hauler truck which had been fully loaded, tied down, and which was ready to leave the field (RT 104, 105, 115, 578-583, 834). At that time, all members of the crew (except for the decedent's son, who was next to the stitcher), were working in the area north and north east of the hauler truck. As there were crew members and uncut lettuce to the north of the hauler, the driver of the truck, Mr. Jefferson Gattes, proceeded to back out of the field at a speed of 4 to 5 mph (RT 530). As he did so, the right rear wheels of the truck passed over decedent.

Between the time that the truck started to back up and the time that it reached the decedent, approximately 1.6 seconds elapsed (RT 583). This extremely short interval of time was established by engineering analysis that was based upon the following: (1) the truck backing at a speed of 4.5 mph (RT 530); (2) Mr. Diaz walking at a speed of 3 feet per second (RT 533); (3) the truck backing 11 feet before striking Mr. Diaz (RT 579-582); and (4) Mr. Diaz walking across the path of the truck at an angle of approximately 40° (RT 597). All of the assumptions were supported by the evidence and the elapsed time of the 1.6 seconds was computed by plaintiffs' engineering expert, Dr. Blythe (RT 579-582).

No one testified that, had a back-up device been installed, Mr. Diaz would have been able to avoid the accident in the 1.6 seconds available (RT 564, 608-613, 817).

Four experts testified concerning time intervals needed for a person to perceive a stimulus, to decide what to do in response to the stimulus, and to set the body in motion. All of the experts, including plaintiffs', agreed that 1.6 seconds was an inadequate amount of time for Mr. Diaz to perceive the danger, decide what to do about the danger, react to the danger, and to move out of the path of the backing truck (570-576, 832, 904-906).

Comment: The jury had answered "No" to the question, posed in the special verdict, whether Kelsey-Hayes was negligent in the design or manufacture of the truck. In their opening brief the Kelsey-Hayes attorneys argued that this was the only reasonable answer to the question because audible back-up signals were not normally installed on farm trucks at the time the truck in question was built. They summarized the evidence bearing on this point as follows.

2. *The Evidence Showed That the Standard of Care in the
   Agricultural Equipment Industry in 1968 Did Not Call
   for the Installation of Audible Back-Up Devices.*

The evidence presented by plaintiffs in an effort to establish a standard of care came through the testimony of witnesses called as experts by plaintiffs.

Mr. Lawrence Ingram was superintendent of equipment maintenance for Bud Antle, Inc., a large agricultural grower headquartered in Salinas (RT 191). In 1968, Bud Antle, Inc., converted standard truck cabs and chassis to equipment suitable for use in the lettuce fields (RT 192-193). They purchased trucks manufactured by other companies (RT 206). According to Ingram, Bud Antle, Inc., installed audible back-up devices on the vehicle conversions they made in 1968 (RT 199-200).

Mr. Ingram and his employer were not *designing* lettuce hauling vehicles (RT 209). Bud Antle, inc., purchased conversion "kits" and installed them on standard cabs and chassis (RT 192-193). Bud Antle, Inc., was an owner-grower of lettuce. Consequently, its decision to install back-up devices on some of its equipment cannot establish a standard of care for the manufacturing industry. Mr. Ingram's testimony could not establish the existence of a standard of care in the agricultural equipment industry. Mr. Ingram was not a truck designer. He repaired and serviced equipment built by others (RT 208).

Mr. Ingram testified that while many trucks were purchased by Bud Antle, Inc., prior to 1968, not a single truck came equipped with an audible back-up device:

> *Q.* You never bought a truck prior to 1968 that was sold to you with a back-up device, did you?
> *A.* No.
> (RT 206)

His testimony, though lacking in foundation and competence, established the very point made by the appellant. The standard of care prevailing in the agricultural truck design and manufacturing industry in 1968 *did not* call for the installation of audible back-up warning devices.

Plaintiff also called Mr. Sewell Knapp, a safety engineer. Mr. Knapp testified that he was thoroughly familiar with the accepted practice in the agricultural equipment manufacturing industry and that it was common practice in that industry to have agricultural equipment equipped with such devices in 1968. However, on cross-examination, Mr. Knapp was unable to name a *single* manufacturer of agricultural hauling equipment that installed back-up devices in 1968:

> *Q.* . . . back in 1968, can you give me the name of a single manufacturer of a hauling piece of equipment that sold that piece of equipment with a back-up device on it for use in agriculture?
> *A.* I would say Peterbilt, probably. White . . . . . .
> *Q.* Are you familiar with a Peterbilt truck built in 1968 to be used in the field in agriculture that was sold with a backup device?
> *A.* No, I am not. I was just saying that devices were available. . . .
> *Q.* You are not aware of any White built truck that was sold in 1968 for use in agriculture that was sold with a back-up device on it, are you?
> *A.* Not particularly, no.
> (RT 300-301)

A standard of common practice in an industry cannot be established in the absence of evidence that *someone* in the industry conformed with the purported standard. Manufacturers of argicultural equipment in 1968 did not install back-up warning devices and there was no evidence of a standard of care to support an argument that they should have done so.

The testimony of other witnesses also established that there was no prevailing practice in the industry to install audible back-up devices. Saturnino Diaz, the decedent's son, testified that he had never heard a back-up device on a lettuce hauler or on any other piece of agricultural equipment prior to the subject accident.

> *Q.* Did you work in areas other than Salinas?
> *A.* *Yes.* . . .
> *Q.* . . . Any other areas, sir?
> *A.* Its a lot of years, Those are the ones I can remember. And lately I worked in other places.
> *Q.* Before the date of your father's accident, had you ever heard a back-up buzzer on any hauler in any field?
> *A.* No.
> *Q.* Prior to the date of your father's injury, had you ever heard a back-up buzzer on any farm equipment in the field?
> *A.* No.
> (RT 129)

Jefferson Gattes, the driver of the truck in question, had never seen a lettuce truck with such a device prior to the subject accident.

> *Q.* Now, prior to the date of this accident, there were no hauling trucks operating in the field to your knowledge with back-up devices, were there?
> *A.* Not to my knowledge, no, sir.
> *Q.* You had never seen a lettuce truck with a back-up warning device installed prior to the date of this accident, had you?
> *A.* No sir.
> (RT 382)

Elmer Fahey, service supervisor for Bruce Church, Inc., for 18 years, testified that back-up warning devices were not installed on haulers owned by Bruce Church, Inc., or by other growers in the lettuce harvesting industry until after 1974 (RT 388, 389, 400, 406, 407).

Joe Warden, who had 20 years of experience as a truck driver and as an equipment supervisor in the lettuce harvesting industry, knew of no hauler trucks operating in the Salinas Valley that were equipped with back-up devices. (RT 651, 664):

Q. Prior to the date of this accident, in June 1974, were you aware of any hauling trucks in the Salinas Valley that had back-up devices on them?

A. No, I wasn't.

(RT 664)

The only *reasonable* inference that the jury could have drawn from the evidence presented was that there was no standard of care in 1968 requiring the installation of back-up devices on agricultural equipment. The jury reached this conclusion and answered Issue No. 5 in the negative.

Comment: On the strict liability issue, the jury had been instructed that a manufacturer was liable for reasonably foreseeable injuries resulting from its defective product and that "a product is defective in design if the product failed to perform as safely as an ordinary consumer of the product would expect when used in a manner reasonably foreseeable by the defendant." The jury had then answered "No" to the question posed in the special verdict as to whether there was a defect in the design or manufacture of the truck. In their brief the Kelsey-Hayes attorneys argued that the answer was clearly correct: Because audible back-up signals were not normally supplied, consumers did not "expect" them, and the product was not "defective." The evidence pertinent to this argument was summarized in the following passage.

A. In 1968 the Truck in Question Met the Expectations of an Ordinary Consumer.

The evidence showed convincingly that the truck manufactured by appellant met the expectations of the ordinary consumer.

Burton Anderson, safety director for Bruce Church, Inc., testified that no equipment purchased by Bruce Church, Inc., was factory equipped with a back-up device. Mr. Anderson saw no need for the installation of such devices prior to the accident in question (RT 282-285).

Jefferson Gattes had never seen such a device on a lettuce truck prior to the accident (RT 382). Joe Warden, a man with 20 years experience in lettuce harvesting, had never seen or heard of a lettuce hauling truck equipped with an audible back-up device prior to the accident in 1974 (RT 664).

Saturnino Diaz, who worked with his father harvesting lettuce in Greenfield, Salinas, Wasco and other places, could not remember ever seeing a hauler truck equipped with an audible back-up device. He was unaware of such a device on *any* agricultural vehicles prior to his father's accident in 1974 (RT 129).

None of the expert witnesses called by plaintiffs could identify a *single manufacturer* of agricultural hauling equipment that installed back-up devices on its vehicles in 1968.

Plaintiffs' counsel submitted and the court gave a proper instruction on the product liability cause of action. There was no dispute in the evidence concerning what an ordinary consumer would have expected with reference to a back-up warning system. Neither grower nor worker "expected" the product to perform more safely than it did, in fact, perform. Mr. Diaz had obviously spent thousands of hours in the lettuce fields during harvesting operations and he could not have expected a warning horn or bell to sound when the truck in question began to back out of the field.

A car manufactured in 1960 without seatbelts could not be found defective in 1979 by applying the instruction given in the instant case. The ordinary consumer's expectation of safety in 1960 did not include seatbelts in passenger cars even though seatbelts were available and used in automobile racing. Similarly, the consumer's expectations of safety in 1968 did not include back-up warning devices on trucks manufactured for use in hauling lettuce from the fields. Hindsight and experience gained from the passage of time cannot be substituted for the "expectations of an ordinary consumer" in determining whether a product is defective.

It is manifestly clear from the evidence summarized above, and from the entire record, that *no one* connected with the lettuce industry in 1968 — corporate growers, safety directors, drivers, field hands, or other employees — expected a lettuce truck to be delivered with a back-up device installed. The evidence was insufficient to support a verdict in favor of plaintiffs and it was clearly an abuse of discretion for the court to order a new trial.

Comment: Later in their brief, after dealing with the breach of warranty theory by means of a legal argument, the lawyers for Kelsey-Hayes argued that the trial judge had failed to consider the issue of proximate cause, and that in fact there was no evidence to show that any negligence or product defect had caused Diaz's death. Their discussion of the evidence pertinent to this issue follows.

The trial court's duty, under section 657, to discuss all of the issues was stated in *Previte v. Lincolnwood, Inc.* (1975) 48 C.A.3d 976, where the trial court's order granting a new trial was reversed:

> An order granting a new trial in which the trial court sets out adequate reasons for finding the jury wrong on only one issue of several submitted to the jury, is erroneous. To grant a new trial in such a situation, the trial court must adequately specify reasons why the evidence is insufficient on all issues presumably found by the jury to support a verdict. *Previte, supra,* at p. 987.

The mandate of *Devine* and *Previte* is clear. Where the jury's verdict could have been based on one or more of several issues, the trial court must specify, in its order, the respects in which the evidence was legally inadequate to support the verdict on each of the issues. It was therefore encumbent upon the trial court to discuss the evidence as it related to the issue of causation.

A. The Absence of an Audible Back-Up Device Was Not the Proximate Cause of the Accident in Question.

The plaintiff must establish that there is a significant probability that the injury complained of would not have occurred in the absence of the claimed defect. A defendant does not have the burden to prove the negative. (*Endicott v. Nissan Motor Crop.* (1977) 73 C.A.3d 917, 926-928).

Appellant contended at trial that the lack of a back-up device on the vehicle would not have prevented the accident. The only reference to proximate cause in the trial court's specification of reasons appears in connection with the court's discussion of the testimony of one of plaintiffs' expert witnesses:

> Dr. Blythe . . . concluded that had the truck been equipped with an audible back-up safety device, decedent, no matter what his position within the "blind spot" area, would probably have had sufficient warning to have moved to safety. (CT 273)

Appendix B

The court could not have concluded as it did if Dr. Blythe's testimony on cross-examination had been recalled. On cross-examination, Dr. Blythe testified that he was unable to state whether the subject accident would have been avoided by installation of back-up device (RT 608-613).

Saturnino Diaz, the decedent's son, testified that the truck came to rest with its right front tire resting on the decedent. At Saturnino's request, Mr. Gattes moved the truck forward, thereby freeing the decedent (RT 119). The decedent was lying one foot behind the right front tire when Saturnino went to the right side of the truck to assist him.

Based in part upon the testimony of Saturnino, Dr. Blythe concluded that the truck would have reached Mr. Diaz 1.6 seconds if it traveled 10¾ feet before striking him. If the truck traveled 11¾ feet, it would have reached the decedent in 1.8 seconds (RT 579, 588). The two conclusions take into consideration the possibility that Mr. Diaz may have been moved laterally (the south) by the impact with the truck.

Because of the time required for Mr. Diaz to perceive the danger, to decide what to do to avoid the danger, and to begin to react, Dr. Blythe testified that even if Mr. Diaz had been alerted by an audible back-up device at the moment the truck began its rearward movement, he would have had little chance, if any, to escape the oncoming truck (RT 564). He was, according to Dr. Blythe, "trapped", with or without the presence of a back-up warning device (RT 565-566).

Experts called by appellant, whose testimony was based upon the same assumptions and data relied upon by Dr. Blythe, concluded that a back-up device would not have prevented the accident in question (RT 912, 913).

Dr. Rollin Patton, an experimental psychologist, was called by appellant to testify. His qualifications may be reviewed at RT 808-813. Dr. Patton concluded that a back-up device would not have prevented the accident:

Q. Based upon all of the information that I previously enumerated, what is your opinion with respect to whether a back-up warning device would have prevented this accident?

A. Based on the information available to me, I believe that it would not have prevented the accident.

(RT 817, 838, 869)

His opinion was based upon the same assumptions made by Dr. Blythe: (1) that the truck was backing at a speed of 4½ mph (RT 578, 818); (2) that Mr. Diaz was walking at a speed of three to four feet per second (RT 589, 820); (3) that the paths of Mr. Diaz and the moving truck intersected at an angle of approximately 40° (RT 597, 820); (4) that the truck backed up 10¾ feet before reaching Mr. Diaz (RT 583, 822); and (5) that the truck reached Mr. Diaz in 1.6 seconds (RT 583, 824). Dr. Patton, like Dr. Blythe, concluded that 1.6 seconds was an inadequate amount of time to allow Mr. Diaz to perceive the danger of the approaching truck, to decide what to do about that danger, and to move through the muddy field to a position of safety (RT 826-838).

Based upon the foregoing, appellant submits that the jury would have concluded that the absence of a back-up device was not the proximate cause of the subject accident. This conclusion is amply supported by the record generally, and specifically by the testimony of plaintiff's expert, Dr. Blythe. The trial court's failure to discuss causation in its specification of reasons was error and an abuse of discretion. The specification of reasons therefore fails to comply with section 657 and the court's order granting the new trial must be reversed.

Comment: Thus the evidence in the case was appropriately divided into topics and presented in sections related to principal points in the argument. However, there were some significant omissions, as the responding brief writers were quick to point out.

In their responding brief the lawyers for the Diaz heirs, plaintiffs in the trial court, also set forth the facts extensively, first in a general statement and later in sections relevant to a particular argument. They chose, however, to make their first statement substantially complete, even though this required some repetition in later sections.

Statement of Facts

The subject accident occurred on the Bruce Church ranch in Salinas, California, at approximately 1:45 p.m. on June 11, 1974. (R.T. 37:26-38:4; 49:4-7) Decedent Pedro Diaz was working for Bruce

Church, Inc. at the time of the accident as a lettuce cutter. (R.T. 74:3; 75:16-76:10) As part of his job, he would have to stack empty boxes and carry them into the field. (R.T. 77:12-16; 81:21-28; Plaintiffs' Exhibit No. 7) The stack that he would have to carry was 15-16 boxes and was taller than himself. (R.T. 82:16-20) The chassis of this truck was designed and manufactured by the Fabco division of defendant Kelsey-Hayes Company specifically for lettuce harvest (R.T. 231:1-232:2) and was sold by them for use by Mr. Diaz's employer, Bruce Church, Inc. (R.T. 272:15; 280:6-282:5) Bruce Church had nothing to do with what safety features went on the truck. (R.T. 397:19-21) Burton Anderson, general services manager of Bruce Church, Inc., testified that when he ordered the trucks from the Fabco Salinas representative, he relied upon the manufacturer to install the safety equipment which they were supposed to have. (R.T. 281:9-15)

The vehicle designed, manufactured and supplied by the defendant to the decedent's employer had a large blind spot at the rear of the vehicle. Jefferson Gattes, the truck driver employed by Bruce Church who was driving the vehicle at the time of the fatal accident, testified that it was not possible from the driver's seat to see to the rear of the truck when it was fully loaded. (R.T. 361:13-16) You could not even adjust the mirrors in such a way as to be able to see behind the load on the truck. (R.T. 361:17-20) After the cartons are placed on the vehicle, the only thing you can see is the cartons. (R.T. 362:4-7) Mr. Gattes checked in both of his mirrors before he started to back up; but because of the blind spot, he did not see anyone or anything behind him other than the field. (R.T. 377:22-27; 383:4-6)

Lawrence Ingram, Sr., who was employed by Bud Antle Corporation, one of the largest lettuce growers in the country, similarly confirmed that when the Fabco truck was fully loaded and equipped with straight mirrors without a wide-angle lense, there was a very substantial blind spot to the driver of the truck when he was looking back in his mirrors. (R.T. 203:23-28) William Blythe, Professor and Chairman of the Department of Civil Engineering and applied Mechanics at San Jose State University and a Registered Safety Engineer of the State of California, also testified that the rear visibility when the truck is loaded is severely limited by the load. (R.T. 549:16-21) Plaintiff's Exhibits 23-R and 23-L show the view from the right-hand and left-hand mirrors as seen from the driver's seat. Most of the mirror simply shows the side of the truck. (R.T. 549:28-551:28) He determined the limit of visibility by placing traffic cones behind the truck to define the area which could be seen on both sides of the truck; and he measured them to determine the dimensions of the blind spot behind the vehicle. (R.T. 553:4-12) The area that was blind when the truck was loaded started off equal to the width of the load of the truck and went out just under 179 feet. (R.T. 553:18-20) The area measured 95½ inches wide at its widest point, which is the width of the bed of the truck, and 178-179 feet long. (R.T. 554:2-4) There is no mirror that can be designed to show the back of the truck. There will always be a blind spot. (R.T. 599:6-10)

Laine Ainsworth, who was the original designor of the chassis on this truck for the defendant, conceded that a loaded truck would have restricted visibility to the rear and that these trucks would be backing up while workers were working in the field around the truck; but he made no effort to find out how far back the blind spot extended. (R.T. 235:10-239:16) He also conceded that a convex mirror does not help visibility with a loaded truck. (R.T. 266:13-20) Mr. Ainsworth acknowledged that the truck would have been poorly designed if any safety features were left off that were important to the job the truck was to perform. (R.T. 242:2-8)

Terrance Smith, who was product engineer for the defendant in 1968 and was involved in both the design of new products and the maintenance and updating of all designs, testified that they reviewed safety design for their vehicles during the three years prior to 1968; but they never specifically reviewed the safety of the backing operation. (R.T. 751:17-752:25) They did not analyze the safety of the WT-206 truck when it was operating in reverse in the field. (R.T. 753:10-15) No engineer at Kelsey-Hayes analyzed the nature of the blind spot at the rear of the truck when it was fully loaded during this period of time. (R.T. 753:16-754:2) None of the engineers at Kelsey-Hayes even knew how large the blind spot behind the vehicle was when it was fully loaded with lettuce. (R.T. 754:8-10) He would now estimate that the blind spot approached 50 feet. (R.T. 754:15)

Accordingly, there was substantial evidence (indeed, we believe that it was uncontradicted) that the dirver of the truck could not see Mr. Diaz bcause of the blind spot; and Mr. Diaz could not see the truck because of the boxes which he was carrying. The design of the vehicle and the nature of the work made it impossible for either the truck driver or Mr. Diaz to see each other or to realize the impending danger and consequent fatality which would occur when the truck driver backed up as Mr. Diaz was crossing in back of the vehicle. The evidence showed that there was a relatively inexpensive safety device, which could have been installed on the vehicle to furnish a warning before the vehicle started to back up; but the defendant did not install such devices on its vehicles, notwithstanding the existence of the blind spot which made the installation of a back-up warning device an absolute necessity if safety was given *any* consideration.

Mr. Smith, product engineer for defendant, testified that there [were] no back-up warnings of any kind on the truck when it was sold in 1968. (R.T. 755:1-8) He had heard of back-up warning devices in 1968 and knew that they were available as components for trucks of one kind or another. (R.T. 750:23-751:3) He knew that such devices were available which would go on the back of the truck and could be turned on by an electrical impulse that could be effectuated by a switch connected to the gear-shift lever, so that when the truck was moved into reverse, the switch would go on. (R.T. 760:20-28) If you had such a device, you will get sound before the truck begins to move. (R.T. 761:1-12) However, there were no back-up warning devices on any of the trucks sold by the defendant in 1968. (R.T. 755:1-14) Nobody at Kelsey-Hayes made any evaluation with regard to back-up warning devices before August 1968. (R.T. 762:14-16) Indeed, Mr. Ainsworth, who designed this vehicle, testified that he didn't even investigate the question of whether or not a back-up warning device should be installed. (R.T. 254:13-16) They got some of the ideas for this vehicle from cement trucks; but he didn't have the faintest idea whether cement trucks had back-up warning devices on them. (R.T. 257:4-14)

Dr. Blythe testified that when this truck was manufactured and sold in 1968, it was deficient because it did not have a back-up warning signal. (R.T. 556:1-6) Such warning signals were available at the time (R.T. 556:7-11); and it was the job of the safety engineer to be aware of the requirements for the performance of a warning device and recognize when such device was warranted by the use of the equipment. (R.T. 556:17-21) Indeed, as early as July 1967 there were specifications prepared by the American Society of Automotive Engineers for the evaluation and testing of electronic devices as opposed to the bell type; and given the traffic pattern irregularity and the blind spot, an electrical warning device activated by shifting to reverse should have been considered and installed by the defendant. (R.T. 557:1-15) The truck was a rather quiet truck at idle; and while the engine noise would increase when the truck began to move, this sound would not tell a person whether the truck was going to move forward or backward, and accordingly, any increase in engine speed as a warning was questionable. (R.T. 560:17-28) Slade Hulbert, a psychologist who testified for the defendant, agreed that the sound of a motor can be ambiguous but the sound of a back-up warning device is not. (R.T. 960:22-961:1)

Dr. Blythe did studies of back-up warning signals; and he determined that the time from the start of the alarm to the start of movement of the truck would range from 1-3 seconds with an average of two seconds. (R.T. 561:1-22) This additional premovement warning should change the almost fatal situation into something that could be escaped quite easily. (R.T. 565:19-23) The truck sold and manufactured by the defendant in 1968 was deficient in not having an audible back-up warning device. (R.T. 565:24-566:1) In his opinion, such a warning device would most probably have enabled Mr. Diaz to escape the difficulty he was in. (R.T. 566:2-6) If Diaz had had a premovement warning, he would have started his reaction time before the truck even began to move (R.T. 574:16-24); and it is highly probable that the accident would have been avoided. (R.T. 608:4-8) With the presence of such a warning device in this case, it would probably have prevented this kind of an accident. (R.T. 613:7-11)

Dr. Blythe also testified that in the normal course of events Mr. Diaz had no way of receiving a warning that the truck was a danger to him without a back-up warning device or unless the driver yelled at him. (R.T. 617:3-20) No matter how far the truck traveled, whether it was 10 feet or 16 feet, until it hit him, there was no way that Mr. Diaz could have gotten any warning that the truck was coming to him before it started to move that distance. (R.T. 617:22-28) If there had been an electrical warning device, he could have had a warning that the truck was coming before it started to move. (R.T. 618:1-4) He could have reacted to the situation (R.T. 618:5-10) and most probably would have escaped the difficulty he was in instead of being killed. (R.T. 566:5-6)

Sewell Knapp, an expert safety consultant who had been in charge of all training and education for the State of California safety engineers and had written safety rules, brochures and booklets and was one of the founders of the California Agricultural Safety Committee, similarly testified that at the time this vehicle was manufactured and sold by the defendant, it was not good safety practice to manufacture and sell a truck to be used in lettuce harvest that did not have a back-up device. (R.T. 292:20-293:4) At that time, it was common practice to use such sound warning safety devices on equipment that was being used to haul produce out of a field where men were working. (R.T. 293:5-21) These devices were available in 1968 and were not complicated. (R.T. 293:24-27) They were successful safety devices which were available for use in all industry and had helped to avoid accidents. (R.T. 294:26-295:25) When the back-up safety device is wired to the transmission, the alarm sounds before the truck moves and this gives an added safety advantage. (R.T. 298:2-27) It furnishes an added warning that the vehicle is going to move before it begins. (R.T. 298:28-299:1) In his opinion, such devices are necessary on vehicles that are used in an area where people are working. This covers agriculture, construction work and forklift trucks in factories where people are constantly moving back and forth. (R.T. 299:2-20)

Mr. Knapp further testified that the standard truck-type mirrors do not provide visibility immediately behind the truck when it is loaded. (R.T. 308:14-309:22) In 1968 trucks used in the harvesting of lettuce should have had back-up warning devices. (R.T. 314:26-315:4) In his opinion, it was not good safety practice to sell or manufacture a truck at that time without such a device. (R.T. 315:5-22) If there had been a back-up horn, it would have given Diaz a fighting chance to jump out of the way. (R.T. 316:17-21)

Mr. Ingram also confirmed that back-up alarms were used on lettuce-hauling trucks in 1968. (R.T. 199:22-201:26) Without a wide-angle mirror and with a truck fully loaded, the driver would have a very substantial blind spot when looking back (R.T. 203:28-28); and Mr. Ingram, who was converting vehicles to use in lettuce harvesting in 1968 for Bud Antle Corporation, testified that in his opinion, a truck that was manufactured or sent out for use in the field without such an alarm was inadequate and not complete. (R.T. 200:11-17) In 1968 if a truck didn't have a back-up alarm, he would not consider it ready to do the job out in the field. (R.T. 215:20-24) The trucks he was redesigning were for naked lettuce harvesting (R.T. 196:16-197:4) and he took into consideration the fact that these trucks would be moved both forward and backward in the field with working men around them. (R.T. 197:3-198:21) They installed both convex mirrors to give a wider range of vision to the rear of the vehicle and a back-up alarm system to warn people when the truck was backing up. (R.T. 198:2-200:10) The back-up alarm would to on before the truck began to move to the rear; and he felt that this was an important part of the design that there be some advance warning before the vehicle began to move. (R.T. 201:17-23) The trucks they used were similar to the defendants' trucks shown in Plaintiff's Exhibits 4 and 12. (R.T. 202:4-5) It would take about 1½ hours to hook up an alarm system; and they cost between $40 and $90. (R.T. 211:6-13)

At the time of the accident, the lettuce truck was fully loaded. (R.T. 330:6-28; 111:23) Gattes checked the mirrors before he started backing; but he couldn't and didn't see anything behind him because of the blind spot. (R.T. 355:2-6; 361:13-362:7; 377:22-27) He put the truck into reverse; and as it moved backwards, it did not make any loud noise of any kind. (R.T. 255:11-17) The truck was moving backward at a maximum of five miles per hour when Mr. Gaddes saw Mr. Diaz's son (who was also working in the field at the time of the accident) waving his arms and yelling and at the same time Gattes felt his wheels bump over something. (R.T. 355:19-356:3) Gattes stopped the truck within two to three seconds. (R.T. 356:7) The right rear portion of the truck struck Mr. Diaz. (R.T. 64:25-26) Gattes told the investigating officer that he had backed up six to ten feet before striking Mr. Diaz. (R.T. 47:15-16; 60:23-61:6)

Saturnino Diaz Velazquez, Mr. Diaz's son, who was also working for Bruce Church at the time of the accident, testified that his father had picked up the boxes from S-3 and was walking in the direction of S-4. (R.T. 86:15-88:1) He was carrying the boxes in the normal way that cutters carry boxes. (R.T. 89:1-4) The truck was stopped when his father started walking in the direction of S-4. (R.T. 92:26-28) They were getting prepared to cut the lettuce to the right side of the truck (R.T. 91:16-22); and his father crossed in back of the truck in order to place the boxes down in the furrow before they cut the lettuce. (R.T. 90:24-91:25) Saturnino did not know whether the truck was going to start moving when his father started to walk away from him; and prior to the time that he saw the truck running over his father, he didn't know which direction the truck would move out of the field. (R.T. 107:1-16) It was an instinct that caused him to look up as the rear wheels ran over his father. (R.T. 93:7-94:27) The truck was backing about twice as fast as his father was walking. (R.T. 123:27-126:27) Saturnino screamed and got the truck driver to stop. (R.T. 95:7-11)

Arnold Siegel, a research engineer who appeared for defendant, testified that the vehicle moved 8 to 12 feet prior to contact. (R.T. 901:17-28) He claimed that there was no way that Diaz could have avoided the accident had a bell or alarm sounded when the truck began to move or if it gave a one-second warning before movement. (R.T. 912:13-913:8) The trial court discounted Mr. Siegel's testimony in his specification of reasons:

> The expert witness called by the defendant was not persuasive to me and I give little or no credence to his testimony. His demeanor and the manner in which he testified, and the reasons given for his opinions, if any, did not inspire confidence in his testimony. (C.T. 275:20-24)

Indeed, Mr. Siegel acknowledged that he was not even familiar with the kind of back-up warning devices that go on when you put a truck into reverse. (R.T. 929:14-17) Moreover, his calculations did not take into account the fact that the driver would take additional time in various actions before the truck would begin to move. Mr. Gattes testified that it takes two to three seconds to depress the clutch and get the stick set in place (R.T. 354:26-355:1); and additional time would be taken in checking the mirrors before he started to back up. (R.T. 355:2-8) Accordingly, the whole process would have taken substantially longer than Mr. Siegel projected in giving his questionable opinion.

Defendant's witness, Rollin Patton, testified that based on his re-creations and calculations, Diaz got within ten inches of safety. (R.T. 882:9-13) Later, he testified that Mr. Diaz had to move three to four feet to avoid the accident. (R.T. 889:21-890:2) He concluded, however, that the point at which Mr. Diaz and the truck came together was only ten inches from one side of the truck. (R.T. 890:3-6)

Whether it was ten inches or four feet, the evidence indicated that with even a minimal warning time prior to movement of the truck, the accident would have been avoided. Dr. Blythe concluded that the truck moved about 16½ feet before striking Mr. Diaz. (R.T. 528:1-26) He felt that it was probable that the truck started to move after Diaz stepped behind it. (R.T. 567:2-18) He felt that the truck probably traveled at 4½ miles per hour or 6.7 feet per second. (R.T. 530:7-16) A reasonable estimate of Mr. Diaz's walking speed was three to four feet per second. (R.T. 532:16-27) Accordingly, one additional second of delay through the medium of a back-up warning device would have enabled Mr. Diaz to have gotten to a position of safety. In Dr. Blythe's opinion, the presence of a back-up warning device in this case would most probably have enabled Mr. Diaz to escape the danger and would have prevented this accident. (R.T. 566:2-6; 574:16-24;

608:4-8; 613:7-11) As noted in the specification of reasons set forth above, the trial court referred to and accepted Dr. Blythe's testimony on this matter (C.T. 273:21-274:25) and fully and amply specified its reasons for granting a new trial where the evidence showed that "the truck in question when used in the manner and for the purposes intended, was an extreme danger to persons working near it when it was manufactured and sold without the available devices that could cheaply and efficiently have eliminated that danger."

Comment: In the Argument that followed, the Diaz attorneys led off with the legal principles that the trial judge was entitled to disbelieve witnesses, reweigh the evidence, and draw reasonable inferences contrary to those drawn by the jury, and that his order for a new trial must be upheld if supported by substantial evidence. They then reviewed the evidence supporting the order in the passage quoted below, from which has been omitted a legal argument on the implied warranties issue.

A fair review of the evidence would, we believe, compel the conclusion that there is more than ample or sufficient evidence to support the trial court's order. There is absolutely no merit in appellant's contention that there is "no evidence that appellant breached an industry standard of care" (Appellant's Opening Brief, omitted above) or that:

> The evidence showed conclusively that appellant's conduct was, in all respects, consistent with the appropriate standard of care prevailing in the agricultural equipment industry in 1968. (Appellant's Opening Brief, omitted above)

These assertions thoroughly ignore the very substantial evidence to the contrary. As noted by the trial court in its specification of reasons:

> I believe from the testimony of witnesses whom I found to be reliable that when the truck in question was built there was available to manufacturers at least two types of inexpensive, efficient, and effective back-up warning devices that could have been installed on the truck to give audible warning to persons working in the vicinity of the truck that it was backing or was about to back up. Those witnesses, Dr.

William Blythe, Mr. Sewell Knapp, and Mr. Lawrence Ingram, testified that it was not a good safety practice to manufacture or sell a truck for use in the lettuce fields without such a back-up warning device. Their testimony was creditable and believed by me. (C.T. 272:16-26)

If appellant had been at all candid with this Court, it would have set forth Mr. Knapp's testimony:

Q. Were you, and are you now, acquainted with what was good safety practice in the sale and manufacture of farm equipment, with regard to safety, in April through August of 68?
A. Oh, yes.
Q. Were you acquainted with what was going on with what the common accepted practice in the industry was, in addition to what good safety practices were with regard to the manufacture and sale of equipment being used in the agricultural industry?
A. Yes.
Q. Based on your training and your education, your experience in this field, do you have any expertise or knowledge about such things as backup sound safety devices?
A. Oh, yes.
Q. You are acquainted with them?
A. Certainly.
Q. And how they operate?
A. Yes.
Q. And how they are used?
A. Yes.
Q. Number one, in the period April through August of 1968, was it good safety practice to sell or manufacture a truck to be used in lettuce hauling out of a field in the area where workmen were working without such devices?
A. No.
(R.T. 292:11-293:4)

Mr. Knapp not only testified that it was common practice in the industry to have agricultural equipment equipped with such devices in 1968 (R.T. 293:5-16) but that it was against the applicable standards of care to manufacture and sell trucks to be used in lettuce hauling out of a field in an area where workmen were working without such devices. (R.T. 293:4) Mr. Ingram testified that his employer, Bud Antle Corporation, one of the largest lettuce growers in the country, had such devices installed on its vehicles; and it was his opinion that in 1968 if a truck didn't have a back-up alarm he wouldn't consider it ready to do the job in the field. (R.T. 215:20-24) Floyd Griffin testified that he had heard back-up warning devices on agricultural trucks similar to the Fabco truck prior to this accident. (R.T. 162:4-163:10) And if appellant had wished to be fair in reciting the testimony of Billie Joe Warden (see Appellant's Opening Brief, page 258), appellant would have set forth Mr. Warden's testimony that he really wasn't sure if back-up warning devices were being used in the agricultural industry at the time of the accident (R.T. 668:18-21) and that they may have been on the Fabco trucks on which the wrap machines were installed. (R.T. 668:15-670:6) Contrary to appellant's assertion, there was abundant evidence to show that back-up warning devices were being used on trucks in the agricultural industry in 1968 and there was very substantial evidence to show that the defendant breached the standard of care in furnishing a truck, which had a large blind spot, without such a device which could have saved the life of Pedro Diaz.

Indeed, we find this contention to be a bit absurd in light of the testimony of defendant's own product engineer, Terrance Smith. Mr. Smith testified that there was no standard in the industry pertaining to the design of the truck that was involved in the accident at the time it was built. (R.T. 734:2-5) Yet, Mr. Smith didn't even know whether other manufacturers were building a truck like this at that time. (R.T. 735:18-21) The evidence showed quite conclusively, we believe, that defendant totally ignored the danger presented by a backward movement of its vehicles when they were fully loaded. Mr. Ainsworth, who designed this vehicle for the defendant, testified that he made no effort to find out how far back the blind spot extended (R.T. 235:10-239:16); and he didn't even investigate the question of whether or not a back-up warning device should be installed. (R.T. 254:13-16) Mr. Smith, defendant's product engineer, testified that nobody at Kelsey-Hayes made an evaluation with regard to back-up warning devices before it sold this vehicle for use by decedent's employer. (R.T. 762:14-16) If they had bothered to check, they would have found such devices were available, relatively inexpensive and being used in the agricultural industry. The reason why they were not installed in defendant's vehicles is because no one at defendant gave any thought to the safety of the backward movement of its trucks.

Appellant argues that its truck "met the expectations of the ordinary consumer." (Page 259 *supra*.) The evidence showed that Bud Antle, one of the largest growers in the country, had audible back-up devices installed on its vehicles. Apparently, what appellant means by the "ordinary consumer" is either the consumer who relied upon the manufacturer to install necessary safety equipment or the consumer who did not care about safety. The evidence in the instant case was that Bruce Church, Inc., the consumer of this vehicle, had nothing to do with what safety features went on the truck. (R.T. 397:19-21) Burton Anderson, general services manager for Bruce Church, Inc., testified that when he orderd the trucks from defendant's Salinas representative, he relied upon the manufacturer to install the safety equipment which they were supposed to have. (R.T. 281:9-15)

Appellant argues, "There was *no* evidence that the truck, as manufactured by appellant, was an 'extreme danger' to persons working near it. Plaintiffs produced no testimony to support such a conclusion." (Omitted from Appellant's Opening Brief) This argument is absurd. There was ample testimony which appellant has chosen to ignore which supported the trial court's conclusion in this regard. Dr. Blythe, Mr. Ingram and Mr. Knapp all testified that the truck supplied by defendant was defective and deficient and fell below the standard of care; and the evidence which demonstrated that the briefest of warnings would have saved Pedro Diaz's life furnishes ample justification for the trial court's conclusion that defendant's truck was "an extreme danger" to persons working near it. . . .

Finally, appellant argues that the trial court failed to address the question of proximate cause; and it further contends that the absence of an audible backup device was not a proximate cause of the accident. Both contentions are spurious. As we have set forth above, there was asbundant evidence that the absence of a backup warning device was a proximate cause of the accident. The trial court recited this evidence in its specification of reasons; and it adequately dealt with the question of proximate cause in its specification. The trial court found the defendant's expert "not persuasive" and stated that it gave "little or no credence to his testimony." The court further stated that, "his demeanor and the manner in which he testified, and the reasons given for his opinions, if any, did not inspire confidence in his testimony." (C.T. 275:20-24) By contrast, the court recited that the testimony of Dr. Blythe, Mr. Knapp and Mr. Ingram "was creditable and believed by me" (C.T. 272:26); and it further stated:

> Dr. Blythe also testified to the speed of the truck in reverse, and the sound of its motor was not much louder when backing than when idling, the walking speed of workers on uneven ground similar to that at the scene, and concluded that had the truck been equipped with an audible back-up safety device, decedent, no matter what his position within the 'blind spot' area would probably have had sufficient warning to have moved to safety. This testimony was creditable, based on facts and observations of the witness, and substantially diminished the negligence, if any, of decedent in walking behind the stopped truck as a proximate cause of his death. (C.T. 273:21-274:3)

The trial court quite properly specified on the basis of substantial evidence that the failure of defendant to furnish an audible back-up safety device was a proximate cause of the decedent's death.

Comment: Thus the attorneys for the Diaz heirs highlighted the evidence in their favor and at the same time showed how the trial judge disbelieved contrary evidence, as he was entitled to do. In the following short closing brief, the Kelsey-Hayes lawyers essentially reemphasized what they regarded as critical points in the testimony.

On appeal respondents argue, as they did at trial, that the failure to install a back-up warning device on a truck to be used in the "nacked-pack" lettuce harvesting process constituted negligence. The evidence demonstrated conclusively that appellant did not breach an existing standard of care. No manufacturer of agricultural hauling equipment installed such devices when the subject truck was sold.

Respondents rely upon the testimony of Sewell Knapp to establish that appellant breached an industry standard of care when the truck was sold without a back-up warning device. (Respondents' brief, pages 267-268). As set forth in appellant's opening brief (page 272), although Mr. Knapp testified he was "thoroughly familiar" with the agricultural industry and that the common practice of the industry in 1968 allegedly called for installation of audible back-up devices, Mr. Knapp was unable to name a *single* manufacturer that installed back-up devices in 1968. Mr. Knapp failed in his attempt to establish that appellant breached an industry standard of care, and it was an abuse of discretion for the trial court to rely on his testimony as a basis for its order granting plaintiff's motion for new trial (CT 272).

The only other effort to introduce evidence on standard of care came through the testimony of Mr. Lawrence Ingram, Superintendent of Equipment Maintenance for Bud Antle, Inc. Mr. Ingram's testimony was also discussed in appellant's opening brief (pages 256 and 257). It is significant to note, however, that Mr. Ingram was not a designer or manufacturer of lettuce hauling vehicles. Bud Antle, Inc. was an owner-grower of lettuce. Its conduct does not establish a standard of care for manufacturers or designers. Bud Antle, Inc. *modified* trucks purchased from manufacturers. The trucks sold to Bud Antle, Inc. did not have audible back-up devices installed (RT 206).

Respondents suggest that appellants have been less than candid with respect to Mr. Warden's testimony (Respondent's brief, page 273). Although Mr. Warden testified that back-up devices may have been installed on wrapper machines *prior to 1974*, he testified as follows with respect to the relevant time period:

> *Q.* Mr. Warden, prior to 1968, were you aware of any piece of harvesting equipment, including a wrapper, that had a back-up device on it?
> *A.* No.
> (RT 670)

Respondents assert that there was "abundant evidence" to show that back-up warning devices were being used on trucks in the agricultural equipment industry in 1968 and "very substantial" evidence showing that appellant breached the industry standard of care (Respondents' brief, page 273). It is respectfully submitted that an examination of the record will not support respondents' assertions.

Respondents argue that the design of the vehicle and the nature of the work to be performed by Mr. Diaz made it impossible for the driver and Mr. Diaz to see one another and, thereby, avoid the accident (Respondents' brief, page 265). Respondents also argue that Dr. Blythe's testimony establishes that the accident would probably have been avoided if an audible warning device had been installed

(Respondents' brief, pages 266 and 267). Respondents ignore the obvious as well as the evidence.

It is obvious that the decedent could easily have held the cardboard boxes on his right hip, thus avoiding the obstruction to his visibility. He could then have seen the truck as he approached it. Dr. Blythe, relied upon by plaintiffs to establish proximate cause, testified that he *did not know* whether the accident could have been avoided if there had been a back-up device on the truck (RT 608). Dr. Blythe admitted that the sound of the engine noise would serve as a warning and that the louder the engine noise, the more obvious the warning (RT 611 and 619). He testified that the likelihood that a back-up device would have prevented the accident was dependent upon the speed of the truck, the timing of the alarm, if any, and the speed and direction that Mr. Diaz was walking (RT 608).

Utilizing various assumptions, Dr. Blythe stated that if Mr. Diaz were in a position at the centerline of the truck and if he perceived the danger when the truck began to move, "the likelihood of him escaping here, even if he hears the truck at the moment it begins to move, is low." (RT 564).

Dr. Blythe's best estimate as to the distance the truck traveled before striking Mr. Diaz was fifteen (15) feet (RT 562). The truck would travel this distance in approximately two seconds (RT 562). Dr. Blythe, on *direct* examination, testified that it would take one and one-half seconds for the average person to perceive the danger and tense his muscles to the point where movement could begin (RT 565). An additional one-half second would elapse while the person turned to see where the truck was coming from (RT 574-575).

If Mr. Diaz perceived the danger of the oncoming truck the *instant* it began to move, the truck would still have traveled fifteen (15) feet, impacting Mr. Diaz before he could have *started* to move out of the path of the truck. The impact would have occurred sooner and with less notice to Mr. Diaz if the truck traveled a shorter distance before striking Mr. Diaz (Opening brief, pages 255, 261-263).

Mr. Knapp, also called by respondents, had no opinion regarding whether the absence of a back-up device had a causative effect on the accident (RT 316-317).

It is submitted that had the jury considered the issue of proximate cause, that issue would have been decided in favor of appellant. The evidence, including that presented by respondents' experts, was insufficient as a matter of law to support a finding in favor of respondents.

Comment: As the reader will have noticed, the authors could point to much favorable testimony, but were unable to avoid some highly pertinent contrary evidence.

The Court of Appeal affirmed the order granting a new trial in an unpublished opinion. With the aid of the carefully prepared briefs submitted the Court summarized the evidence and stated its principal conclusion as follows:

The Evidence

Since the basis for each of the three theories of recovery advanced by plaintiffs in their complaint relates to the failure of defendant to have an audible safety device installed on its product, we will direct our review of the evidence to those portions relevant to this question, as reflected in the trial judge's statement of reasons for granting the new trial.

Terrance M. Smith, engineering manager for the Fabco Division of Kelsey-Hayes, testified that he had complete design responsibility for defendant's products. In 1968 he was product engineer and was involved with the design of new products. At that time he knew there were back-up warning devices available that could be activated by a switch connected to the gear shift lever. He knew that there is always a blind spot at the back of the WT-206 truck, but no studies or evaluations were made in the three-year period prior to 1968 regarding the safety of the truck in the field during a backing operation. There were no back-up warning devices on this truck when it was sold in 1968.

Three witnesses testified that the WT-206 truck did not meet safety requirements for use in the field in 1968. These were (1) Lawrence L. Ingram, Sr., a member of the engineering department with Bud Antle Corporation, one of the largest growers and shippers of lettuce in the country; (2) Sewell Knapp, a retired safety engineer for the State of California; and (3) William Blythe, Ph.D., Professor and Chairman of the Department of Civil Engineering and Applied Mechanics at San Jose State University.

Ingram's testimony was based on his experience of 16 years in work with lettuce hauling trucks. His opinion was that the field conditions in lettuce harvesting made it necessary to have an alarm device on them to warn the workers. Such a device, which was readily available, would sound the alarm as soon as the gear was shifted to reverse and before the truck began to move.

Knapp's testimony was based on his experience of 36 years as an occupational safety engineer. He was acquainted with back-up sound safety devices and testified that it was common practice to use them in the truck farming industry, and that it was not good safety practice to sell or manufacture a truck to be used in lettuce hauling out of a field in the area where workmen were working without such devices.

Dr. Blythe had made extensive tests related to the functioning of the subject vehicle at the time of the accident. He studied the traffic patterns of the truck and the pedestrians in the field and the visibility from the cab of the truck rearward when the truck was backing. He backed the truck up with and without the warning device, making noise measurements. He measured the area of visibility to the rear of the truck from the driver's seat.

Dr. Blythe had also found that as early as 1967 there were specifications prepared by the American Society of Automotive Engineers for the evaluation of electronic backup warning devices.

Based on the extensive tests made by this witness, he testified that had there been an audible backup warning device in operation at the time of the subject accident, "[i]t probably — I think most probably would have enabled him [decedent] to escape the difficulty he was in." In response to the defense question on cross-examination, "Dr. Blythe, you don't know whether this accident would have been avoided if there had been a back-up device on the truck, do you?" this witness responded, "I can't say that for certain, certainly. I think it's highly probable it would have."

Dr. Blythe also testified that if the subject truck had been equipped with the audible warning device which was available on the market, the deceased would have had a warning that the truck was coming before it started to move.

Arnold W. Siegel testified for defendant on the issue of alleged defects in the subject truck. He testified that he was a research engineer doing consulting work in the field of automotive collisions and other kinds of vehicular and pedestrian accidents.

The following quoted testimony fairly summarizes the opinions of this witness:

> Q. Did anybody ask you to determine whether this truck had any deficiencies in it when it was manufactured in 1968?

A. No, sir.

Q. Did you reach any conclusions about whether this truck was deficient in any way when it was manufactured?

A. I found no deficiences [*sic*] at all. It was an operating truck, doing its job. . . .

Q. The absence of a back-up warning device was not a deficiency that you found?

A. I considered that quite—in fact, I took a look at the frequency—the best I could, the frequency of how much lettuce has been picked in the last—well, I got 16 years of data from the State Agricultural Department and I am aware that there was one injury in a previous lettuce truck, and this fatality, and I tried to determine any other injuries— . . .

A. . . . But, I did determine the frequency factor and tried to make an understanding that if there was a deficiency in terms of the loading process, and based upon the limited—well, the two accidents that I was aware of, and just the literally billions of tons of lettuce that have been harvested, I just could not find any deficiency.

On the issue of proximate cause, Siegel testified that there was no way that decedent could have avoided the accident had an alarm sounded when the truck started up in reverse. This answer was based on his calculations of the truck speed and the perception, decision, and reaction time of decedent.

Dr. Blythe had made extensive measurements and speed calculations on the ground where the accident occurred, and, as noted, reached a different conclusion regarding the probable impact which a warning device would have had in all of the circumstances involving decedent's activities at the time of his death.

There is no conflict in the testimony regarding the time and place of the death of decedent. There is also no conflict regarding the operating instrumentality which was the immediate cause of his death. Saturnino Diaz Velazquez, son of decedent, who was working in the field near his father, testified that he had seen his father walking in the normal way. The truck was stopped when his father started to walk into the area to its rear. Saturnino did not know whether the truck was going to move or whether it would be going forward or backward. About a minute later he looked at the truck and saw that his father had been run over. The truck was fully loaded. It was backing up about twice as fast as his father was walking.

The Review

1. We first consider the sufficiency of the evidence to support the granting of the motion for new trial.

The testimony of Ingram, Knapp, and Blythe clearly supported a finding of defective design. The testimony of Blythe supports the finding that this defective design was a proximate cause of the accident which resulted in the death of decedent.

As was stated in *Buccery v. General Motors Corp.* (1976) 60 Cal. App. 3d 533, 547, "any product so designed that it causes injury when used or misused in a foreseeable fashion is defective if the design feature which caused the injury created a danger which was readily preventable through the employment of existing technology at a cost consonant with the economical use of the product."

Ingram testified that sound warning systems available in 1968 could be readily purchased for a cost of between $40 and $90 and could be installed in about two hours.

The trial judge clearly and amply stated his reasons for concluding that the evidence, which he believed and which he found to be reliable, established that the subject truck was defective in design and that such defect was a proximate cause of decedent's death. He further concluded that the preponderance of the evidence was contrary to the jury's findings.

Comment: The Court of Appeal accordingly concluded that the order granting a new trial was not an abuse of discretion.

SELECTED
BIBLIOGRAPHY

Basic Writing Texts

The most useful texts on basic writing techniques that I know are W. Strunk and E. White, The Elements of Style (3d ed. 1979) and J. Williams, Style: Ten Lessons in Clarity & Grace (1981). Two other books by talented authors, each offering helpful insights on writing techniques, are C. Brooks and R. Warren, Modern Rhetoric (2d ed. 1958) and W. Zinsser, On Writing Well: An Informal Guide to Writing Nonfiction (1976).

Texts on Legal Writing

More generalized texts on legal writing that I have found helpful are D. Mellinkoff, Legal Writing: Sense and Nonsense (1982); H. Weihofen, Legal Writing Style (2d ed. 1980); and R. Wydick, Plain English for Lawyers (1979) (first published in 66 Cal. L. Rev. 727 (1978)).

Texts on Appellate Advocacy

For many years the most useful text on oral and written advocacy in the appellate courts has been F. Weiner, Briefing and Arguing Federal Appeals (1961). R. Stern and E. Gressman, Supreme Court Practice (5th ed. 1978) includes useful sections dealing with Supreme Court petitions and briefs.

Articles and Lectures by Judges

The most authoritative suggestions on effective brief writing derive from the judges themselves. I found the following addresses and articles particularly helpful.

Breitel, A Summing Up, in Counsel on Appeal 193 (A. Charpentier ed. 1968).

Friedman, Winning on Appeal, 9 Litigation 15 (Spring 1983).

Godbold, Twenty Pages and Twenty Minutes — Effective Advocacy on Appeal, 30 Sw. L.J. 801 (1976).

Goodrick, A Case on Appeal — A Judge's View, in A Case on Appeal (4th ed. 1967).

Gurfein, Appellate Advocacy, Modern Style, 4 Litigation 8 (Winter 1978).

Jackson, Advocacy Before the Supreme Court: Suggestions for Effective Case Presentation, 37 A.B.A.J. 801 (1951).

Kaufman, Appellate Advocacy in the Federal Courts, 79 F.R.D. 165 (1978).

Marshall, the Federal Appeal, in Counsel on Appeal 139 (A. Charpentier ed. 1968).

Peters, The Preparation and Writing of Briefs on Appeal, 22 Cal. St. B.J. 175 (1947).

Pollack, The Civil Appeal, in Counsel on Appeal 29 (A. Charpentier ed. 1968).

Prettyman, Some Observations Concerning Appellate Advocacy, 39 Va. L. Rev. 285 (1953).

Rifkind, Appellate Courts Compared, in Counsel on Appeal 163 (A. Charpentier ed. 1968).

Rutledge, The Appellate Brief, 28 A.B.A.J. 251 (1942).

Stewart, Reflections on the Supreme Court, 8 Litigation 8 (Spring 1982).

Tate, The Art of Brief Writing: What a Judge Wants to Read, 4 Litigation 11 (Winter 1978).

Vanderbilt, Forensic Persuasion, 7 Wash. & Lee L. Rev. 1 (1950).

Articles and Lectures by Practitioners

A classic lecture on appellate advocacy is Davis, The Argument of an Appeal, in A Case on Appeal (4th ed. 1967). Other useful articles by practitioners include the following:

Bonner and Appler, Interlocutory Appeals and Mandamus, 4 Litigation 25 (Winter 1978).

Christensen, How to Write for the Judge, 9 Litigation 25 (Spring 1983).

Cooper, Stating the Issue in Appellate Briefs, 49 A.B.A.J. 180 (1963).

Kester, The Law Clerk Explosion, 9 Litigation 20 (Spring 1983).

Purver and Taylor, Writing the Brief: The Realities of a Criminal Appeal, U.S.F.L. Rev. 31 (1980–81).

Randolph, Certiorari Petitions in the Supreme Court, 4 Litigation 21 (Winter 1978).

Seligson, Ideal Appellate Judges, 9 Litigation 11 (Spring 1983).

Background Reading

Other sources, less directly pertinent to the subject matter but still of background interest, include the following:

W. Brandt, The Rhetoric of Argumentation (1970).

The Writer's Art by Those Who Have Practiced It (R. Brown ed. 1921).

P. Carrington, D. Meador, and M. Rosenberg, Justice on Appeal (1976).

Selected Bibliography

R. Flesch, the Art of Plain Talk (1946).

E. Gowers, Plain Words: Their ABC (1972).

R. Graves and A. Hodge, The Reader Over Your Shoulder: A Handbook for Writers of English Prose (2d ed. 1979).

The Writer's Craft (J. Hersey ed. 1975).

D. Mellinkoff, The Language of the Law (1963).

F. Philbrick, Language and the Law: The Semantics of Forensic English (1949).

INDEX

Index